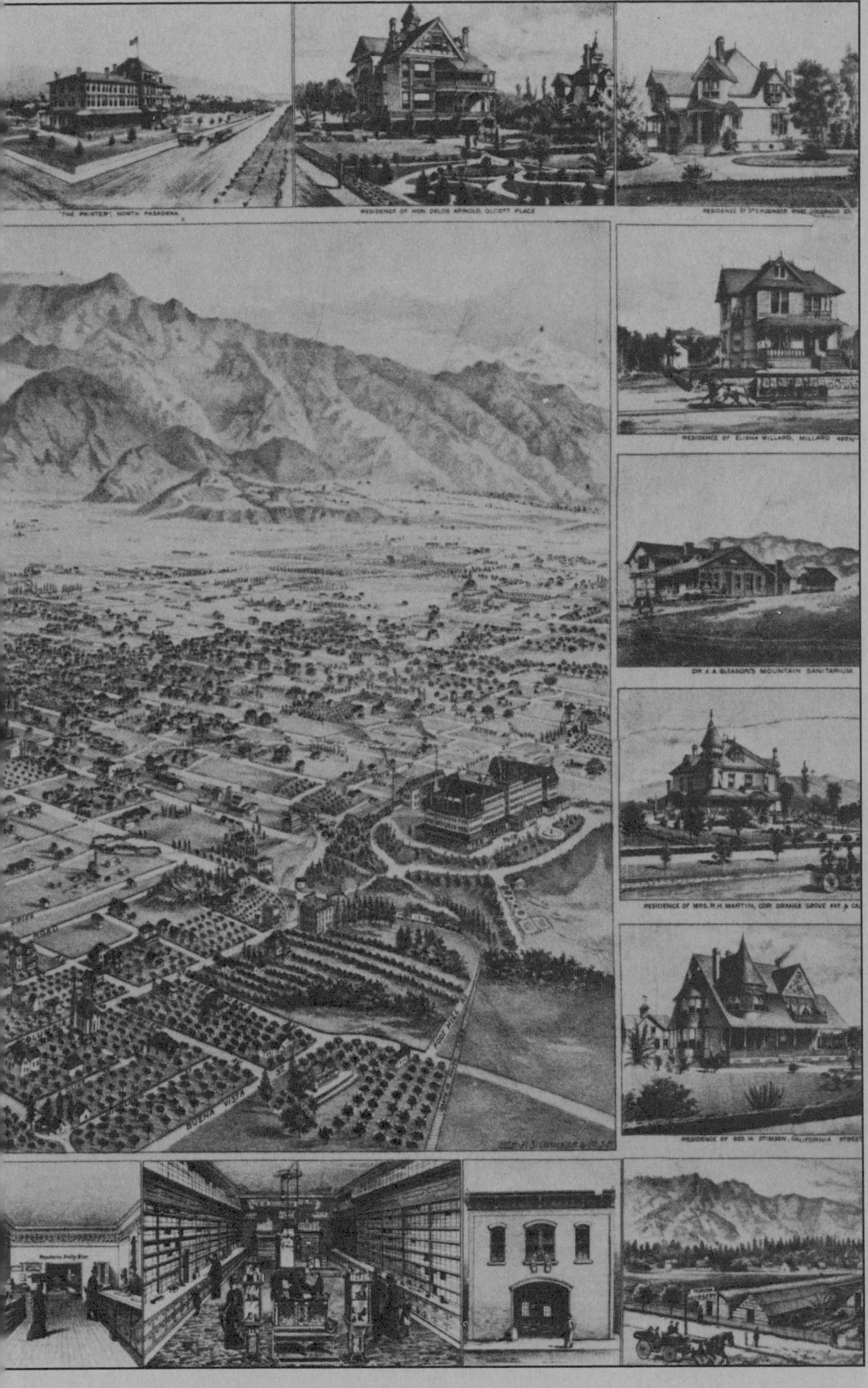
"THE PAINTER", NORTH PASADENA
RESIDENCE OF HON. DELOS ARNOLD, OLCOTT PLACE
RESIDENCE OF ELISHA MILLARD, MILLARD
DR. A. A. GLEASON'S MOUNTAIN SANITARIUM
RESIDENCE OF MRS. R. H. MARTIN, COR. ORANGE GROVE AVE. &
RESIDENCE OF GEO. H. STIMSON, CALIFORNIA
BUENA VISTA

Pasadena

Pictorial Research by Dan Dunkelberger
and Ann Scheid
"Partners in Progress" by Robert J. Kelly

Produced in Cooperation with the
Pasadena Chamber of Commerce

Windsor Publications, Inc.
Northridge, California

Pasadena

Crown of the Valley

An Illustrated History

By Ann Scheid

Endpapers: *This bird's eye view of Pasadena in 1889 depicts the growing town at the close of the 1880s land boom. The fruit orchards shown in the foreground soon gave way to the mansions of millionaires along Orange Grove Avenue. Courtesy, Urban Conservation, City of Pasadena*

Frontispiece: *Built in 1927, Pasadena's City Hall has always been a favorite subject for artists. This circa 1930 painting by New Zealand born mural painter Chris Siemer (1874-1940) hangs in Pasadena's main post office. Courtesy, Pasadena Post Office*

Acknowledgments: *This tinted panorama from the 1890s shows the small town of Pasadena from behind the elegant balustrade of an Orange Grove mansion. Courtesy, Pasadena Historical Society*

Windsor Publications, Inc.—History Book Division
Publisher: John M. Phillips
Editorial Director: Teri Davis Greenberg
Design Director: Alexander D'Anca

Staff for Pasadena: Crown of the Valley
Senior Editor: Pamela Schroeder
Director, Corporate Biographies: Karen Story
Assistant Director, Corporate Biographies: Phyllis Gray
Editor, Corporate Biographies: Judith Hunter
Editorial Assistants: Kathy M. Brown, Laura Cordova, Marcie Goldstein, Marilyn Horn, Pat Pittman, Sharon L. Volz
Designer: Christina McKibbin
Layout Artist: Ellen Ifrah

Library of Congress Cataloging-in-Publication Data

Scheid, Ann, 1940-
Pasadena: crown of the valley.

"Produced in cooperation with the Pasadena Chamber of Commerce."
Bibliography: p. 276
Includes index.
1. Pasadena (Calif.)—History. 2. Pasadena (Calif.)—Description. 3. Pasadena (Calif.)—Industries. I. Dunkelberger, Dan. II. Kelly, Robert J. Partners in progress. 1986. III. Pasadena Chamber of Commerce. IV. Title.
F869.P3S34 1986 979.4'93 86-4023

Published 1986
Printed in the United States of America
First Edition
ISBN: 0-89781-163-1

CONTENTS

Acknowledgments 6

Chapter I
The Fertile Valley 8

Chapter II
A Village of Orchards 24

Chapter III
The Flourishing Resort 52

Chapter IV
The Roots of Greatness 94

Chapter V
Pasadena's Golden Age: "The City Beautiful" 130

Chapter VI
Depression and World War II 154

Chapter VII
Postwar Pasadena: New Directions 170

Chapter VIII
Partners in Progress 200

Bibliography 275

Index 277

ACKNOWLEDGMENTS

Any author setting out to write a history of Pasadena faces an almost impossible task. Although every city has made important contributions to this nation's history, few cities of Pasadena's size have made their mark in such diverse fields as science, architecture, theater, and sport. The challenge of presenting the diversity of the community in a manuscript of 200 pages has forced me to concentrate on certain themes and to pass over subjects already thoroughly covered in earlier publications. With few exceptions, the city limits of present-day Pasadena also form the limits of this book. Certain eras, people, and events are poorly documented, if at all, and so this book necessarily treats only that part of Pasadena's history for which sufficient information was readily available. Many areas remain tantalizingly obscure, but the recent surge of interest in local history holds promise for an increase in knowledge about the community.

Wherever possible, this book relies on primary sources, referring to earlier histories only when information was unavailable elsewhere. Letters, diaries, oral histories, personal papers, and newspaper articles were the principal source materials. Personal interest and the sources available determined many of the themes presented: city government, civic beautification, arts and culture, scientific achievements, education, minority histories, and architecture.

Ironically, the oldest history of Pasadena is also the longest; Hiram Reid's *History of Pasadena* (1895) runs 600 pages and covers twenty years. Later histories were less ambitious, but each has made contributions to the cumulative knowledge of the city, most recently, Manuel Pineda's *Pasadena Area History* (1972). The present work surveys the history of the city from prehistoric times to the present, with a strong emphasis on the period 1900-1930, which has been less documented than both the nineteenth century and more recent times. The focus has been on those events, people, and achievements that have made Pasadena well-known or have had a far-reaching influence.

Many people have contributed to this book. I wish to thank William Cross for the loan of his collection of materials on Pasadena history. Margaret Meriwether, who has contributed her vast store of information from the early newspapers and has also reviewed the manuscript, deserves special thanks, not just from this author but from all future writers and researchers interested in Pasadena's history. Members of the staff of the Huntington Library, especially Virginia Rust, as well as Brita Mack, Doris Smeeds, and Mary Wright, have provided invaluable information and service. Similarly, I wish to express appreciation for the exceptional services of the reference staff of the Pasadena Public Library, especially Carolyn Garner, Elaine Zorbas, and Laurie Whitcomb. Sue Schechter of the Pasadena Historical Society has lent her personal support and that of her staff from the very beginning of this project. The Historical Society's black history collection, compiled by Robin Kelley, was a significant resource. Oral histories from Hugh Anderson, Mary Borgerding, Margaret Fleming, Nobu Kawai, Benjamin McAdoo, Keith Marston, Robert Oliver, and Stephen Reyes, made available through the Pasadena Oral History Foundation under the direction of Brooke Garlock, provided unique source material for the later chapters.

A number of persons knowledgeable in various areas of Pasadena history have read all or parts of the manuscript: Jane Apostol, Karen Blair, Edwin Carpenter, Alson Clark, David Leary, Robert Oliver, and Robert Winter. I wish to thank them for their helpful criticism. Others who have contributed information or source material include Mary Borgerding, Nancy Impastato, Lorraine Melton, Kennon Miedema, and Midge Sherwood. Karen Smith and April Durem patiently typed the introductory chapters.

The author's colleagues in the Urban Conservation office at City Hall—Paul Gleye, Denver Miller, Linda Dishman, Phyllis Cozad, and Arthur Lowy—have given sympathetic and unfailing support, as has John Scheid, without whose encouragement and patience this book could not have been written.

ANN SCHEID
ALTADENA, CALIFORNIA

Chapter I

Grazing sheep and native oaks dotted the lands of the San Gabriel Valley during the mission period. Irrigation and cultivation of the fertile soil began under the Franciscan fathers, but the vast majority of the land lay fallow until the arrival of large numbers of settlers in the second half of the nineteenth century. Courtesy, Western History Collection, Natural History Museum of Los Angeles County

The Fertile Valley

"There is no frost to bind up the face of nature–
& all the herbage annually springs
anew from the seed, self sown–
Hence the farmer never encounters a tough and
obstinate greensward in the tilling of his grounds,
but only a soft and yielding surface."

–George Yount, 1826

The Spanish rancheros called it "llave del valle" (key of the valley); later Midwestern settlers coined the phrase "crown of the valley." Both described the high land of the San Pasqual Ranch, bounded by the bold face of the San Gabriel Mountains on the north, overlooking the broad San Gabriel Valley to the east, and guarding the narrow Eagle Rock pass to the west. When the settlers came to choose a name for their village, they wanted "some long Indian word," and sent a list of phrases—"crown of the valley," "peak of the valley," "key of the valley," and "hill of the valley"—to a Midwestern missionary who had worked among the Chippewa in Minnesota. His suggested phrases all proved to be too long, and so the settlers decided on the last four syllables common to all four phrases—Pa/sa/de/na—meaning "the valley" or "of the valley" in a Chippewa dialect. Thus Pasadena took its name from the topography of the region and the Midwestern origins of its first settlers.

Yount's description of the fertility of the land around the San Gabriel Mission prophesied the agricultural development of the San Gabriel Valley. But fertile soil was only one prerequisite for bountiful harvests; even more important, in arid Southern California, was plentiful water. Father Cruzado, who in 1775 selected the present site of the San Gabriel Mission near a dependable water supply, reported to his superior: "the soil is not of the best quality . . . but with the irrigation ditch . . . the land will fructify."

Situated at the western end of the valley, the future site of Pasadena enjoyed an especially abundant supply of water due to the geological formations underlying it. Pasadena sits on an alluvial fan, deposited by stream systems which eroded the bedrock of the mountains to the north. The primary stream carved out the great gorge, the Arroyo Seco, near the western edge of the city. Recognizable bedrock outcroppings poking up above the alluvium are the San Rafael and Linda Vista hills, Devil's Gate in the Arroyo, Monk Hill in north Pasadena, and Raymond Hill in South Pasadena.

Above: *Wilson Lake, also known as Kewen Lake, lay below the Raymond dike (see ridge in background), a geological formation running along the southern boundary of Pasadena. The dike retains water in a vast underground reservoir known as the Raymond basin, which provided well water for early Pasadena settlers and is still drawn upon today. Courtesy, Western History Collection, Natural History Museum of Los Angeles County*

Opposite: *The mountain stream and wooded slopes of the Arroyo Seco offered the Gabrielino Indians an abundant harvest of acorns, their chief source of food, and a plentiful water supply. Evidence of Indian life in the Pasadena area has been found primarily along the banks of the Arroyo and in the smaller wooded canyons along the Raymond dike. Courtesy, Western History Collection, Natural History Museum of Los Angeles County*

Beneath the alluvium is the Raymond basin, a vast underground reservoir of water held back by the Raymond dike. This dike, created by an earthquake fault, is an easily recognized feature—a series of wooded hills and canyons stretching eastward from Raymond Hill. The Huntington-Sheraton Hotel, Oak Knoll, the Huntington Library and Art Gallery, and El Molino Viejo are all situated on or near this wooded escarpment. Leaks in the dike are the sources for numerous springs along the scarp, which fed Wilson Lake (now drained and renamed Lacy Park), and the lake on Lucky Baldwin's ranch (now Los Angeles County

Arboretum). North of the dike, wells fifty or sixty feet deep would bring forth water, while south of it, a depth of 250 feet was required. This accessibility to water in the form of wells, springs, and mountain streams, made Pasadena a favorable place to settle and found an agricultural community.

Before the arrival of the Spanish and Americans in Southern California, earlier peoples had found the Pasadena area a favorable location. The earliest inhabitants of the valley were the Gabrielino Indians, so named because of their later attachment to the San Gabriel Mission. The Gabrielinos lived throughout the Los Angeles Basin within a semicircle drawn roughly from Topanga Canyon to San Bernardino to Aliso Creek near Laguna, and including the islands of Santa Catalina, San Clemente, Santa Barbara, and San Nicholas. They were a prosperous tribe, living in one of the richest regions of Southern California. Of Shoshonean stock, they formed a wedge between the Hokan tribes to the north and south, and their influence was felt as far east as the Colorado River.

Their language, of the Uto-Aztecan family, relates them to the Hopi Indians of the Southwest and to the Comanche Indians of the Great Plains. Virtually the only traces of the Gabrielinos remaining today are in the place names ending in "-nga" so familiar in Los Angeles County. The ending denotes "place of" or "place where," and names such as Cahuenga ("place of the mountain") or Topanga ("place where mountains run out into the sea") remind us of the original inhabitants of Los Angeles.

The Gabrielino Indians built circular domed huts thatched with fern, reeds, or tule, a native grass. These buildings were used as dwellings or sweathouses, and some were large enough to hold fifty people. This modern representation depicts how the Gabrielinos might have gone about constructing a typical dwelling. Courtesy, Southwest Museum

Archaeological evidence of the Gabrielinos is scanty. The primary source of information has been the accounts of Europeans, who viewed the Indians as an uncivilized race.

The first Spanish explorers, of the Juan Rodriguez Cabrillo expedition in 1542, were struck by the nakedness of the Indians as well as by their lack of embarrassment at their primeval state. The men wore no clothing, while the women wore short skirt-like garments made of the inner bark of trees and of plant fibers. Robes fashioned of animal skins such as otter, deer, or rabbit offered protection in cold or wet weather and at night, and sandals of yucca fiber were used for walking on rough terrain. Men wore their hair long, often braided or caught back in a "horse-tail," while women wore their tresses long and loose, usually with bangs. The hair was kept clean and glossy by applying clay, which was allowed to dry and then broken off. Short hair denoted a state of mourning; the long locks were singed off upon the death of a spouse or other close relative.

The Spaniards were also struck by the fair skin of the Gabrielinos, which gave rise to the legend of a race of "white Indians." The women protected their skin from the sun and weather by coloring themselves with red ochre paint; younger women used the paint as a decorative cosmetic. Part of the daily ritual of all the Gabrielinos was the morning bath, after which they dried off around the breakfast campfire.

Their principal food, the acorn, was gathered in great quantities from the oak woodlands which once covered large portions of the Los Angeles area. The acorns were pounded into a meal, which was then leached to make it more palatable. Other plants and seeds also formed part of their diet, especially tender shoots of yucca. Small and large animals were hunted by the men; deer, antelope, rabbits, gophers, and rats were snared or hunted and eaten. Insects such as grasshoppers and caterpillars were also part of the diet.

Metates (flat grinding stones) and mortars and pestles were used to prepare food. Pottery was

uncommon, as the Gabrielinos preferred to use cooking utensils made from steatite (soapstone), a valued commodity obtained from Catalina Island. Soapstone was also used for pipes and ceremonial carvings. Other implements, such as saws, fishhooks, and needles, were fashioned from animal bones, while baskets were utilized for countless purposes and reflected a high degree of artistry.

Early accounts describe circular domed dwellings, framed in willow and thatched with tule, a kind of reed grass, grouped together to form villages which were concentrated along streams or near springs. The Raymond dike, with its oak-forested canyons, streams, and springs, provided abundant food and water. Settlements located

Following secularization of the missions, the large complex of adobe buildings around the San Gabriel Mission decayed and the Indian population dwindled. This late nineteenth-century photograph shows a rudimentary Indian dwelling which still remained in the shadow of the massive church building. Courtesy, Southwest Museum

along it were Aleupkingna, near the lake on the Santa Anita Ranch; Acurangna, near La Presa Street and Huntington Drive; Sisitcanongna, in a wooded area near the present San Gabriel Mission; and Sonangna, on the present-day grounds of San Marino High School.

In Pasadena itself, the banks of the Arroyo Seco were favorable sites for Indian settlements. Oak groves provided acorns, and the Indians probably also harvested wild grains from the flat plain east of the riverbank. Archaeological remains have been found in Pasadena in areas near the Arroyo.

The Gabrielinos remain one of the least-documented of Southern California Indians, because by the time systematic studies of the region's Indian culture had begun, most of the Gabrielinos were extinct. During the 200 years that passed between the first contact with the Spaniards in 1542 and the colonization of 1769, the decimation of the people by diseases to which they had no immunity had already begun. The estimated population at the time of the arrival of the Spaniards was a mere 5,000; by 1900, the Gabrielinos had disappeared, destroyed by disease, dietary deficiencies, and forced reduction of their population.

Although Cabrillo first landed at Santa Catalina Island in the sixteenth century, it was not until 1771 that the Spanish established themselves in the San Gabriel Valley with a mission located near what is now Whittier Narrows. Named by Father Junípero Serra as *La Misión del Santo Arcángel San Gabriel de Los Temblores,* the San Gabriel Mission was moved to its present site in 1775 under the leadership of the Franciscan priest, Antonio Cruzado, who selected a site just south of the Raymond dike, where streams and springs were plentiful.

When the de Anza expedition passed through in 1776, Father Pedro Font, who was traveling with de Anza, reported that three buildings "partly adobe, but chiefly logs and tule" existed: one long shed housed the missionaries and also contained a storehouse and granary; a separate shed served as a chapel; and a third shed as a guardhouse for the eight soldiers. Five hundred Indians lived in traditional tule huts, separated from the mission buildings by an irrigation ditch. Father Font also reported on the rich pasturelands and the fine herds: "The cows which they have are very fat and they give much and rich milk, with which they make cheese and very good butter." Sheep and hogs were also raised, and George Yount reported that the pastureland was covered with wild oats,

Mission San Gabriel is depicted here in an 1832 painting by Ferdinand Deppe. It is the earliest painting of the mission, and is considered one of the best renderings of a California mission.

which kept the animals fed continuously, except for a month or two at the end of the dry season. Wheat was the preferred crop at the mission in the early years; corn, beans, squash, and grapes were also raised, with the Indians providing the labor.

Father Font described the conversion of the Indians as voluntary but noted that if converted they were obliged to live at the mission and that they were chased and punished if they attempted to leave. Occasionally the Indians were allowed to leave to visit relatives or harvest acorns, and they often returned with new converts. Font related that the Indians liked the Spanish *pozole* (porridge) better than their native foods "and so these Indians are usually caught by the mouth."

As the mission expanded its agriculture and land holdings, destroying the oak groves and wild plants, diverting the water from its natural

This photograph by pioneer Los Angeles photographer Frederic Hamer Maude gives an idyllic view of the mission church at San Gabriel. Its distinctive campanario *(bell tower) and pyramid-capped buttresses enhance the monumentality of the building in its rural setting. Courtesy, Southwest Museum*

courses, and introducing cattle and sheep, it became more difficult for the Indians of the valley to survive, dependent as they were on acorns and other wild plants, and on game for food. The superior weapons of the Spaniards ensured that they would control the territory they chose, pushing the Indian population out onto less desirable lands, and disrupting their trade routes. Eventually most of the Indians were forced to join the mission in order to survive. Their conversions, therefore, were not necessarily genuine.

Mission San Gabriel's only Indian revolt occurred in 1785. It was led by a young Indian woman, Toypurina, said to be a witch and to possess magical powers. She persuaded warriors from surrounding villages to attack the mission by night to rid the land of the invaders. The Spaniards learned of the plot, however, and the attack failed. Toypurina was exiled to Mission San Carlos Borromeo, and ironically, a few years later she married a Spanish soldier, by whom she had four children.

As time passed and the prosperity of the mission increased, more and more buildings were added to the mission compound. In 1795, the present mission church was begun. It was the third church building on the site, following the original chapel of tule and a later adobe church. The new church was considerably more ambitious, for it was built of stone and mortar and had a barrel-vaulted roof. It took some twenty years to construct this massive building, which was partial-

The Gabrielinos developed a high degree of artistry in the design of objects for everyday use, especially baskets. Here a Gabrielino woman displays a basket she has made. Courtesy, Southwest Museum

ly destroyed in the great 1812 earthquake. Its most unusual feature is its picturesque campanario, a "pierced-wall" bell tower with five bells.

Shortly after the blessing of the church in 1805, Father José María de Zalvidea took charge of the mission, and it was during his tenure (1806-1827) that the mission experienced its greatest productivity and economic growth. Father Zalvidea has been variously characterized as "austere," a man of "great managerial ability," "a severe and rigid disciplinarian," "harsh," "cruel," and a "man of iron." There is no doubt that Zalvidea resorted to the whip whenever the Indians infringed on his stringent regulations regarding work and behavior. An ascetic himself, Zalvidea is reported to have worn a belt of iron spikes next to his skin and to have indulged in self-flagellation. Despite the considerable human cost, Father Zalvidea developed the already prosperous San Gabriel Mission into one of the most productive and richest missions in Alta California.

At the height of its prosperity, the mission produced much more than it needed to support its own population, so it sought other markets for its products, especially the ships landing at San Pedro, the growing settlement at Los Angeles, and the many surrounding ranches. According to a traveler passing through in 1826, the mission herds could be seen at pasture for a distance of seventy miles around the mission. While this may be exaggerated, nevertheless the hides, tallow, dried beef, candles, soap, shoes, and saddles derived from the cattle and sheep produced a good income for the mission. According to an 1827 report from the mission fathers, the mission owned 34,000 animals and had an Indian population of nearly 1,500.

Wheat, corn, and barley were grown on mission lands, and extensive vineyards were planted. Fruits in the mission gardens included oranges, citrons, limes, apples, peaches, pears, pomegranates, and figs. At first, flour was made by the Indian method of grinding with metates, but in 1816 the first gristmill in California was built in the canyons above the mission where a plentiful supply of water drove the mill wheel. Known as *El Molino Viejo* (the old mill), it now serves as the regional headquarters of the California Historical Society.

During this prosperous period, the mission functioned like a well-organized village, with Indians trained in various trades useful to the mission economy. Woodcutters brought logs to the sawmill, where timbers were sawed for building. Indian carpenters, wheelwrights, cartmakers, box makers, and fence builders produced goods for trade or to serve the needs of the mission. Coopers made the barrels needed for wine production. Wood was converted to charcoal for the fires of the blacksmiths, who fashioned parts for carts, mill gears, plows, harrows, farm implements, and harnesses. Wood and charcoal fired the kilns of the brick and tile makers, who made building material for the mission and for other buildings in the area. Masons laid brick and stone for buildings and dams, while limeburners quarried lime to produce mortar and cement.

Indian women spent their days as spinners and weavers, turning the wool from the flocks into clothing and blankets for their own use and for sale. Women also became tailors and dressmakers, fashioning garments for their once-naked people. A report from Father Zalvidea in 1814 notes that "although [the Indians] are quite given to nudity we are ever making every effort to have them go about decently covered. To this end the clothing given them consists of a blanket, a short tunic which we call a coton and a narrow cloth which serves as a covering for the men called a taparrabo. The women are supplied with a coton, blanket and skirt."

Father Zalvidea's attitude toward the Indians is clearly expressed in his 1814 report, which reflects the conflict between the two cultures. Responding to a question about how the Indians treated their children, Zalvidea wrote: "Their parents love them to such an extent that we might say they are their little idols. As a result, the education the children receive amounts to nothing. Consequently, they as well as their fathers lack any inclination towards work or towards the arts." Zalvidea was no less critical of the Spanish ranchers near the mission:

With regard to the education of their children, with very few exceptions, they act in the same manner as the Indians. . . . They are so given over to idleness and are so disinclined to better their status that they are satisfied with merely planting enough to produce a year's crop. . . . They hire pagan Indians to do this as well as for whatever work is to be done around the house. . . . The one activity they engage in is to go about on horseback from one rancho to another.

Once they had satisfied their basic needs, the Indians traditionally saw no necessity in laboring further, but Zalvidea reported that he had succeeded in regulating them so that they worked a certain number of hours each day. Yet, according to Zalvidea, "all the Indians live in the most wretched poverty."

As for the health of the Indians, Zalvidea revealed that they were a dying race, for the number of deaths was double the number of births. The Indians were rapidly succumbing to venereal diseases, tuberculosis, and "dysentery of the blood." Infant mortality was high with three out of four of all children born dying of the effects of venereal disease and most dying before age twenty-five. Under Zalvidea a hospital was established at the mission to provide the disease-ridden Indians with some care and comfort. But, he predicted, "if the government does not supply doctors and medicine, Upper California will be without Indians at all."

In 1826, Zalvidea suffered a nervous collapse, and he retired to Mission San Juan Capistrano. His successor, Father José Sánchez, had assisted Father Zalvidea for some time in the management of the mission, but he was regarded as more lenient with the Indians and was also better-liked by the travelers who stopped at the mission.

Secularization of the missions occurred in 1833. The Mexican government issued a decree transforming the missions into parish churches but failing to specify the disposition of church properties. Early settler Hugo Reid, in writings based on the memory of his Indian wife, Victoria, who had lived at the mission, described the fate of the imposing and wealthy institution. Timber roofs were dismantled and became firewood, cattle were slaughtered, goods were handed out to the Indians. Reid wrote that "the vineyards were ordered to be cut down, which, however, the Indians refused to do. It did not require long to destroy what years took to establish." Local ranchers helped themselves to cattle. Food supplies were scarce for the Indians, who had become dependent on the mission for their livelihood. According to Reid, most of the Gabrielinos left their native region and moved north, while other tribes from the south moved into the San Gabriel Valley, creating a glut of cheap labor. Old and frail Indians were kept at the mission by the padres, while others sought work on the ranchos in the area.

After secularization, the Mexican government carved up the mission lands into ranches; portions of two of these ranches, Rancho San Pasqual and Rancho Santa Anita, make up part of present-day Pasadena. Rancho San Pasqual, the westernmost part of the mission lands, was deeded in 1835 to Juan Mariné, husband of Eulalia Pérez de Guillén, who claimed she had received the land for her long service to the Indians at San Gabriel Mission. Rancho San Rafael comprised that part of present-day Pasadena west of the Arroyo Seco, as well as Highland Park, Glendale, and Burbank. San Rafael was given to José María Verdugo, a Spanish soldier, in two Spanish land grants in 1784 and 1798.

Scotsman Hugo Reid gained possession of Santa Anita Ranch through his wife, Victoria, and received provisional title to it in 1841. Reid and his family had lived in an imposing two-story house in

Leonard J. Rose's Sunny Slope vineyard and winery was one of the largest and most prosperous in California. The brick buildings, shown here in about 1890, housed modern crushers, tanks, and rooms full of casks. They were the earliest large brick buildings in the Pasadena area. Courtesy, The Huntington Library

the settlement of San Gabriel near the mission, but after acquiring Santa Anita, they began spending more and more time on the ranch. Their one-story adobe house was built at the edge of a lake and shaded by tall trees (now part of the Los Angeles County Arboretum). William Heath Davis, who visited the Reids a number of times, wrote glowingly of the comfort, hospitality, and fine food that the Reids provided for their guests:

Reid was a cultivated and educated man, a big-hearted man, a thorough accountant, and bred as a merchant in his own country. . . . The hospitality shown to McKinley and myself, not only by Reid himself but by his Indian wife, was sumptuous. A Castilian lady of standing could not have bestowed on us any greater attention or graciousness.

Moreover, Davis wrote that the ranch of 8,000 acres "was then the most picturesque spot of Southern California, with mountains, valley, springs, and running silvery streams. You would observe in riding over the 'rancho' its having more than its 'pro rata' of towering and overspreading live oak trees, 'manzanita,' laurel and other forest in comparison with other 'ranchos.' "

After several years of financial reverses and mounting debts Reid was forced to sell his ranch in 1847, and it eventually passed to investors William Corbitt and Albert Dibblee in 1858. Dibblee, a New Yorker who had become prominent in San Francisco business circles, and Corbitt, a Los Angeles trader, sold the ranch in two parts to William Wolfskill and Leonard Rose in the 1860s. Wolfskill, a pioneer trader and early citrus grower, had long had his eye on Santa Anita. He bought the eastern portion of the ranch (later owned by E.J. "Lucky" Baldwin), now the site of the city of Arcadia. Rose, a German immigrant, purchased about 1,300 acres of the western portion of Santa Anita, in what is now east Pasadena. Calling his new ranch "Sunny Slope," Rose proceeded to plant extensive vineyards and orchards.

According to Rose's son, Leonard Jr., his father chose to locate in the San Gabriel Valley because of the accessibility of water, especially the constant springs that rose from the formation of the Raymond dike, and the fact that wells of only fifty to sixty feet deep would bring forth plentiful water.

Rose was an energetic and ambitious man, who created one of the most outstanding vineyards in Southern California. His other great passion was fine racehorses, which he stabled and bred on the southern portion of his ranch. Initially, Rose dared to plant his vines without relying on irrigation, thus obtaining a sweeter crop than that grown on irrigated lands, although his yield was not so great. Although at first he planted the common mission grape, Rose soon imported cuttings from France and Germany. There were about thirty-five distinct varieties of grapes at Sunny Slope, and Rose produced all types of wines, both red and white as well as brandy, sherry, port, and other dessert wines. In 1867, he began shipping to New York, and shortly thereafter, Rose himself began to make annual trips east to market his wine. Rose's brandy was very successful, and in a time when brandy was believed to have strong curative powers, druggists across the country stocked Rose's Sunny Slope Brandy.

Originally, Rose employed about a dozen Indians from the "rancheria" or Indian village called Acurangna near the south end of his property. During the 1870s, however, Rose expanded his operations greatly, and he began using Chinese laborers. He purchased an additional 640 acres of the Santa Anita Ranch, which he planted with more vines, as well as 200 acres of oranges and 100 of English walnuts and fruit trees. Rose also expanded his vineyard operation by offering cuttings for sale and buying the grapes of other growers. Rose supplied railroad industrialist Leland Stanford with a million cuttings for his 2,000-acre vineyard near Sacramento. By 1880, his goal of 1,000 acres in vines was nearly reached and his workers were kept busy with orange shipments in the spring, preparations for the vintage during the summer, and wine-making in the fall.

Perkins and Stern, Rose's New York dealers,

took over the business side of Sunny Slope in the mid-1870s and sent a German wine-maker to the ranch to take charge of the wine-making. In the late 1870s Rose built a new distillery and steam crushers, making Sunny Slope the largest winery in Southern California if not the state. The original capacity had grown from 5,000 gallons annually to a daily capacity of 5,000 gallons. All this was housed in an impressive complex that included two brick buildings, two and three stories in height. Several large frame warehouses, some wine-makers' cottages, and a large cooper shop completed the establishment.

During the 1870s, Sunny Slope became a tourist attraction. Tourists came to view the prize horses that Rose was raising, to pick oranges at fifty cents a dozen, and to taste the wines. Rose's passion for racehorses was so great, however, that he eventually decided to sell Sunny Slope in order to devote himself completely to his horse ranch, called "Rosemeade," located on 500 acres he had purchased near El Monte.

Shortly before selling Sunny Slope, Rose subdivided a portion of the ranch, naming it "Lamanda Park," a combination of his wife's first name, Amanda, and his own first initial, "L." Lamanda Park remained a small village, a railroad stop where tourists headed for the Sierra Madre Villa Hotel alighted and growers shipped their products to the East. Sunny Slope was sold in 1887 for over a million dollars to a British syndicate; at the time the ranch employed over 150 workers—more than a hundred Chinese, thirty Mexicans, and twenty whites—and claimed a net profit of $275,000 annually from wine, grapes, and oranges.

As for Rancho San Pasqual, it was apparently not especially desirable land, as its early owners made little effort to use it for either grazing or agriculture. The first grantee, Juan Mariné, died before obtaining full title, and despite his wife Eulalia's claim that the land was actually hers, Mariné's son, Fruto, sold his claim to José Pérez for the sum of six horses and ten head of cattle. Pérez and a comrade, Enrique Sepúlveda, were granted the ranch in 1840, and they built two small houses near the Arroyo Seco. Pérez died shortly thereafter, and Sepúlveda abandoned the property, opening the way for Manuel Garfias, a prominent Los Angeles citizen, to obtain the land in 1843 by a grant from Governor Manuel Micheltorena. Garfias' claim for 13,500 acres was confirmed by the American government in 1854 and formally granted in 1863.

Garfias built a large hacienda on the ranch, which attracted much attention in the area for its magnificence. Judge Benjamin S. Eaton visited the ranch in 1858 and wrote: "It was a one and a half story adobe building with walls two feet thick, all nicely plastered inside and out, and had an ample corridor [porch] extending all around. It had board floors, and boasted of green blinds [shutters]—a rare thing in those days. This structure cost $5,000—in fact, it cost Garfias his ranch, for he had to borrow money to build it."

Garfias had borrowed the money from Dr. John S. Griffin, an army surgeon who had come to California during the Mexican-American War. In 1854 Griffin settled in Los Angeles, where he started a medical practice. He also invested in banking and water enterprises as well as in large tracts of land. He had many business dealings with Benjamin D. Wilson, a former trader and trapper who had come to Los Angeles in 1841 and who lived near the San Pasqual Ranch. When Garfias forfeited his ranch in 1858 to pay his debt, Griffin acquired the land for the amount of the debt and the accumulated interest, plus $2,000. In 1859, Wilson was named as the titleholder to the land for the recorded sum of $1,800, probably in settlement of a debt that Griffin owed him. A year later Griffin gained back a one-half interest in the San Pasqual Ranch for $4,000. Because of this joint ownership by Griffin and Wilson, Pasadena settlers were to have a difficult time getting both partners to agree to sell part of the San Pasqual Ranch in 1873.

While Griffin lived in Los Angeles, Wilson lived on his Lake Vineyard Ranch, purchased from Victoria Reid in the 1850s. A prominent figure in

Left: *Benjamin D. Wilson, seated here with his family, came to California in 1841. A prominent figure in early Los Angeles history, Wilson was the city's second mayor and acquired much of the San Pasqual ranch, part of which was later sold to the Indiana colonists. Courtesy, Security Pacific National Bank Photograph Collection, Los Angeles Public Library*

Opposite: El Molino Viejo *(the old mill) remains as a romantic reminder from California's Spanish past, attracting artists, as in this photograph. The Southern-style wooden porch at the left was added by a Mississippian, Colonel Edward J.C. Kewen, who lived at the mill from 1859 to 1879. Courtesy, California Historical Society/ Ticor Title Insurance (Los Angeles)*

early Los Angeles history, Wilson served as the city's second mayor, and as a state senator. Like Rose, Wilson developed his ranch into vineyards and citrus trees, with smaller acreages devoted to walnuts and olives. In 1874, a visitor to Lake Vineyard reported that over a million oranges were expected to be shipped that season from about 2,000 orange trees on both Lake Vineyard and Mt. Vineyard estates (the latter being the adjacent property of J. De Barth Shorb, Wilson's son-in-law).

Wilson and Griffin built ditches from Devil's Gate along the Arroyo and out onto the mesa of the San Pasqual Ranch in what is now north Pasadena. This was the first attempt to irrigate the high land that lay north and east above the Raymond dike and the Arroyo Seco, the two principal sources of water on the ranch. These ditches had

cost Wilson and Griffin $10,000, and were to be an important asset in the sale of part of the San Pasqual to early Pasadena settlers; the existence of the ditches reassured the settlers that irrigation of this arid upland was indeed possible.

At various times, Wilson and Griffin did sell off portions of the San Pasqual Ranch. One of the earliest sales was to Mrs. Albert Sidney Johnston, widow of a Civil War general. Mrs. Johnston was also the sister of Dr. Griffin, and she named her ranch after the old Griffin plantation in Virginia, "Fair Oaks." Mrs. Johnston built a modest home there, but stayed only a short while. In 1865, Judge Benjamin S. Eaton took over her ranch, which comprised about 260 acres now in northeast Pasadena and Altadena west of Eaton Canyon. The ranch house, moved and remodeled, still stands in Altadena. In 1868 or 1869 Wilson and Griffin sold 5,000 acres to James Craig, who was acting as agent for Alexander Grogan of San Francisco. This Grogan Tract was bordered on the east by Santa Anita Avenue (now Altadena Drive), and originally extended west of Lake Avenue, but a portion of that was repurchased by Wilson later to make up his Lake Vineyard Tract. Craig carved out for himself about 150 acres of the eastern portion of the land, naming his ranch "L'Hermitage." Craig built an adobe farmhouse on the property; it still stands on Monte Vista Street in east Pasadena and is the oldest house standing within the city limits. In 1870, Wilson, at Griffin's behest, sold a large acreage in north Pasadena to Henry G. Monk of Boston. This property included Redmont or Prospect Mount, now known as Monk Hill, the highest point in north Pasadena (now the site of Washington School).

After the conclusion of the Mexican-American War in 1848, when the United States gained control of Alta California, more and more Americans from the East and Midwest migrated to Southern California, gradually acquiring the former Spanish lands. The land that had been so hospitable to the Indians, and had proved adaptable to the grazing and agriculture introduced by the Spanish missionaries and ranchers, was further developed by the newcomers. Hugo Reid, Leonard Rose, and Benjamin Wilson planted extensive orchards and vineyards, using the plentiful water supplies to irrigate portions of their large acreages. During the third quarter of the nineteenth century, portions of the large ranches, Santa Anita and San Pasqual, were sold off. The western portion of Rancho San Pasqual, used only for sheep grazing, remained untilled, but promised to be as productive as the Reid, Rose, and Wilson lands. It awaited only settlers to develop its water supply, to till the land, and to plant vines and citrus trees, in order to produce a rich agricultural bounty.

Chapter II

This view of Pasadena looking west in 1884 shows the beginnings of the town center. A school, two hotels, and a store and community hall are clustered around the intersection of Colorado Street and Fair Oaks Avenue. Courtesy, The Huntington Library

A Village Of Orchards

"Knowest thou the land

where the citron and olive

is fairest of fruit,

And the voice

of the meadowlark

never is mute?

It is Pasadena."

–Thomas Balch Elliott, 1876

In May 1873, following an especially harsh winter in the Midwest, a group of friends in Indianapolis gathered to discuss the possibility of moving to a more favorable climate. According to their leader, Dr. Thomas Balch Elliott, they considered Texas, Florida, and Louisiana but finally settled on Southern California as "the spot uniting the blessings of the tropics without their heat, malaria and enervating influences." Calling themselves the California Colony of Indiana, the group advertised for additional investors, and before long, Elliott wrote in his *History of the San Gabriel Orange Grove Association,* "flocks of letters came snowing in" from hopeful immigrants all over the northern states and even Canada. Over a hundred families eagerly joined the colony for a small sum, pledging a larger investment once land was found.

Using some of the funds thus raised, the officers sent Elliott's brother-in-law, Daniel Berry, a teacher and journalist, and General Nathan Kimball to California to prospect for land. They were to look for 50,000 acres of level land (at five dollars an acre), suitable for fruit growing. Believing that California was flat like Illinois or Indiana, the colonists stipulated that every acre should be alike, with equal exposure and equal access to water. Once west of the Rockies, Kimball left the expedition to take up a surveying job in Utah, but Berry, accompanied by his young son, Fred, arrived in California in the summer of 1873 and began at once his search for suitable land. Every few days, Berry reported on his progress by letter to Elliott, leaving a detailed record of his activities.

Much of Berry's information about California came from a book by Charles Nordhoff titled *California for Health, Pleasure and Residence.* In it Nordhoff described the successful colony at Anaheim, which may have served as a model for the Indianans. Inspired by Nordhoff's descriptions, Berry went first to San Diego, where he looked at a number of ranches, but he left after a week, declaring that San Diego land was overrated and overpriced.

Proceeding to Los Angeles, where he settled down at the Pico House in the heart of the town, Berry began to scout the surrounding region by horseback, stagecoach, and wagon. His first trip was to the San Gabriel Valley, where Leonard Rose of Sunny Slope showed him the eastern portion of Santa Anita Ranch, which was available for twenty dollars an acre. Berry was impressed: "It is the first thing we have seen that has plenty of water in sight." Sunny Slope "is more than Nordhoff said it was. It is a kingly place," Berry enthused. Rose's orange trees would pay $2,000 an acre the following year, and the railroad was expected to come through the valley soon, making the land even more valuable. But unfortunately, Santa Anita was far too expensive for the Indianans.

Searching out the other places described by Nordhoff, Berry visited Anaheim, which was a disappointment—too sandy and full of mosquitos and "dutchmen." His report from San Fernando was somewhat more favorable: 53,000 acres of good land at a reasonable price, but water was not easily available. As for San Bernardino, the land was cheap at $2.50 an acre, but it was too hot: "Your face and nose get scalped with the sunshine and you need new hide about twice a week on your countenance." Moreover, it was three days' time for a loaded team to travel from Los Angeles, and after his trip, Berry complained, "My back is broken with 120 miles of villainous stage riding, but I still live."

Berry's descriptions of the rigors of travel in Southern California form some of the most colorful passages in his letters. After only ten days of scouting, Berry wrote: "You have no idea of the extent and labor of these trips. We have been on the move vigorously all the time, and if it were not for the charm of the climate I would be tired out." After a month of this, Berry had had enough: "I wish you were here just to knock around day and night for a week in canjons, cactus nettles, jungles, dry river bottoms, etc. I have been at it 35 days and going again Monday. It is no longer funny. I want to resign."

As for the people, Berry found those in San

Above: *Daniel M. Berry, teacher and journalist from Indianapolis, searched Southern California for land as the official representative of the California Colony of Indiana. His final selection of the western portion of the San Pasqual Ranch determined the future development of Pasadena. Courtesy, Pasadena Public Library*

Above, right: *Dr. Thomas Balch Elliott and his wife Helen were the initial organizers of the California Colony of Indiana, which was supplanted by the San Gabriel Orange Grove Association, formed to purchase land for the settlement. The Elliotts were important investors, purchasing 165 acres together with Daniel Berry. Courtesy, Pasadena Public Library*

Bernardino likeable, but the people of the San Gabriel Valley he described as a special "aristocracy who work and raise fruit." According to Berry, the valley was peopled with Harvard graduates, judges, lawyers, generals, and ex-senators, all running vineyards or herding sheep in the healthful air. Chinese and Indians lent an exotic aura—and did most of the work.

Impressed with Berry's description of Santa Anita, Elliott authorized an offer of fifteen dollars an acre for the ranch. In the meantime, however, Berry had returned once again to the San Gabriel Valley and found another tract which was cheaper and just as fine: "Found a tract of 2,800 acres at $10 an acre about 4 miles from town, about 500 acres a wooded and watered canyon, suitable for wood and cattle grazing. The wood is plenty, the water delicious and cool, leaping out of the rocks on the side in little cascades."

This idyllic place, Berry wrote, was

> *right in line with all the best orange orchards and vineyards here and just as good,* with more water. . . . *I slept over there last night in the clear transpicuous air and awoke to the music of a thousand linnets and blackbirds in the evergreen oaks. It was the sweetest sleep of years. The land is not on the market, but the brother-in-law of the owner lives near and wants us over there. . . . I am just agonizing to buy the whole thing, but can't do it.*

That brother-in-law was Judge Benjamin Eaton of Fair Oaks Ranch and agent for the sale of Dr. Griffin's portion of the San Pasqual Ranch. Eaton was related to Griffin through his first wife, sister of Dr. Griffin's wife. Berry, who suffered from asthma, had spent the night with Eaton at Fair Oaks, and in the dry, warm air of San Pasqual, high above the fog of Los Angeles, he was able to sleep the whole night through. That night's sleep may have been the decisive factor in Berry's choice of San Pasqual. In any case, Berry wrote glowing letters to Elliott about the land, and no property that he saw afterward compared to it.

Berry foresaw more than fruit-growing in the future of the settlement. He wrote to Elliott:

Send along . . . [an] enlightened man to build a sanatarium next to the mountains. It would be filled in a day and every visitor would be an advertiser of our fruit to all sections of the country. . . . Then we want a Polytechnic School. The mountains form a natural observatory in a clear air, and then for geology send Dr. Fletcher.

In an uncanny way, Berry's words prophesied the future of Pasadena as a health resort, the establishment of Throop Polytechnic (later California Institute of Technology), the founding of Mt. Wilson Observatory, and the role of Caltech as one of the foremost geologic research centers in the world.

It was on September 12, 1873, that Berry discovered the land he wanted, but on September 18 a financial panic swept the nation, and most of the potential colony investors disappeared. Berry was deeply discouraged, but instead of giving up, he opened an office in Los Angeles and became an agent himself, taking potential investors out to San Pasqual or "Muscat" (named for the grapes the colonists expected to grow), to convince them to join in the undertaking. (Berry and Elliott had devised a code for telegraphic messages, referring to San Pasqual as "Muscat," which should be remembered as the first name for Pasadena.) Despite the uncertainty of the financial situation, Berry pushed ahead in negotiating for Muscat, concealing from its owners the dire straits of his Indiana backers.

Berry's first obstacle was Wilson, who owned the land jointly with Griffin and was not particularly enthusiastic about selling. Boundaries were drawn and redrawn, water rights were negotiated and renegotiated, all with the help of Eaton and J. De Barth Shorb, Wilson's son-in-law, who were eager to facilitate an agreement. Griffin helped by easing the terms of payment for the settlers and paying Wilson an extra $1,000 to get some squatters off the land. Shorb worked out a water plan with Berry and tried to bring Wilson round to accepting it.

Eaton, arguably Pasadena's first real estate agent, was willing to go in with Berry and Elliott to help close the deal and offered to provide the colony his experience with waterlines and irrigation systems. (Eaton had superintended construction of water systems in Los Angeles.) Thomas Croft, an investor with ready cash, arrived from Indiana in October and was delighted with the land Berry had chosen. John Baker of Indiana was already in Los Angeles, working as a blacksmith. Other investors in Los Angeles that Berry recruited were William Clapp, a businessman from Massachusetts, A.W. Hutton, city attorney of Los Angeles, and Albert O. Bristol of Chicago.

Gathering these and several others together, Berry finally formed the San Gabriel Orange Grove Association on November 11, 1873, which was incorporated under the laws of the state of California. The name was chosen, according to Berry, because of the good reputation of San Gabriel Valley oranges; Berry thought it would help the settlers market their fruit. Besides, Berry wrote, "the name Indiana sounds too much like colds, coughs, chills, etc. to suit us here."

It took several weeks to get Wilson's agreement on the division of the land and the water, but finally on December 18, Griffin and Wilson signed the bargain. Croft wrote in his diary, "we all feel good," but Berry was overjoyed, for the deal included almost 4,000 acres, stretching northward to the base of the mountains. "That is enough for our little $25,000 in the fairest portion of California," Berry exulted. The price was only $6.31 an acre, close to the original $5 an acre that the colonists were willing to pay. The only disadvantage was that the settlers would have to bring in their own water from Devil's Gate, instead of using Wilson's ditch.

After weeks of stalling, why did Wilson finally agree to the bargain, even throwing in an extra 1,100 acres? Berry wrote: "Wilson assured me today that he consented to our new lines giving us 1,100 acres extra solely to get us there to develop the land." The clever Wilson knew that his own land adjoining the association's would be worth far more once the new settlement was established.

During the protracted negotiations for the land, there were many times when it seemed that the scheme would almost certainly fall apart. Berry, however, kept working both sides, bargaining with Wilson while trying to maintain enthusiasm for the land in Elliott and the Indianans.

At one point, seven of the major Indiana investors pulled out, believing that Berry was trying to make a commission for himself on the sale. This nearly killed the negotiations, and Thomas Croft wrote despairingly in his diary: "I can't [expect] any help from them. I must buy it myself or fail. Berry and Elliott will never close any deal. . . ." But Berry kept his own counsel, continuing to

This circa 1890 view of Orange Grove Avenue shows one of the native oaks spared by the settlers when they laid out their main street. The photograph is by noted Los Angeles photographer Frederick Hamer Maude. Courtesy, Western History Collection, Natural History Museum of Los Angeles County

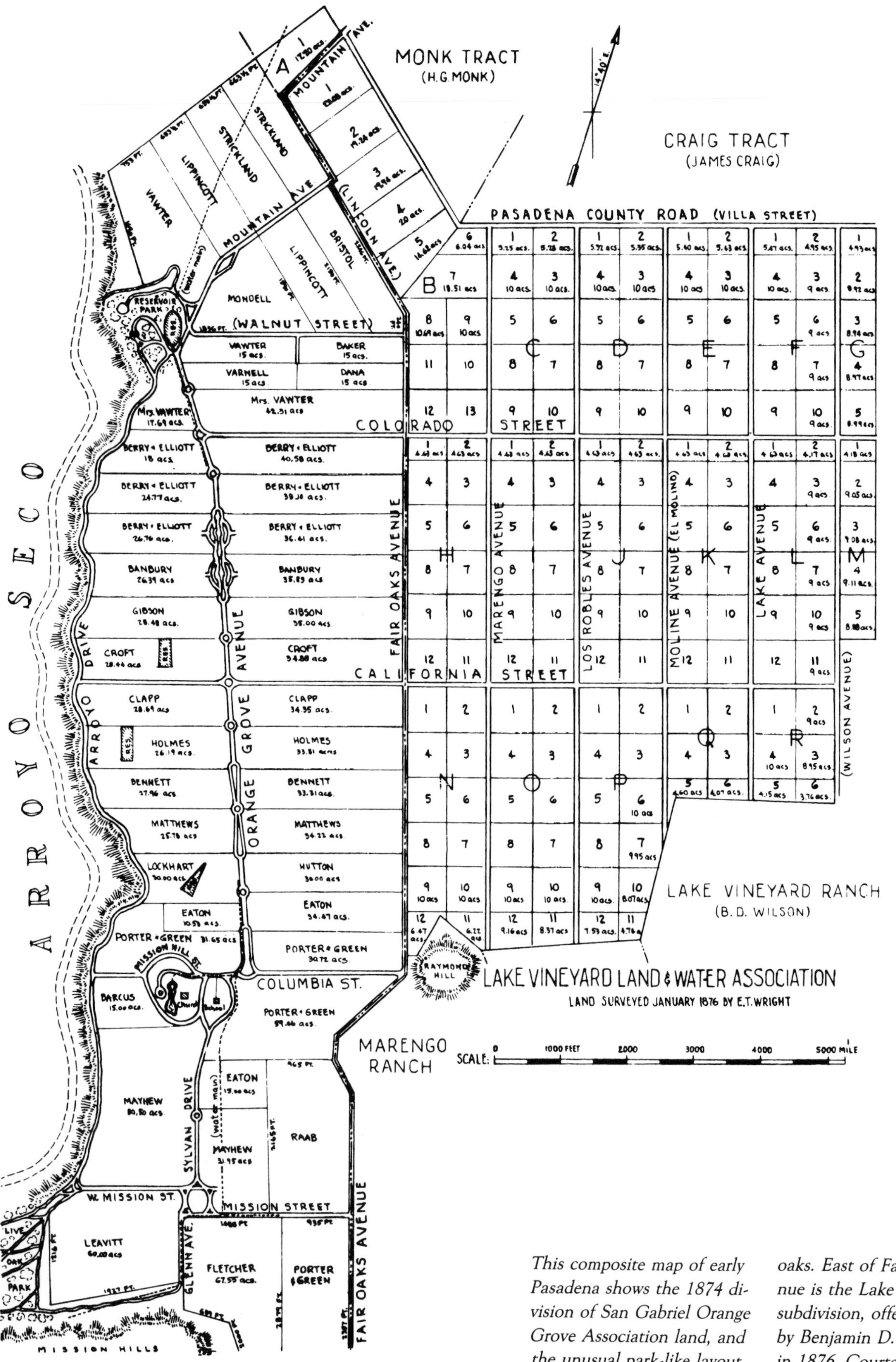

This composite map of early Pasadena shows the 1874 division of San Gabriel Orange Grove Association land, and the unusual park-like layout of Orange Grove Avenue, designed to save the native oaks. East of Fair Oaks Avenue is the Lake Vineyard subdivision, offered for sale by Benjamin D. Wilson in 1876. Courtesy, Mrs. Robert H. Peterson

The first of the Orange Grove mansions was the Edwin F. Hurlbut house, built in 1882. Named Casa Propia, *the graceful Italianate structure was situated on the east side of Orange Grove between Bellefontaine and Columbia streets. It was the scene in 1885 of a major social event: the marriage of Jessie Banbury to Dr. F. DeW. Crank, which united two of Pasadena's most prominent pioneer families. Courtesy, Pasadena Historical Society*

deal with Wilson as though nothing were amiss, and meanwhile reassuring the Indianans of his honesty. In the end, the deed for the land was finally made to Thomas Croft on the day after Christmas, 1873, for $6,250 cash down, with $18,750 to be paid within a year. Croft's diary laconically records the following days: "December 28: Attended Church. December 29: Make deed San Pascual Rancho to San Gabriel Orange Grove Association. January 2: Got wagon at $2.00." The new settlement had begun.

Once the land had been purchased, the next step was to divide it equitably among the various investors. Calvin Fletcher, member of the original California Colony of Indiana, arrived from Indianapolis the day the land was deeded to Croft and began at once to survey and subdivide. Elliott credits Fletcher with laying out the streets and lots as "a charming landscape garden with all the evergreen trees reserved on the avenues and the roads and parks diverted to save the live oaks." Fletcher's drawing served as Pasadena's first city plan.

The principal north-south street, named Park Avenue (now Orange Grove Boulevard), was laid out at an angle to save two large live oak trees in the middle of the street. Fletcher's plan called for a series of parks down the middle of the street, to be planted with orange trees. All lots fronted on Park Avenue and ran east to Fair Oaks or west to the Arroyo. At the foot of Park at Columbia Street was the school site and farther south at Mission Street was a park named Sylvan Square. The live oaks to the southwest along the banks of the Arroyo were set aside as Live Oak Park, to be used by the community as a whole. Land to the north, beyond present-day Lincoln Avenue and including Altadena, was also owned communally.

On January 27, 1874, those investors who were in California gathered on the knoll southwest of the present intersection of Walnut and Orange Grove to choose their land. Other investors, including Dr. Elliott, sent proxies. Two years later Dr. Elliott described the scene: "The day was, as is usual in this climate, pleasant. Good cheer, bread, cakes and meats were in full force; so were the members of the Association and their families, also some guests from the city and the Fruit Belt." The smallest shareholders were given first choice, and as the land was spoken for, an unusual harmony prevailed. Everyone seemed to be satisfied with his share, making an auspicious beginning to the new settlement.

Even before the division of the land had been completed, work had begun on laying the water system. In January, Berry, Fletcher, and two other Indianans, A.O. Porter and Perry M. Green, were planting grape cuttings and laying pipe. Instead of relying on the more common ditch irrigation system, the settlers decided to use pipe, which would be much more reliable and save water besides. This water system, supplied from springs and mountain streams, was an important factor in Pasadena's early prosperity.

Thomas Croft is credited with having turned the first furrow with his new plow, and houses began to spring up almost immediately. Albert O. Bristol's house, a board and batten cottage at the corner of Orange Grove and Lincoln Avenue, was the first house completed. It was finished within two weeks after the division of land. John Baker's house on Fair Oaks was completed within a month and Colonel Jabez Banbury's more elaborate dwelling was finished in early March. About this time the harmonious spirit of the settlement was clouded by complaints about their land from newly-arrived Indiana investors Vawter and Leavitt. Berry's patience had worn thin, for he wrote, "and now [they] want a new deal after a month had passed, and three houses are up and there is [sic] 100 acres plowed." Both investors soon sold their land at a good profit and were apparently satisfied.

Berry and a number of the other landholders subdivided and sold off considerable portions of their holdings during that first year, in part to meet the payments due to Griffin and also to help pay for the water system, the cost of which was assessed to property owners. Building and planting also required capital, and investments in fruit trees and grape cuttings could not be expected to pay off for several years. The settlers needed other sources of income to live on until their orange trees and grapevines began to bear.

By the close of 1875, less than two years after the founding of the village, forty houses were up and 10,000 young orange and lemon trees had been planted. Several thousand deciduous fruit trees had been set out, as well as olive trees and 150,000 grapevines. The roads were bordered by ornamental trees—pepper trees, Monterey cypress, and eucalyptus—demonstrating the villagers' concern for the beautification of their town.

In 1876, with only a few parcels of the San Gabriel Orange Grove Association lands remaining for sale, Benjamin Wilson subdivided the Lake Vineyard Land and Water Company Tract, a portion of his land east of the original settlement. Wilson priced his land at $75 an acre, more than ten times the price the San Gabriel Association had paid. The land extended east from Fair Oaks almost to present-day Wilson Avenue, and was referred to by the settlers as the "east side." Water was brought in from Wilson's ditch to serve the new lands.

Orange growing had been the dream of the Indiana settlers, and it became the mainstay of the

Early San Gabriel Valley settler Abbot Kinney raised blood oranges, an exotic variety, and sold small trees for others to plant. Here workers harvest a crop. Courtesy, The Huntington Library

new community. The San Gabriel Valley was already known for producing premium oranges that brought the highest prices at market. The rich sandy loam retained moisture, providing ideal growing conditions, and the climate was dependably frost-free. The San Gabriel Valley orange kept well when shipped over long distances. Shorb boasted of oranges he had sent to London in 1875 arriving in good condition, and at about the same time, an article in the *New York Evening Post* praised the firmness and flavor of Sunny Slope oranges.

An orchard of only ten acres was considered enough to provide a net income of about $10,000 a year, after expenses. While seedlings took ten to twelve years to mature, older trees could be planted, shortening the time from planting to harvest. The groves were cultivated regularly during the summer months, and plowed twice, in the spring and in the fall. There was much controversy over irrigation methods, but two methods seemed to be most popular. The first was a type of drip irrigation, which fed water slowly and evenly to each tree through a small hole in the irrigation pipe. The second required digging a basin around the tree at the drip line and flooding the basin with water at regular intervals. Pasadena's pipe water system was recognized as the most efficient in the county, using the least amount of water to achieve maximum growth and production.

While waiting for trees to mature and bear fruit, the farmer could plant and harvest crops such as corn, pumpkins, squash, or melons. Or he could plant half of his land in orange trees, using the other half to grow grain or other cash crops. Insects, gophers, and rabbits were threats to the young trees, and various sprays made of tobacco, kerosene, or brine were used to ward off the pests.

Author Jeanne Carr, shown here with her husband Dr. Ezra Carr, was the leading cultural figure in the early days of the Pasadena settlement. An expert in horticulture, Jeanne Carr planted numerous exotic plants and trees on the grounds of her home, Carmelita. Courtesy, Pasadena Public Library

A mixture of animal blood and water applied to the base of the trees was said to be offensive to rabbits, and gophers were combatted with traps and by flooding the ground two or three times a year.

The small farmer could do most of the work himself on his ten-acre plot, but when picking time came, he had to rely on hired help. The well-known artist, Charles Walter Stetson, who lived in Pasadena some time later, described the scene on an April morning in 1889:

Early this morning the gang of Chinese and Mexicans came here to pick the oranges. It was wonderful to see the Chinamen pack them. The Mexicans picked and carried them in bags to the Chinese. A boxer made the boxes in the grove and the Chinamen took each orange and wrapped it in tissue paper and put it in the box. The rapidity with which they did it was something wonderful.

Larger growers employed women in packing-houses that were often located near the railroad line. Although soil and climate were eminently well-suited to wine grapes, the early Pasadenans planted mostly raisin grapes, probably because they frowned on alcohol consumption. Other fruits, such as apricots, peaches, pears, figs, prunes, nectarines, plums, and cherries were grown, as well as nuts, especially walnuts and almonds. Barley grew as a volunteer [self-seeding] crop, especially on the San Rafael hills and north of the village on the flat mesa land near Woodbury Road east of Devil's Gate. Stetson described the stacks of barley as enormous. "They use a kind of derrick for hauling the straw to the top. Some of the stacks must be a hundred and fifty feet long."

Besides growing crops, many of the early settlers planted magnificent gardens, beginning a tradition that was to give Pasadena its reputation as a "city of gardens." One of the most famous gardens in

Carmelita, Dr. and Mrs. Carr's estate at Orange Grove Avenue and Colorado Street, was the cultural center of early Pasadena. Mrs. Carr's gardens and her literary salons drew many visitors, including naturalist John Muir and author Helen Hunt Jackson. Mrs. Carr also took in boarders, but she was finally forced to sell the property in 1892 for financial reasons. Subsequent owners built a new house at Carmelita, which served as the home of the Pasadena Art Institute for many years. Courtesy, The Huntington Library

the early years was Carmelita, which was planned and planted by Jeanne Carr, horticulturist and leading cultural figure in early Pasadena. A native of Vermont, Mrs. Carr had moved to Oakland, California, with her husband, Dr. Ezra Carr, a noted physician, chemist, and geologist at the University of Wisconsin, who accepted an appointment at the University of California in 1869. Dr. Carr became superintendent of Public Instruction for the state of California in 1875, and shortly thereafter, on a trip to Southern California, the Carrs became enchanted with the new settlement on the San Pasqual Ranch.

An old friend, Dr. Orville H. Congar, had settled in Pasadena, and urged the Carrs to do the same. Mrs. Carr had spied a forty-two-acre plot, belonging to Mrs. Vawter, at the northeast corner of Colorado and Orange Grove Avenue and stretching east to Fair Oaks, which she thought would make a fine homestead. Convinced that the Carrs

Abbot Kinney's imposing mansion looked out across his fruit orchards, vineyards, and the ranch he named Kinneloa. He and his wife raised a large family on the ranch and the subdivided property still carries the name Kinney gave it in the 1880s. Courtesy, The Huntington Library

would be an important asset to the village, Congar did all he could to facilitate the purchase of the land. In his letters to Mrs. Carr, Congar called the community "intelligent and enterprising" and relayed offers by Los Angeles nurserymen to provide fruit and other trees gratis to Mrs. Carr. He offered the Carrs use of water from his own reservoir and guaranteed to buy their land from them at no loss, should they change their minds. Congar completed the negotiations for the sale in February 1877, but a stroke suffered by Dr. Carr caused the Carrs to delay their move to Pasadena.

As early as 1877, however, Jeanne Carr made a complete map of Carmelita, determining the location of roads, house, orchards, vineyard, flower beds, hedges, and shade trees on the weedy sheep pasture. The first house was built in 1880, a four-room barn, but five years later she was able to sell her Fair Oaks frontage for $2,000 an acre, realizing enough to build a fine house on the high ground at Orange Grove and Colorado. By 1883, Jeanne Carr had fifty-six varieties of grapes, more than a thousand citrus trees, over a thousand fruit trees of various kinds, two hundred nut trees—including walnuts, almonds, butternuts, beechnuts, chestnuts, hickory nuts, pecans, and filberts—and twenty mulberry trees for silk culture. The estate boasted specimens of all the coniferous trees of the Pacific Coast as well as numerous exotics, which lined the drives and roadways. Jeanne Carr was instrumental in convincing Pasadenans to plant hedges instead of fencing their property, and she herself had the most interesting hedges in town. Along Orange Grove Avenue she planted Mexican limes behind the row of pepper trees lining the street, and along Colorado Street roses and grapevines climbed in profusion over a row of four-foot Monterey cypress trees. The effect was to create, in her words, "a touch of wildness, as well as to secure plenteous bloom in spring and color for autumn thoughts."

A great lover of trees, Jeanne Carr planted pines first of all, to remind her of her Vermont childhood, and to listen to them "whisper" to her while she worked. The Spanish name *carmel* (grove) became *Carmelita* (little grove), an appropriate title for her magnificent collection of trees and plants, said to be the best in Southern California. Friends from all over the world sent or brought her seeds or seedlings to add to her collection, and John Muir was one of those who contributed to her stock. Jeanne Carr was the famous naturalist's mentor, and the two carried on a lively correspondence until her death in 1903.

Other notable early gardens were those of Abbot Kinney at Kinneloa and Charles Hastings at Hastings Ranch. Kinney, a tobacco millionaire, came to California for his health in 1880 and purchased 500 acres of dry mesa land near Eaton Canyon, naming the estate "Kinneloa" *(loa* means "hill" in Polynesian). Well-traveled, educated in the great European universities, and well-connected in Eastern political and social circles, Kinney proceeded to create a country estate in the grand manner. He tunneled into the mountainside to obtain water, planted thousands of fruit trees and grapevines, as well as exotic plants from all over the world. He was especially fond of the eucalyptus, experimenting with new varieties and also writing a book about the species. He attributed its introduction to California to his friend Jeanne Carr. An ardent conservationist, Kinney served as chairman of the State Board of Forestry and of a state commission on Yosemite Valley. In Southern California, Kinney is best remembered as the visionary developer of Venice.

Charles Houston Hastings inherited Hastings Ranch from his father, a department store magnate, in 1884. The younger Hastings, a graduate of Cornell University in horticulture, turned the ranch into a garden of rare plants, many imported from India. Hastings was also a collector of fine horses and dogs, which he kept on the ranch.

Early social life in Pasadena centered around the churches. The Presbyterians founded the first church, constructing a small frame building in 1876 near California and Orange Grove, which was developing as the center of the village. In 1877, the Methodists finished their church just north of the intersection. By the mid-1880s, most

Below: *Pasadena's second school, Central School, was built in 1878 on the corner of Fair Oaks Avenue and Colorado Street on property donated by Benjamin Wilson. This building and a store across the street became the nucleus of Pasadena's business district. Courtesy, Security Pacific National Bank Photograph Collection, Los Angeles Public Library*

Right: *Pasadena's first schoolteacher, Jennie Clapp, held classes in her parents' home on Orange Grove Avenue in the fall of 1874. In one month, her class grew from two to nineteen students. Courtesy, Pasadena Public Library*

Students and faculty of Miss Orton's Classical School for Girls pose in front of the school on South Euclid Avenue in about 1895. A Vassar graduate and daughter of a Vassar professor, Anna B. Orton prepared her students for entrance to prestigious Eastern colleges. Courtesy, The Huntington Library

of the major denominations were represented in Pasadena; the Episcopalians, Society of Friends, Baptists, Disciples of Christ, Universalists, Congregationalists, Catholics, and African Methodist Episcopalians all had organized churches.

The first concern of the settlers, however, was to establish a school. In the fall of 1874, Jennie Clapp, the daughter of William Clapp, began formal instruction at the Clapp home on Orange Grove. A small one-room schoolhouse, located on the Clapp property, was finished in January 1875, and in 1876 it was moved to a new five-acre site at Colorado and Fair Oaks, donated by Benjamin Wilson. The new location, however, was deemed too far by those living on the south end of town. The "southsiders" formed their own school district, building a school on Columbia Hill, which became the nucleus of the new community of South Pasadena.

Pasadenans were not long content with a simple school, however. The steady growth of the community led to the building of a two-story school building with a bell and an upstairs community meeting hall in 1878. In 1884, a group of residents, including Abbot Kinney, Judge Eaton, and Charles C. Hastings, decided to establish Sierra Madre College. The Columbia Hill school was offered by the people of the school district as a location, and the college operated there from 1885 to 1887 before failing due to financial difficulties. Despite this failure, the founding of the college had important historic consequences for Pasadena. Professor Charles Holden, who had come to Pasadena to be on the Sierra Madre faculty, became a professor at Throop University and later founded the Tournament of Roses. Professor M.M. Parker, another faculty member, founded a college preparatory academy that eventually merged with Throop, the forerunner of Pasadena's most renowned educational institution, the California Institute of Technology.

The relocation of the village school and the settling of Wilson's Lake Vineyard Tract moved the center of the community from the intersection of California and Orange Grove to Colorado and Fair Oaks. This was further reinforced by the establishment of L.D. Hollingsworth's general store near the northeast corner of Fair Oaks and Colorado. An earlier store on Colorado near Orange Grove had been forced to close when its owner, Moritz Rosenbaum, began selling liquor. Rosenbaum then rented the empty building to Yuen Kee, who operated a laundry there, the first Chinese-owned business to be founded in Pasadena.

Hollingsworth originally wanted to build his store and post office on the high ground of his property at Marengo and Colorado, but pressure from those on the "west side" along Orange Grove Avenue convinced him to move it farther west, near the corner of Fair Oaks and Colorado. The store and post office opened in September 1876, with Hollingsworth's son, Henry, as postmaster. At the same time, Benjamin Wilson made his gift of five acres for a school across Colorado Street, and the nucleus of Pasadena's business center was established. Named for the newest state in the Union, Colorado Street was destined to become the principal commercial artery of the town.

With the opening of the post office, the name Pasadena was officially recorded. In April 1875, the name was voted on and accepted by the members of the San Gabriel Orange Grove Association. The name "Indiana Colony" persisted, however, and Jennie Giddings claims in her memoirs that at the time of the establishment of the post office a petition was circulated, again offering a choice of names for the village. Pasadena was the choice of the majority once more, and the issue was finally settled.

Abbot Kinney was the principal force behind the organization in 1882 of the Pasadena Library and Village Improvement Society, which was formed to establish a library and to discuss such questions as the planting of trees and construction of walks and drives. Pasadena was not yet an incorporated community, so public improvements were achieved by persuasion and cooperation among the villagers. The reasons given for founding a library were outlined in an 1885 Citrus Fair

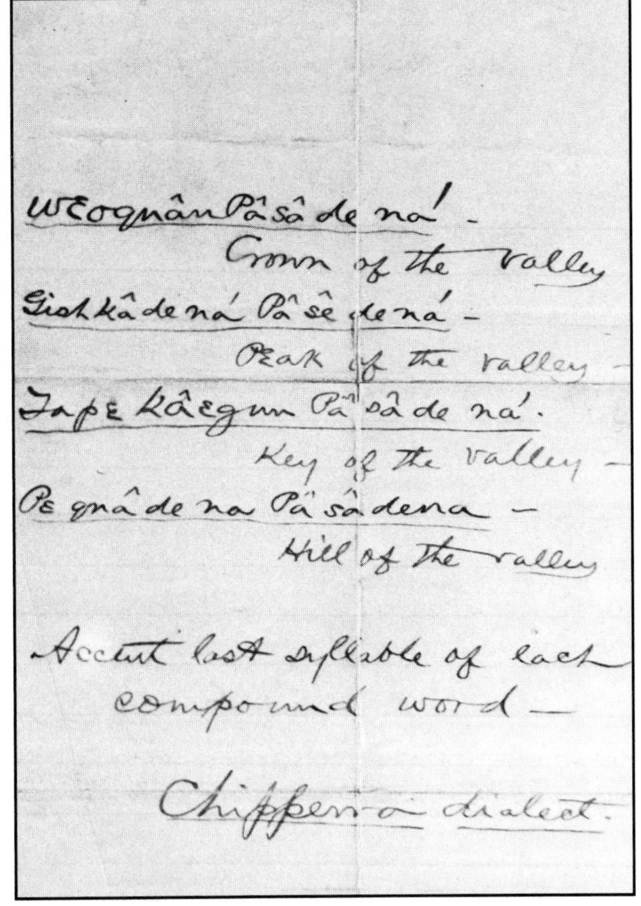

Weoqnân Pä sâ de na! -
Crown of the valley
Gishkâ de ná Pä sê de ná -
Peak of the valley -
Tapekâegun Pä sâ de ná.
Key of the valley -
Pe quâ de na Pä sâ dena -
Hill of the valley

Accent last syllable of each compound word -

Chippewa dialect.

Left: *This fragment of a letter preserved in the Pasadena Historical Society library records the origins of the name Pasadena. The fragment is a copy, written in an unknown hand, on the reverse of the original letter sent by Midwestern missionary George Smith to the Indiana colonists. Smith provided the colonists with the Chippewa translations of their proposed names for the new town: Crown of the Valley, Peak of the Valley, Key of the Valley, and Hill of the Valley. In the end, only the final element, "Pa sa de na,"* meaning *"the valley"* was chosen. Courtesy, *Pasadena Historical Society*

Below: *Taken shortly before the boom of the 1880s, this photograph of South Fair Oaks Avenue shows the typical small frame buildings of the time. By 1888, many of these would be replaced by substantial brick buildings constructed during the optimistic boom period. Courtesy, Pasadena Public Library*

pamphlet, and they testify to the values and interests of the community. As few had the resources to acquire large personal libraries, the founding of a common library was deemed "a good business move." Periodicals and newspapers would help the villagers keep up with the world. The library would be a pleasant place for women and children and for "those young men who, having some leisure . . . too often drift into resorts of pernicious influence morally and physically." For the tourists and invalids who were already coming to Pasadena in significant numbers, it would provide a pleasant place to visit, and since they were important to Pasadena's prosperity, "anything that would attract and retain them seemed a good business investment."

Part of Wilson's school lot was donated for the two-story frame library building, erected in 1884. Money was raised from contributions and from fund-raising events, such as the Art Loan Exhibition, which featured local collections and work by local artists. When the library opened it had just over 300 volumes, but by the time of the Second Citrus Fair of 1885, held to raise funds for the library, there were 1,700 volumes, many of them donated by members of the community.

The Literary Society, formed in 1875, provided an outlet for reading and discussion in the early days. It also spawned Pasadena's first newspaper, *The Reservoir,* a handwritten collection of humorous tales based on events and people in the village. The Pomological Society, a scientific society of a sort, was organized in 1876 to exchange information on the best methods of orange culture and fruit growing. The first paper, given by Perry M. Green, was on the topic of irrigation, and later papers covered other subjects of interest to growers.

This exchange of information was important, for as Jeanne Carr noted about the settlers: "There was not a professional, and hardly a practical, horticulturist or farmer among them; but the spell of the neighboring orchards and vineyards soon transformed them into enthusiastic culturists of the orange and the vine." An early settler, Jennie Collier, writing home to Iowa, reported, "Doctors, lawyers, mechanics, Colonels and Majors are plentiful, but they can all don blue overalls and turn the soil for their fruit trees as if 'to the manner born.'" An Eastern visitor was heard to remark: "What a highly educated lot of farmers you have out here. Do they all talk so learnedly?"

Cultural life in the colony centered around Carmelita, where Mrs. Carr received distinguished guests and where she produced numerous articles on a variety of subjects: horticulture, conservation, botany, American Indians, and history. After visiting Mrs. Carr and his college-mate, Dr. Congar, in 1877, John Muir wrote:

The Pasadena Colony . . . is scarce three years old, but it is growing rapidly into importance, like a pet tree, and already forms one of the best contributions to culture yet accomplished in the county. . . . There is nothing more remarkable in the character of the colony than the literary and scientific taste displayed. The conversation of most I have met here is seasoned with a smack of mental ozone, attic salt, which struck me as being rare among the tillers of California soil. People of taste and money in search of a home would do well to prospect the resources of this aristocratic little colony.

Besides John Muir, Helen Hunt Jackson, author of the California romance *Ramona,* visited Pasadena, staying at Carmelita. Mrs. Jackson traveled the countryside with Mrs. Carr and with Abbot Kinney, taking some of the inspiration for her book from the people and scenery around Pasadena.

Another notable writer who settled in Pasadena in 1876 was Margaret Collier Graham. Mrs. Graham, who came to Pasadena because of her husband's poor health, wrote stories and articles for national magazines such as *Atlantic Monthly, Century, Scribner's Monthly,* and *Overland Monthly.* Her husband, Donald Graham, an attorney, ran the mail service between Los Angeles and Pasadena for a time, astonishing his passengers with his knowledge of Greek, Hebrew, and Latin.

Author and sportsman Charles Frederick Holder was an important figure in early Pasadena. Together with Dr. Francis F. Rowland, he founded the Tournament of Roses. An avid hunter and fisherman, he also authored many pamphlets and articles extolling Pasadena. Courtesy, Pasadena Public Library

Abbot Kinney was also an author, writing on such varied subjects as political economy, eugenics, education, and horticulture. Fluent in several languages, he served as Spanish interpreter for Helen Hunt Jackson as she interviewed California Indians, and translated a book from the French on the American Civil War for President U.S. Grant. Horatio N. Rust of Chicago, a leading abolitionist and collector of American Indian artifacts, wrote on such topics as the Southwest Indians, the family of John Brown, and horticulture in Southern California. Charles Frederick Holder was a distinguished zoologist, and the author of several important scientific works as well as articles for scientific journals and the popular press. Noted artist William F. Cogswell, whose portrait of Abraham Lincoln hangs in the White House, settled just east of Pasadena on an estate which he named Sierra Madre Villa and which eventually became the Sierra Madre Villa Hotel.

Although the village had only one store, a blacksmith's shop, a school, two churches, and a Chinese laundry in 1876, growth was stimulated by the increasing stream of health-seekers and tourists. Tuberculosis was a feared incurable disease at the time, and the pure dry air of Southern California was believed to be beneficial. Popular literature also ascribed cures of other respiratory ailments to the sunny California climate. The San Gabriel Valley had acquired a reputation as the "Great Orange Belt and Sanatarium," according to John Baur in his book *The Health Seekers.* Invalids were already in the valley in 1874 when Berry described "a Boston man who came here with hemorrhage of lungs, nearly dead, also his aunt in the same condition. Both got well and think of returning to Boston to get sick again."

Berry himself probably came to California for health reasons, as he suffered from asthma and had been sick with respiratory problems in the winter of 1868-1869. In his letters he intimates that his wife, Marcia, died of a respiratory ailment in Indiana. Some of the earliest letters preserved from Pasadena, written by Margaret Collier Graham and her sister, Jennie Collier, record the lives of the invalids in the little village. The Grahams, who first boarded with Mrs. R.C. Locke in Pasadena, later rented part of a house, where they also began to take in boarders, invalids from the East.

The Grahams socialized with their guests, prepared them special food such as boiled milk and toast, made excursions with them into the canyons, and read to those lying in bed to help them keep up their spirits. Jennie Collier described a curious croquet game: "The boarders, sick and well, turned out and tramped down a ground in front of the house. They are a 'spooky' looking set when they are all out together but we try to have at least two well men on the ground just to keep up the credit of the house." She also described the scene around the post office as the invalids congregated, sitting "coughing upon the steps or leaning against the walls with eager anxious faces,

Sierra Madre Villa Hotel opened in 1887 as the first real hotel in the Pasadena area. Several prominent residents of the hotel found Pasadena so enchanting that they returned to live permanently in the area. Among them was Abbot Kinney, who purchased a ranch west of the hotel. Courtesy, The Huntington Library

waiting, hoping for letters from home." Most were men and alone. If wealthy, they lodged in boarding-houses or hotels. Some, however, lived in rude cabins in the hills, fending for themselves, while others bought small farms, and settled in.

An Eastern writer, quoted by Baur, described the invalids as "a combination of ill-health, intellectuality, and comfortable circumstances. Orange culture is eminently adapted to their condition and circumstances. They can sit on the verandas of their pretty cottages . . . inhaling the pure air of the equal climate, reading novels or abstruse works of philosophy . . . and waiting from year to year for their oranges to grow." Some early accounts seem to indicate that many were also escaping the stress and physical confinement of traditional

Lucky Baldwin (second from right) purchased the eastern portion of the Santa Anita Ranch, including Hugo Reid's adobe ranch house, in 1875. Baldwin had made his fortune in a legendary silver mine, the Comstock Lode. Today his part of Santa Anita Ranch encompasses the site of the Los Angeles County Arboretum, Santa Anita Race Track, and the city of Arcadia. Courtesy, Pasadena Historical Society

middle-class occupations in the East, and actively seeking a simpler rural life. It was believed that farmwork in the pure clean air would cure the lungs of disease and relieve nervous tension in the overworked businessman.

The first real hotel in the area was Sierra Madre Villa, which began as a large house set on 500 acres on the mesa just east of Kinneloa. The land was purchased by William Porter Rhoades and his father-in-law, artist William F. Cogswell, in 1874. They built a comfortable house, planted the grounds in orchards and vineyards, and landscaped with rose gardens and ornamental trees. The house remained a private home until 1877, when the James F. Crank family arrived from Denver, seeking a healthful climate for the ailing Mrs. Crank. The Cranks stayed with the Rhoades, and during this time, a twenty-room addition with a long glass-enclosed veranda transformed the ranch house into a full-fledged hotel.

The hotel soon became an important social center, attracting guests from around the world. Famous for its hospitality, beautiful site, and eminent clientele, the hotel was also known for its fine foods and genial host, William Porter Rhoades. Activities for the guests included horseback riding or driving through the surrounding countryside, hunting and fishing, and, in the evenings, dancing parties and musicales. Guests came for a week, for a month, or for the whole season, and their ranks included such names as Ulysses S. Grant, Collis P. Huntington, the Crocker and Mark Hopkins families of San Francisco, as well as English financiers with interests in Southern California. When tobacco millionaire Abbot Kinney visited Sierra Madre Villa in 1880, he put up a sleeping tent in a eucalyptus grove on the grounds, filling it with beautiful rugs and furnishings. Like many health-seekers, Kinney believed that sleeping in the open air would cure his respiratory ailments. He was so enchanted with the setting that he soon decided to purchase the mesa to the west, which became his ranch, Kinneloa.

In the early 1880s, large excursion groups from Boston sponsored by Raymond and Whitcomb Travel Agents began arriving in Los Angeles. They made regular excursions out to the San Gabriel Valley, taking lunch at Sierra Madre Villa and then visiting Lucky Baldwin's ranch and winery, Rose's Sunny Slope, Shorb's winery, and the San Gabriel Mission. This greatly increased business at the hotel, and fifty more rooms were added. But the intimate home atmosphere was gone, and for Mr. Rhoades, who had reveled in socializing with his guests, the place had become too big. The Rhoades sold the hotel to William G. Cogswell, brother of Mrs. Rhoades. It later changed hands again, and was converted into a sanatarium, which was operated until 1923. A remnant of the hotel still stands on Old House Road in northeast Pasadena.

Besides literary and cultural pursuits and avid gardening, early Pasadenans enjoyed the out of doors, hunting, fishing, and camping in the local mountains. One of the first persons to hike in the local mountains was John Muir, who described the Sierra Madre as one of the most inaccessible ranges he had ever seen. Walking was difficult because of the dense growth of chapparal. A highlight of his hike was Eaton Falls, which he described as "a charming little thing, with a low sweet voice, singing like a bird as it pours from a notch in a short ledge some thirty-five or forty feet into a round-mirror pool." The falls were surrounded by delicate ferns and mosses, and overhung with sycamore trees. Muir, famous for his hardiness, camped in the canyon, sleeping on a bed of "smooth cobblestones."

The Indians had developed a network of trails in the mountains, and the Spaniards, Mexicans, and early American settlers had penetrated the mountains primarily to hunt and for timber. Benjamin Wilson, needing wood for fences and wine barrels, had a trail built up through Little Santa Anita Canyon to Wilson's Peak. Although not used much by Wilson, this trail became the main route used by hikers and riders for outings in the early days.

In her memoirs, Jennie Hollingsworth Giddings describes a trip up Wilson's Trail by horseback

Campers relax at Strain's camp atop Mt. Wilson in the early 1890s. Camps like Strain's, Martin's, and Switzer's offered meals and accommodations in tent cabins to hikers and riders. Later Strain's and Martin's housed astronomers and construction workers in the early days of the Mt. Wilson Observatory. Strain's finally closed in 1914. Courtesy, Pasadena Public Library

with some friends in 1880. The first part of the trail, from Sierra Madre to Halfway House, was steep and dusty. Halfway House, a small one-room shack, had been built by Wilson's men as a construction camp, and Mrs. Giddings describes the settlement as having an abandoned blacksmith shop and a neglected apple orchard. The trail led up from Halfway House "through slopes and vales of bosky beauty." Later the riders made their way over a slide area of loose stones. "Beyond this shaly portion the trail curved around huge mountain shoulders crossing steep escarpments where we gazed down thousands of feet into the depths of Eaton Canyon . . . . Farther up our way led through more open country." The hikers spent the night at the top in a log cabin, cooking on a campfire. Telling stories round the campfire at night and feasting on freshly caught trout were high points in this early camping experience.

Mrs. Giddings' brother-in-law, Eugene Giddings, had a ranch up near Millard Canyon. He eventually built a toll road to Millard Falls, a popular destination for picnickers in the early days. One early resident recalled that Pasadenans drove up into the canyons in lumber wagons to picnic beside the rushing streams and waterfalls.

Brown Trail, named for Jason and Owen Brown, sons of John Brown of Harper's Ferry fame, was also a gateway to the mountains. The brothers had a ranch at Las Casitas (above the present Loma Alta Drive in Altadena), where they kept pack animals and served as guides for tourists. Owen, the last surviving member of the Harper's Ferry raid, was a celebrated figure in Pasadena, and his mountain grave is still visited by hikers.

The rugged but beautiful Arroyo Seco Canyon was opened up for tourists in 1884, when Commodore Perry Switzer established a camp above what is now known as Switzer's Falls. According to John W. Robinson, whose book *The San Gabriels* provides a wealth of information on early resorts and camps, Switzer's was the first tourist resort in the San Gabriel Mountains and one of the most popular. Tourists traveled by stage to Las Casitas and there hired horses or burros for the trip to the camp. The visitors slept in tents or rough cabins and spent their days hiking, fishing, or just plain loafing in the sylvan glade. The Arroyo Seco was a favorite stream for trout fishing, and meals in the camp's log cookhouse often featured trout. Although Switzer's was probably far too civilized for his tastes, John Muir visited it in the 1880s, noting that "here one may sleep on a bed of fragrant fir branches," no doubt more comfortable than the stones of Eaton Canyon.

Hunting was a popular sport, and in some cases a necessity, in the 1870s and 1880s. Eugene Giddings described shooting a grizzly bear that had been robbing his honey stands. Black bears and cinnamon bears were also listed in Professor Holder's catalogue of local fauna which appeared in Hiram

Above: *Jason and Owen Brown, sons of abolitionist John Brown, settled in the Pasadena foothills in the 1880s. Owen fought with his father at Harper's Ferry. Affectionately called the "Brown Boys," they were welcomed as heroes in Pasadena, home of many abolitionists and Union veterans. Courtesy, California Historical Society/Ticor Title Insurance (Los Angeles)*

Opposite: *"Getting away from it all" in Pasadena's early days meant camping in the neighboring mountains. Here the Elliott-Bandini family poses in front of their tent in 1889. Left to right are Arturo Bandini, his wife Helen Elliott Bandini, her mother Mrs. Thomas Balch Elliott, Ralph Bandini (child in foreground), Whittier Elliott, and Agnes Elliott. Courtesy, The Huntington Library*

Reid's *History of Pasadena* (1895). In an essay on hunting and fishing, Holder listed deer, mountain lion, wildcat, badger, fox, and coyote as big game animals for the huntsman in the early 1880s. Smaller quarry included quail, pigeon, dove, and water birds, as well as cottontails and jackrabbits.

Rabbit coursing had begun in the Mexican period, and its popularity continued under the Americans. Raymond Hill was the site for meets attended by Mexican and American gentry of old Los Angeles, who set their greyhounds on the numerous jackrabbits there. Mary Agnes Crank recalled that "there were no fences and few cultivated fields to prevent a good run across country." The hunters were led by Arturo Bandini, a local sheep rancher who had married Dr. Elliott's daughter, and the popular pastime was eventually institutionalized by the founding of the Valley Hunt Club in 1888.

The founding of Pasadena in 1874, and its development by the industrious settlers, had not only increased the value of Benjamin Wilson's land to seventy-five dollars an acre, it had also created great interest in surrounding tracts. In 1880 Caspar T. Hopkins of San Francisco purchased the Olivewood Tract, a parcel of eighty acres bounded by the present-day streets of Colorado, Lake, El Molino, and Villa. An attempt was made to develop Olivewood in the boom of 1886, but it did not really experience growth until the early 1900s. In 1881, John H. Painter and Benjamin F. Ball purchased 2,000 acres, the old Henry G. Monk property, which comprised all of north Pasadena between Lake Avenue and the Arroyo. The tract, known as the Painter and Ball Tract, was purchased for fifteen dollars an acre, with no wa-

The Valley Hunt Club was formed by early settlers who enjoyed riding to hounds, a tradition made popular in Southern California in the Mexican period. Today the club is chiefly remembered for its role in the founding of the Tournament of Roses in 1890. Courtesy, Pasadena Tournament of Roses Licensing

ter on it. Painter and Ball built the water supply system, and sold off parcels for three times their original investment.

In 1883, the San Rafael Ranch lands west of the Arroyo were purchased by the Campbell-Johnston family, and by Professor J.D. Yocum (present-day San Rafael and Linda Vista). Yocum cleared the land, put in water and streets and sold off some parcels. However, Linda Vista was far from the town center, and suffered from poor road and transportation connections. It remained largely rural until the 1920s. San Rafael Ranch was run as a ranch until about 1920. Vineyards were planted and a winery was established. The most notable building on the property was the Church of the Angels, a beautiful stone church designed by English architect Arthur Edmund Street. It was built by Mrs. Campbell-Johnston as a memorial to her husband, Alexander, who died at the ranch in 1888. The church still remains on Avenue Sixty-four south of La Loma Road, one of the few stone buildings in Pasadena.

During its first decade Pasadena had grown from a settlement of twenty-odd families to a village of several hundred persons. It was known by various names, first the California Colony of Indiana, later Muscat, then the San Gabriel Orange Grove Association, and, popularly, the Indiana Colony. The adoption of the euphonious Indian name, Pasadena, in 1875, and the establishment of the Pasadena post office near Fair Oaks and Colorado the following year, were the initial steps in creating the city. The school and the library, as well as several churches, furthered the cohesiveness of the community. Tourists and health-seekers had already discovered the San Gabriel Valley, and a number of them settled in Pasadena. Well-educated and sometimes well-to-do, some of these newcomers contributed much to the cultural life of the community. For the most part, however, Pasadena was a quiet village of orchards (as citrus groves were then called), its residents unprepared for the great land boom of the mid-1880s that would permanently change the life and economy of the community.

One of Pasadena's most noted early authors, Margaret Collier Graham, poses here with her sister Jennie (center) and her nephew Will on an outing to Echo Mountain. Courtesy, Mary Collier Wayne

Chapter III

Known as the "Royal Raymond," the Raymond Hotel was the largest and most elegant of Pasadena's early hotels. Many of its guests were New Englanders, brought to Pasadena by Raymond and Whitcomb tours, a Boston travel firm. Courtesy, Pasadena Public Library

The Flourishing Resort

"The town makes me think of a bee-hive.
It is all bustle and business and building.
Such an enterprising, striving place it is;
one can see it grow daily.
It seems bound to be a city
and even now to assume the dignity of a city,
as children love to play 'grown up.'"

–Amy Bridges, 1887

In the mid-1880s Pasadena changed, almost overnight, from a sleepy agricultural village of orange groves into a bustling resort town, replete with sophisticated hotels, fancy brick commercial buildings, railroad connections and trolley lines, and a number of elaborate mansions. Pasadenans also gained control over their own affairs by incorporating as a city "of the sixth class" in 1886. The great Southern California land boom of 1886-1888 reached a fever pitch of speculation in Pasadena, stimulating the growth of the city far beyond the wildest dreams of the early settlers. The population of 392 souls, mostly recorded as orchardists in the 1880 census, jumped to an estimated 12,000-15,000 at the height of the real estate boom before settling at around 5,000 in 1890. The continuing influx of tourists from the East, many of whom bought property in Pasadena, ensured a steady pace of growth throughout the 1890s. By the turn of the century, Pasadena boasted several millionaires among its population of close to 10,000; an opera house; a new university; excellent schools, both public and private; social and cultural clubs; and many imposing churches.

In the early 1880s, Pasadena had already begun to evolve from an agricultural community into a town. In 1883, a newspaper, the *Pasadena Chronicle,* was founded, and the first telephone was installed at Barney Williams' new two-story store on the northeast corner of Colorado and Fair Oaks. (Williams had taken over Hollingsworth's store and post office but built his new store farther west, at the real center of town.) Just across from the store, two frame hotels rose in 1883, the Los Angeles House on the northwest corner and the Pasadena House on the southwest. And in 1883, work began on Pasadena's grandest hotel, the Raymond, a massive five-story structure of 200 rooms, sited on the prominent Bacon Hill south of town. Shortly before ground was broken for the Raymond, James F. Crank got together a group of investors and organized the Los Angeles and San Gabriel Valley Railroad to build a line from Los Angeles to Pasadena. In 1883 Pasadenans also began to feel the need for stronger community organization, for although there was no crime to speak of, a constable was elected to protect the citizenry. In the same year, the San Gabriel Orange Grove Association passed out of existence, its stipulated ten-year lifetime over, leaving no formal community organization to replace it.

In the following year, 1884, Pasadenans were to wish they had more power to regulate affairs in their town. A billiard hall was established on Colorado Street, and shortly thereafter a saloon was opened on the premises. The citizens held a mass meeting in the schoolyard across the street to protest and demand that the saloon be closed, but the saloon-keeper, unmoved by this demonstration, claimed he was abiding by state law and was within his rights. This confrontation raised the issue of local control, and a petition was circulated proposing that Pasadena incorporate as a city.

Prior to incorporation, the boom, and the coming of the railroad, Pasadena was little more than a rural hamlet with only a general store where the most essential provisions could be bought. Nevertheless, Pasadena did have some fledgling industries. One of these was Joseph Wallace's cannery, established in 1881 near present-day Lincoln Avenue west of Orange Grove. In its first year, the cannery packed 10,000 cans of perishable fruits, mostly peaches, and also processed dried fruits. By 1884, production was up to 50,000 cans for the season, and many Pasadena women and girls were employed for the pack. In 1885, however, the cannery burned to the ground, and all that season's pack plus much of the previous year's was lost.

Another early industry was the Pasadena Manufacturing Company, a wood milling company started by Clinton B. Ripley and Harry Ridgway, builders and architects, to turn out moldings and woodwork for the interiors of the houses they were building. The mill also produced doors, windows, fireplace mantles, and frames, and had a local monopoly on such items.

All lumber and other building materials, as well as farm implements, tools, and provisions had to be brought into Pasadena from Los Angeles, either over the Arroyo Seco road, which had many

Below: *The Los Angeles House, at the northwest corner of Fair Oaks and Colorado, was built in 1883. That same year Barney Williams built a new general store and meeting hall across the street on the northeast corner. These two buildings, along with the Pasadena House, another hotel on the southwest corner, became the nucleus of the village center, called "the Corners." Within three years "the Corners" would become the center of the newly incorporated city of Pasadena. Courtesy, California Historical Society/ Ticor Title Insurance (Los Angeles)*

Bottom: *The boom of the 1880s brought prosperity to Clinton B. Ripley's planing mill, which supplied the finished pine and redwood for the new houses going up in Pasadena, while Ripley's partner, Hamilton (Harry) Ridgway, supplied many of the architectural designs. Ripley's mill also provided employment for some of the newcomers, as evidenced by the fifteen workers shown in this photograph. Courtesy, Pasadena Public Library*

The arrival of the Los Angeles and San Gabriel Valley Railroad in Pasadena was celebrated on September 16, 1885, with a banquet held on the Central School lot at Colorado and Raymond. A trellis covered with cypress boughs shaded the elaborately decorated tables. Courtesy, The Huntington Library

steep hills and fords across the sometimes flooded stream, or by way of the adobe or mission road through South Pasadena, which was virtually impassable after a rainstorm because of the thick mud. In order for Pasadena to really grow, it needed a railway connection, at least to Los Angeles.

Since its organization in 1883, Crank's Los Angeles and San Gabriel Valley Railroad had progressed in fits and starts. Construction of the track had begun in late 1884, but was delayed when the contractor went bankrupt in January 1885. Another contractor was hired within a few weeks, but by July only 3,500 feet of track and one of the two major bridges were completed. The company experienced delays in getting equipment and materials from the East, because the Southern Pacific Railroad, over whose lines the goods had to travel, occasionally lost or misdirected the freight. The management of the Southern Pacific viewed any railroad, no matter how small, as a competitor and sought to discourage the enterprise. But the Los Angeles and San Gabriel Valley Railroad refused to be intimidated by the giant, and pressed on, building its track beyond Pasadena as far east as Mud Springs, near present-day San Dimas.

On September 16, 1885, the first passenger train arrived in Pasadena, and the villagers joined in a grand celebration. A large open pavilion roofed with freshly-cut cypress boughs was erected on the schoolhouse grounds. The first passengers, mostly Pasadena and Los Angeles dignitaries, were treated to an extravagant lunch at tables decorated with elaborate centerpieces, including a locomotive and two cars constructed entirely of flowers and fruits. Crank's Los Angeles and San Gabriel Valley Railroad had finally arrived.

Meanwhile, the Atchison, Topeka and Santa Fe Railroad was building its own line to Los Angeles, and within two years it purchased the Los Angeles and San Gabriel Valley Railroad, connecting the line with its track at Mud Springs, thereby gaining a direct route into Los Angeles and incidentally connecting Pasadena directly with Chicago and the East.

By the mid-1880s the Central School at Colorado and Fair Oaks was no longer adequate. In 1885 two new schools were constructed, one on Monk Hill and the other at Colorado and Allen, to serve outlying settlers. That same year also saw the establishment of Pasadena's first bank, headed by Perry M. Green and located in the Pasadena House hotel.

In that same year, a race riot occurred just west of the hotel. Depressed labor conditions fed a strong anti-Chinese sentiment in California in the early 1880s. The Chinese, brought over as laborers to work in the mines and to build the railroads, had moved into other areas of work, such as fruit-picking, and had also established small businesses, mostly laundries. On the evening of November 6, 1885, a group of whites attacked a Chinese laun-

James F. Crank's Los Angeles and San Gabriel Valley Railroad arrived in Pasadena from Los Angeles in 1885. This small steam engine was soon replaced by the engines of the Atchison, Topeka and Santa Fe Railroad, which purchased Crank's road in 1887, thereby linking Pasadena directly with Chicago and points east. Courtesy, Pasadena Historical Society

dry in Mills Place, throwing rocks through the windows and upsetting a lamp, which started a fire. The Chinese managed to barricade themselves in another building, and finally some of the town's leading citizens arrived to quell the disturbance and rescue the Chinese. The aftermath of the riot was not exactly heartening to the Chinese, however, as they were from that time on banned from living or working in the center of town, being exiled to the area south of California Street and east of Fair Oaks Avenue.

By the mid-1880s the community was suffering severe growing pains. Street paving, a sewerage system, streetlighting improvements, fire protection, school expansion, police protection, the liquor question, all of these problems could be solved with more local community control, said the proponents of incorporation. The opponents, who feared tax increases, were a strong voice. They were strongest in South Pasadena, that is, south of Columbia Street. To appease these opponents, the incorporaters at first agreed to a southern boundary of California Street, excluding the South Pasadenans. However, the petition presented to the Los Angeles County Board of Supervisors in the spring of 1886 proposed the boundaries as the Arroyo Seco, the foot of the mountains, Santa Anita Avenue (now Altadena Drive) on the east, and the old Monterey Road on the south. When the petition was heard, protests from opponents resulted in an amendment of the boundaries, making the northern boundary run south of Mountain Street, the eastern boundary run between Catalina and Wilson, and the southern boundary follow Columbia Street.

A referendum was held for those living within those boundaries on June 7, 1886. Of the 232 votes cast, 179 voted for incorporation and 50 voted against. Five men were elected to the first board of trustees, as the city council was called: M.M. Parker (principal of the Parker School); E.C. Webster (manager of the Carlton Hotel); R.M. Furlong; Edson Turner; and Henry J. Holmes. Holmes served as the first chairman of the board (mayor), and the first board meeting was held in Webster's office, over Frank D. Stevens' hardware store.

Early ordinances enacted by the board reflected citizen concerns. Ordinance No. 6 prohibited "loud or unusual noise," "challenging to fight, or fighting," and using profane language "within the presence or hearing of women and children." Ordinance No. 7 prohibited keeping of a "riotous or disorderly house." Ordinance No. 31 prohibited riding or driving any animal or team at a "dangerous rate of speed," while Ordinance No. 74 prohibited fast or reckless driving of bicycles, tricycles, or velocipedes.

But it was Ordinance No. 45, the "whiskey" ordinance, that addressed the most controversial question of the time. It was passed in February 1887, several months after incorporation. The villagers had tried to regulate liquor by imposing excessive business license fees ($100 a month), but the saloon-keepers gladly paid and their establishments remained the source of "brawls, carousals, drunkenness, debauchery, gambling, strumpetry, vagabondage," and "indecent exposure," according to Hiram Reid, a leader of the anti-saloon movement.

Finally, the townspeople passed Ordinance No. 45 to prohibit "places and things of immoral or indecent character." Specifically prohibited were "any tippling-house, dram-shop, cellar saloon, bar, bar-room, sample-room or other place where spiritous, vinous, malt or mixed liquors are sold or given away." But the passage of the ordinance was not the end of the matter. The ordinance was contested by the liquor sellers, only to be finally upheld by the California State Supreme Court. Even that, however, failed to discourage the liquor dealers, who blithely continued to sell liquor in the face of community opposition.

At a mass meeting held in August 1888, one thousand citizens gathered to hear speakers, who vowed to drive "the last rum-hole from our borders." The townspeople raised money to create an enforcement fund and hired an attorney. They filed a statement of violators with the U.S. Revenue Office in Los Angeles, but of the seven violators found, only one, the Carlton Hotel, sold anything stronger than beer. The Carlton, however, was accused of giving wine banquets and serving liquor to guests in their rooms. The issue of serving liquor in hotels was a divisive one, as the community already depended to some extent on tourism.

The movement to enforce the ordinance foundered on technicalities, and meanwhile the "liberals" were gathering their forces. Uncomfortable with the total ban on alcohol which they felt infringed on personal liberty (and might hurt the tourist trade), the "liberals" produced a petition allowing the sale of liquor in hotel dining rooms. Initially, their efforts were unsuccessful, but the 1890 election of the city board proved to be a landslide for the "liberals." Though the ordinance was not repealed, enforcement was lax, if not totally nonexistent. Eventually, in 1892, Ordinance No. 195 was passed, allowing sale of liquor in hotels, restaurants, and boardinghouses, "when sold with and as a part of a regular meal." In the end, the "liberals" had won a partial victory, and the church leaders and Women's Christian Temperance Union, who had led the fight for total prohibition, had to admit defeat.

The beginnings of Pasadena's role as a major resort date from the completion of the railroad and the opening of the Raymond Hotel in 1886. Easterners could now travel by Palace Car, a well-appointed Pullman car, directly from points east to Pasadena. Walter Raymond, of Raymond and Whitcomb excursions, a Boston travel firm which had been organizing travel to Southern California for several years, completed construction of the Raymond Hotel in 1886. Raymond's father, Emmons Raymond, helped finance the project, and since he was one of the forty stockholders in the Santa Fe Railroad, he saw to it that the hotel was served by a station just below Raymond Hill.

The railroad and the Raymond Hotel also contributed to the beginnings of the great land boom in Pasadena from 1886 to 1888. Travelers had easier access to Pasadena, and the Raymond alone boasted a total of 3,500 guests in 1886 and 1887. But the spark that ignited the boom in Pasadena, as Glenn Dumke wrote in his book *The Boom of the Eighties in Southern California,* was the schoolhouse auction, which took place in March 1886. The schoolhouse occupied the five valuable acres of land donated by Benjamin Wilson in 1876 and located at the center of town fronting on Colorado and Fair Oaks. The directors of the San Pasqual School District got permission from Wilson's heirs to sell the property. The land was subdivided into thirty-five lots, which were auctioned off for amounts ranging from $612.50 to $3,700, for a total amount of $44,772. The schoolhouse was moved off to a lot just south of Colorado on the east side of Raymond, where it served for a short time as a city hall. With the proceeds from the sale, the school district purchased land at the corner of Marengo and Walnut streets, where a new school building, named after benefactor Wilson, was erected at a cost of $30,000.

The availability of the school property in the center of town promoted the creation of a substantial business district. Almost immediately building began along Colorado and the few frame buildings of the village center began to disappear. Amy Bridges, a young lady from Massachusetts and a guest at the Raymond Hotel in its first season, described Pasadena's booming downtown in her journal:

At [Colorado and Fair Oaks] is the greatest confusion. The narrow dirty wooden sidewalks are crowded with all sorts of foreign-looking men and children. The little stores are full of goods of all sorts, variety and quality, and seem to do a thriving business, such queer little stores. But there are two or three, even more than that, fine business blocks with neat fronts and gilded signs, especially one bank and the new Hotel Carlton. But all on a small scale. Two other fine buildings are going up on opposite corners of Colorado St. and they are building everywhere, as the sides of the streets are filled with piles of brick and lumber and blocks of stone. They were so very dusty the first weeks, and the horses and carriages and foot passengers seemed to get all mixed up with the bricks, stones

Above: *Built with the money raised from the auction of the schoolhouse property, Wilson School was named for Benjamin D. Wilson, who had donated the land to the school district. Although much larger than the two-room school it replaced, Wilson School was still not adequate to accommodate students during the 1886-1888 boom, when Pasadena had over 1,800 registered students. Courtesy, The Huntington Library*

Opposite: *The Masonic Temple Block was a major building on Colorado Street in the 1890s. It survives today in a truncated form with its top stories removed and its facade moved back fourteen feet to accommodate the widening of Colorado Street in 1929. This view looking south on Raymond also shows the Vandervort Block, which still stands in the heart of Pasadena's historic district. Courtesy, Pasadena Public Library*

and lumber, with the dust and with each other. . .

In an attempt to cope with the building boom, an early ordinance specified that building materials were not to be left on the public right-of-way, but building fever was so high that it became impossible to enforce it. By 1888, at the end of the boom, Colorado Street was lined on both sides, east and west of Fair Oaks, with substantial two- and three-story brick buildings of elaborate design, giving downtown Pasadena a distinctly citified character. Fair Oaks and Raymond north and south of Colorado also had a number of large brick buildings which were joined by other substantial business blocks in the growth years of the 1890s. Plans for an opera house on South Raymond were announced in 1887, creating a great deal of interest in property on that street.

Pasadena's streets were so muddy after a good rain that it was impossible to step from the horsecar to the sidewalk without sinking knee-deep in mud. Gallant men threw planks out over the mud to aid the ladies alighting from the streetcar in their fine shoes and long dresses. Rush-hour traffic was often so heavy at Colorado and Fair Oaks that a contemporary newspaper account warned "it is really dangerous for the pedestrian to attempt to cross . . . the carriages and wagons dash by so rapidly and so close after one another."

Sprinkling the streets to keep down the dust and paving to achieve a more permanent solution were top priorities of early city government. Most houses kept a feather duster outside the front door to brush off dusty shoes and clothes. Amy Bridges described a shopping trip in downtown Pasadena in 1887, at the height of the boom:

The sidewalks of Pasadena are something wonderful. When we first came there was hardly more than ten feet of pavement in two different places. Most of the sidewalks were of wood and after passing over one of these flat low wooden sidewalks for a few yards we step onto the hard-trodden earth for a little distance, then up two wood[en] steps to another wooden sidewalk, down steps to a long plank, then a careful balancing of oneself amidst all sorts of debris and perhaps a ditch on one side, then onto a wooden sidewalk again. . . . Before we left they had begun to lay a broad cement walk on either side of Fair Oaks Avenue and had finished it for some distance, making a beautiful walk.

During the boom, land values escalated at stupendous rates, and property often changed hands daily, sold and resold at ever higher prices. There seemed to be no limit. The library lot on the schoolhouse property which had been bid in at the admittedly low price of $170 at the 1886 auction was sold for $10,000 dollars two years later. Hiram Reid relates in his *History of Pasadena* that Philander G. Wooster, who had purchased ten acres of land on the east side of Raymond between Green and Del Mar for $550 in 1875, sold one and a half acres of it for $36,000 in 1887. Taxes rose proportionately. Wooster's taxes on ten acres in 1878 totaled $7.68; in 1893, he paid $300 on his remaining plot of less than one acre. Although many sales were not recorded, real estate sales for 1886 may have been as high as seven million dollars and those for 1887 were probably twice that.

Speculation mania brought with it sharp practices and shady deals. It was said that some real estate speculators produced maps with fixed prices for lots, only to call them in the following day to double the prices. Purchasers would be convinced to join in with the speculators to double their money, reselling their lots the following day. To counter this sort of activity, the Real Estate Exchange was formed in 1887 with 149 member firms. According to Reid, its stated purpose was "to maintain principles of honesty and fair dealing," and "to stimulate greater activity." The exchange ensured that contracts and deeds were executed in proper form, and set commissions for its members as well. Once the bubble of the boom had burst, however, the Real Estate Exchange disappeared with it, although it did reappear as the Pasadena Realty Board some years later.

Alongside the building boom in the commercial center came a boom in residential buildings, many of them the mansions of those who were making money in the boom. Notable among these were the houses of Theodore P. Lukens on North El Molino Avenue and of Romayne "Barney" Williams on Mountain Street at Hill. These houses, both probably designed by Pasadena's most prolific Victorian architect, Harry Ridgway, contrasted sharply with the board and batten cottages put up by the early settlers. These "boom mansions," both still standing, feature elaborate interior woodwork, stained glass windows, and extensive grounds planted with palm trees and other favorite Victorian landscape features. The Lukens house is notable for its lacey wood trim around the porch and under the eaves, while the Williams house, known as "Hillmont," features green Tehachapi sandstone in the first story, a rare building material in the Pasadena area. Williams sold his land, the site of present-day Central Park, for $200,000 during the boom, in order to build Hillmont. By the end of the boom, Williams had lost his fortune and eventually had to sell his grand mansion. Lukens, a real estate agent who published pamphlets touting Pasadena during the boom, sold $100,000 worth of real estate in May 1886 alone, and probably multiplied that amount manyfold in the following months. Lukens went on to become mayor of Pasadena and one of its most successful and respected citizens.

Houses of all kinds were going up in Pasadena, from small cottages to larger residences to mansions. One of the less than mansion-size houses which nevertheless exhibited fine style and detail was J.C. Rust's house on Garfield Avenue (still standing), a "blending of gothic and Queen Anne

One of the large mansions built in Pasadena's boom period was that of Henry H. Markham, who served as governor of California from 1891 to 1895. Built on South Pasadena Avenue in 1887 to plans by the San Francisco and Los Angeles architects Curlett, Eisen, and Cuthbertson, the house was described in the newspaper as "making a pleasing change from anything like plainness." Courtesy, Security Pacific National Bank Photograph Collection/Los Angeles Public Library

attending into a villa style," according to a newspaper account. Featuring a tower with a witch's cap peak, elaborate interior woodwork, and exterior "gingerbread" trim, Rust's house exemplifies a middle-class residence of the time. Even small cottages, such as those still surviving on Cypress Street, featured gingerbread trim, while the plainest houses, such as Colonel James Place's on Valley Street (still standing) attested to the Midwestern origins of many of Pasadena's settlers.

The building boom created a shortage of workmen, and, despite all the building, a tremendous housing problem, resulting in tent cities in some parts of town where the workmen lived. Amy Bridges described them: "Low dirty white tents, long and narrow, furnish 'Lodging 25 cts.' And many shanties are only a little more respectable." Some early arrivals, like the Marston family who came from Oakland in 1883 and bought property at California and Madison, built a barn to live in while waiting for their house to be built.

Another problem was the lack of a sewerage system. Cesspools connected to the downtown hotels were constantly overflowing, and with the increased population and many new buildings Pasadena was becoming an "odoriferous place," according to Henry Markham Page in his book *Pasadena: Its Early Years.* The beginnings of a sewer system were made during the boom years, but not until the 1890s did the system begin to catch up with the growth of the city.

Water was a limited resource, and a city ordinance was passed which set fines for violation of the water rules. No one had anticipated the growth of the village, and water supplies were not inexhaustible. The two water companies set fees for a family at four dollars per quarter, with thirty cents extra for each horse, cow, mule, or donkey, and seventy-five cents extra for a bathtub or a water closet. Irrigation was restricted to certain times of the day, but since there was no metering system, regulations were unenforceable. Disputes over water continued until meters were installed by the water companies in the late 1890s.

A fire department was also established shortly after incorporation. Wagons were horse-drawn and dependent on local water supplies, which were often unreliable during the summer months. The building of a fire station on Dayton Street in 1889 and the purchase of modern equipment increased the safety of the community. Firemen were largely volunteer, responding to the call of the bell mounted on the station roof. At the sound of the bell the

Above: *Theodore Parker Lukens came to Pasadena in 1880 from Illinois. From small beginnings as a* zanjero, *tending the irrigation ditches of the new settlement, Lukens rose to become a prominent real estate broker and investor, and in the 1890s served as mayor of Pasadena. He was an early promoter of conservation, especially reforestation of the mountains above Pasadena. Courtesy, Pasadena Historical Society*

Opposite: *Pasadena Presbyterian Church, built in 1886 at the corner of Colorado and Worcester (now Garfield Avenue), was demolished in 1906 to make way for the new post office. Parts of the interior were saved and incorporated into the Presbyterian Church in South Pasadena (now Fremont Avenue Brethren Church). Courtesy, Pasadena Public Library*

horses were trained to leap from their open stalls into the traces where they could be harnessed to the engine in seconds. Lack of hydrants in many parts of town and the inexperience of the men resulted in some early mishaps, but the support of the citizenry for the department encouraged growth and increased competence.

Transportation in the form of horse-car trolley lines expanded as the city grew. The first line, completed in 1886, ran up Fair Oaks from the railroad station to Colorado Street. Over the next few years the horse-car lines created a transportation network reaching east to Hill on Colorado Street, north on Fair Oaks to the Painter Hotel and beyond to Mountain View Cemetery, south on Fair Oaks to the Raymond Hotel, and west across the Arroyo into Linda Vista. More complicated routes threaded through the city streets and created connections to Altadena and to Alhambra. Several of these lines failed within a short time; others were bought up, consolidated, and electrified. By the turn of the century, Henry Huntington had begun establishing his Pacific Electric empire, which amalgamated lines throughout Los Angeles

Pasadena High School's second graduating class, the Class of 1891, had twelve students, double the number of the Class of 1890. The Class of 1891 was the first Pasadena class accorded the privilege of entering the University of California or Stanford University without preliminary examination. Courtesy, Pasadena Public Library

and its suburbs, creating a vast network of interurban electric cars, known as the "Red Cars," which continued to serve area transportation needs until 1951.

The schools were stretched beyond capacity by the boom. The *Annual Report of the Pasadena Public Schools* for 1887-1888 noted that the six schools could not accommodate all the new pupils at the beginning of the fall term and a vacant store on South Fair Oaks had to be rented to handle the overflow. The Monk Hill School doubled its teaching staff and thirty-six more seats had to be added at Wilson School. After the winter holiday the situation was even worse; it was necessary to hold half-day sessions and the rooms were still crowded. Enrollment had nearly doubled from 703 in 1886-1887 to 1,354 in 1887-1888, and the school had grown from four rooms to forty in several buildings. Since the background of the students was so diverse it was difficult to place them in the proper grades. Yet the Pasadena schools were trying out the so-called "new education," a method based on "learning by doing," which also added music, drawing, and physical exercises to the academic curriculum.

The 1888-1889 school year saw 500 pupils added to the already strained system, but in the following year the end of the boom brought the number of pupils down to 1,388. Steady growth continued through the 1890s and by 1900 the schools had almost 3,000 pupils. The first high school graduating class was that of 1890, when six graduates received their diplomas, among them Fred Sears, who went on to study astronomy at Berkeley and in Berlin and Paris before returning to Pasadena as the assistant director of Mt. Wilson Observatory. Pasadena High School was one of the few accredited schools in the state, and Pasadena graduates at that time were admitted to Berkeley or Stanford without examination. Most students, however, did not go beyond the eighth grade. By 1900, a free kindergarten had been established at Garfield School and manual training was taught in the fifth through eighth grades. Girls were taught sewing, while boys were taught cooking and woodworking.

Hyper-inflation caused the collapse of the boom in the spring of 1888, meaning tremendous losses for some, and a decline in population, but the effects were also positive. Since the arrival of the railroad, Pasadena had grown to become the third largest city in Southern California in population and the second in wealth. Amy Bridges wrote:

But it is all a new place of hardly more than five years growth, and it is wonderful to see how fast it has grown. Little by little the cheaper, more temporary buildings will be done away with. In another four years I many not know the place. Four years ago, I remember it only as a few cross roads, and a few scattered houses.

Contemporary accounts ascribed many positive developments in the city to the boom, especially the many fine buildings in the commercial district, the new schools, improvements in water and sewerage systems, paving of sidewalks, street lights, the beginnings of a new library building, and new church buildings. Optimists felt that Pasadena could capitalize on these new assets and would return soon to a more healthy rate of growth, based on genuine improvement rather than on mere speculation, and preserving the more stable aspects of the community.

One unfortunate result of the boom was the neglect of the orchards planted so hopefully a few years earlier. Now the fruit lay rotting on the ground, and weeds grew high among the young trees. Although even before the boom it had become clear that much land had become too valuable to be planted in orchards, those orchards already bearing still represented an investment worth saving. The brief excitement of the boom diverted many growers into the "town lot fever," as it was called, but afterwards many of them returned to the cultivation of their land. Orange and deciduous fruit production remained a significant aspect of the local economy for at least the next decade.

With the boom, however, came the realization that the future of the city lay in a tourist-based economy, and some of the negative consequences of the boom had been detrimental to that goal. Civic beautification again became a community effort, for as one newspaper put it, "most of our streets are without shade trees, denuded of those beautiful hedges so celebrated by us some years ago, and [have become] dusty thoroughfares of travel instead of beautiful, shady avenues. The boom did much to make the quiet village of Pasadena a lively, animated city, but, alas! it destroyed much of its original beauty."

Jeanne Carr stated the problem more dramatically:

Satan entered into this Paradise, finding his opportunity in a branch Railroad, and congenial oc-

cupation in the creation of a Boom. The little parks, left in reverence of some grand oak which had not lived out its 'green century', or at the points which commanded the finest views of the mountains, were sacrificed; as also other reservations of priceless value for their wood and water. The ideals of a community of fruit growers, were not those of numbers who came later, to bask in one winter's sunshine. . . .

By March 1888, the boom was virtually over, and in that same month the Board of Trade was organized, one of its principal objectives being to stimulate tourism. The general tone of newspaper articles and "booster" literature of the late 1880s and 1890s was that Pasadena was not pursuing industrial development but was seeking to promote the tourist trade by emphasizing the fine residen-

Above: *This view of Pasadena in about 1895 was taken by Frederick Hamer Maude from the tower of Thaddeus Lowe's mansion on Orange Grove Avenue. The small palms alternating with larger trees and the carefully clipped hedges were inspired by Jeanne Carr to beautify Pasadena. Courtesy, Western History Collection, Natural History Museum of Los Angeles County*

Opposite: *The Hotel Painter was the third of Pasadena's three major resort hotels of the 1890s. Located in the foothills above town, the Painter claimed to have better air and so was popular with tuberculosis sufferers. A streetcar line (tracks in foreground) linked the hotel with downtown Pasadena. Courtesy, Pasadena Public Library*

tial qualities of the city, a healthful climate, and scenic beauty. The first of many Board of Trade pamphlets, published in 1888, took pains to emphasize that Pasadena was no rough Western frontier town, but a civilized and moral community, with imposing buildings, eleven churches, a new school costing $35,000, a public library of 4,000 volumes, many fraternal organizations, three banks, several first class hotels, an opera house, and three newspapers—and, of course, no saloons. By this time, however, reserve was evident in the description of the climate and its benefits for tubercular patients; no longer were all invalids encouraged to come to Pasadena, for "persons well advanced in consumption . . . should think well . . . [before undertaking the trip.] Many consumptives arrive here only to die within a few weeks." Indeed, the early death statistics of Pasadena reveal that from the 1890s at least into the 1920s one-third to one-half of all deaths reported in the city were due to tuberculosis. Plainly, the invalids came in great numbers, but not all were cured.

The 1890s was the era of Pasadena's grand hotels, as Thomas D. Carpenter has noted in his recent book, *Pasadena: Resort Hotels and Paradise.* Construction had begun on the Raymond Hotel in 1883 with the leveling of the top of Bacon Hill, part of the Marengo Ranch then owned by Henry Douglas Bacon of San Francisco. Unfamiliar with the geology of the region, Walter Raymond, the new owner, thought a few mules, men, and scrapers could create the required flat building space in a short time. Unfortunately, the hill proved to be bedrock, requiring Thomas Banbury and his crew to blast and then haul away the heavy rocks, costing Raymond far more than was intended. Work stopped on the project in 1884, until Raymond's father, Emmons Raymond, came to the rescue with additional funds. Finally completed in 1886, the hotel, designed by J.H. Littlefield of San Francisco in the fashionable Second Empire style, featured tall mansard-roofed towers stretching three stories above the eaves, and twenty towering chimneys. Although built of wood, the massive structure on its imposing site dominated the landscape for miles around.

Known as the Royal Raymond, the new hotel also began to dominate the community socially as well. With 200 rooms and several hundred guests, the hotel became the focal point for concerts, balls, and parties. Although not many Pasadenans participated in the life at the Raymond, the hotel was clearly Pasadena's most sophisticated establishment.

Amy Bridges wrote that every evening there was music and dancing for the guests and every Sunday afternoon a concert with printed programs. Sunday dinners had special themes, with elaborate souvenir menus. As guests stayed on for several months and ate their meals together, they became well acquainted. As for the rooms, Miss Bridges wrote: "Our rooms are very pleasant and nicely furnished in red. We have two long windows in each room and the view is magnificent. The hotel is on a hill and we look down over the valleys with their orange groves and vineyards and cultivated fields."

Responding to the continuing stream of booster literature about Pasadena which was circulated throughout the country, tourists began flocking to the hotels and various inns and boardinghouses, which were springing up all over Pasadena. Each hotel had its particular charm or interest and appealed to a particular clientele. The Arroyo Vista Guest House, perched on the bluff of the Arroyo south of Colorado Boulevard, featured the rugged beauty of its Arroyo setting and offered the guest quiet and seclusion away from the bustling town. First opened by Mrs. Emma C. Bangs in 1882, it offered few, if any, of the glittering social events of the Sierra Madre Villa or Raymond Hotel, but it was a much sought-after place of residence, where

On Easter Sunday, April 14, 1895, the Royal Raymond, Pasadena's finest hotel, burned to the ground. Fed by high winds, the flames consumed the wood frame building in less than two hours. Not until 1901 was Walter Raymond able to rebuild and reopen his hostelry in a fire-resistant stucco building. Courtesy, Western History Collection, Natural History Museum of Los Angeles County

reservations were usually necessary to ensure accommodation.

Another even more remote hotel was the Painter, established by John J. Painter in 1887 and located just below Monk Hill at an altitude of 1,000 feet. A three-story building with a central tower, it was surrounded, like the Raymond, by a wide *piazza* (porch) where the guests could take the air. The Painter was touted for its high altitude, guaranteed to be even farther above the fogs than downtown Pasadena. According to Charles Holder's description in *The Highlands of Pasadena* (1889), the Painter was also the scene of "dinners, hops and other entertainments," as well as celebrated banquets. Extensive gardens surrounded the hotel and in front of the hotel was a large vineyard.

The remoteness of the Painter apparently did not detract from its desirability, for it was linked by horsecars and a "dummy" steam car to the center of Pasadena. During the 1888-1889 season, the Painter housed guests from New York, Chicago, Cleveland, Detroit, Pittsburgh, Philadelphia, Baltimore, Washington, D.C., St. Paul, and even Prairie du Chien, Wisconsin. Built of wood like most of the early hotels, the Painter, later named La Pintoresca, burned to the ground in 1912 and was never rebuilt. La Pintoresca Park and Branch Library on the site preserve the name of this early Pasadena hotel.

One of the most advantageously located hotels was the Green, on South Raymond Avenue next to the Santa Fe station. It was no accident that hotel and station were linked, for E.C. Webster, who originally began building the Webster Hotel at that location in 1887, also built the station, a turreted Romanesque building behind the hotel, and gave it to the railroad. This put the Webster on par with the Raymond, which had its own station below Raymond Hill. Unfortunately, Webster did not survive the boom in a financially solvent condition, and the faltering enterprise was taken over by Colonel George G. Green, whose father, Dr. Lewis M. Green, had made a fortune in the patent medicine business. Colonel Green was a man of great resources and great vision. In 1894, he enlarged the original four-story building, which occupied the south end of the lot next to the tracks, into a massive four-story-plus-attic structure stretching from Kansas Street (now Green Street) south to present-day Dayton Street on the east side of Raymond Avenue. The architecture was distinctly Mission Revival, which was echoed by the Mission furniture in the public rooms, but classical columns and plaster work abounded in the interiors. The curved, columned entrance still survives at the corner of Green Street and Raymond Avenue and traces of the plaster work can still be seen in the interior of the one-story remnant of this once grand establishment.

Easter Sunday, 1895, was an important day in the history of Pasadena resort life, for on that afternoon the massive five-story, 200-room wood-frame Raymond Hotel burned to the ground. All that was left standing of the Royal Raymond was a lone brick chimney, but luckily there was no loss of life. Insurance did not cover the loss, and Walter Raymond was unable to rebuild until 1901, when he received financing from Chicago industrialist Richard T. Crane, who had been a regular guest at the hotel.

The Raymond's loss was the Green's gain, and Colonel Green expanded his enterprise in 1898, building an imposing annex across Raymond Avenue where the hotel park had been, linking it to the original building with an arcaded bridge across the street. The new building was elaborately Moorish, built of brick, steel, and concrete, finished in plaster and guaranteed fireproof. The architect was Frederick L. Roehrig, who elaborated on the rather plain Mission Revival design of the 1894 building by designing more prominent towers with distinctive domes, more elaborate balconies, and ornamental plaster panels of organic leaf and tendril design. An interior "Moorish Room," just off the main lobby, carried out this Moorish theme in furniture, tiles, woodwork, and fabrics. It is this 1898 building, with its truncated bridge stretching out to Raymond Avenue, that survives as the Castle Green Apartments today.

As the largest and most elaborate hotel in Pasadena in the 1890s, the Hotel Green became the focus of many social events. Perhaps the most memorable was the visit of President Benjamin Harrison in 1891. It was only the second time an American president had visited Pasadena. President Rutherford B. Hayes had stopped briefly in Pasadena in 1880 to humor his wife, who wanted to see where her ne'er-do-well half-brother, J.M. Matthews, a member of the original colony, had lived. The Hayes were greeted by a few locals on Orange Grove Avenue, and had dinner at the Los Robles Ranch of Governor Stoneman. Reflecting Pasadena's increasing sophistication, President Harrison's welcome was far more elaborate.

Arriving in his own presidential car at the Santa Fe station, the president proceeded to the Green Hotel where a suite of rooms overflowing with flo-

Tourists in a four-horse tally-ho set off from the Hotel Green for an excursion into the surrounding countryside. Perhaps Pasadena's leading hostelry in the 1890s, the Hotel Green profited from its central location near the train station and from the destruction of the Hotel Raymond by fire in 1895. Courtesy, The Huntington Library

This lively scene depicts the Hotel Green after its expansion by Colonel Green in 1894. Stucco walls, red tile roofs, towers, and arcades were reminiscent of California's mission architecture and seemed exotic to tourists from the East. The Green's central location near the railroad station made it a popular tourist destination and the center of Pasadena social life. Courtesy, Pasadena Historical Society

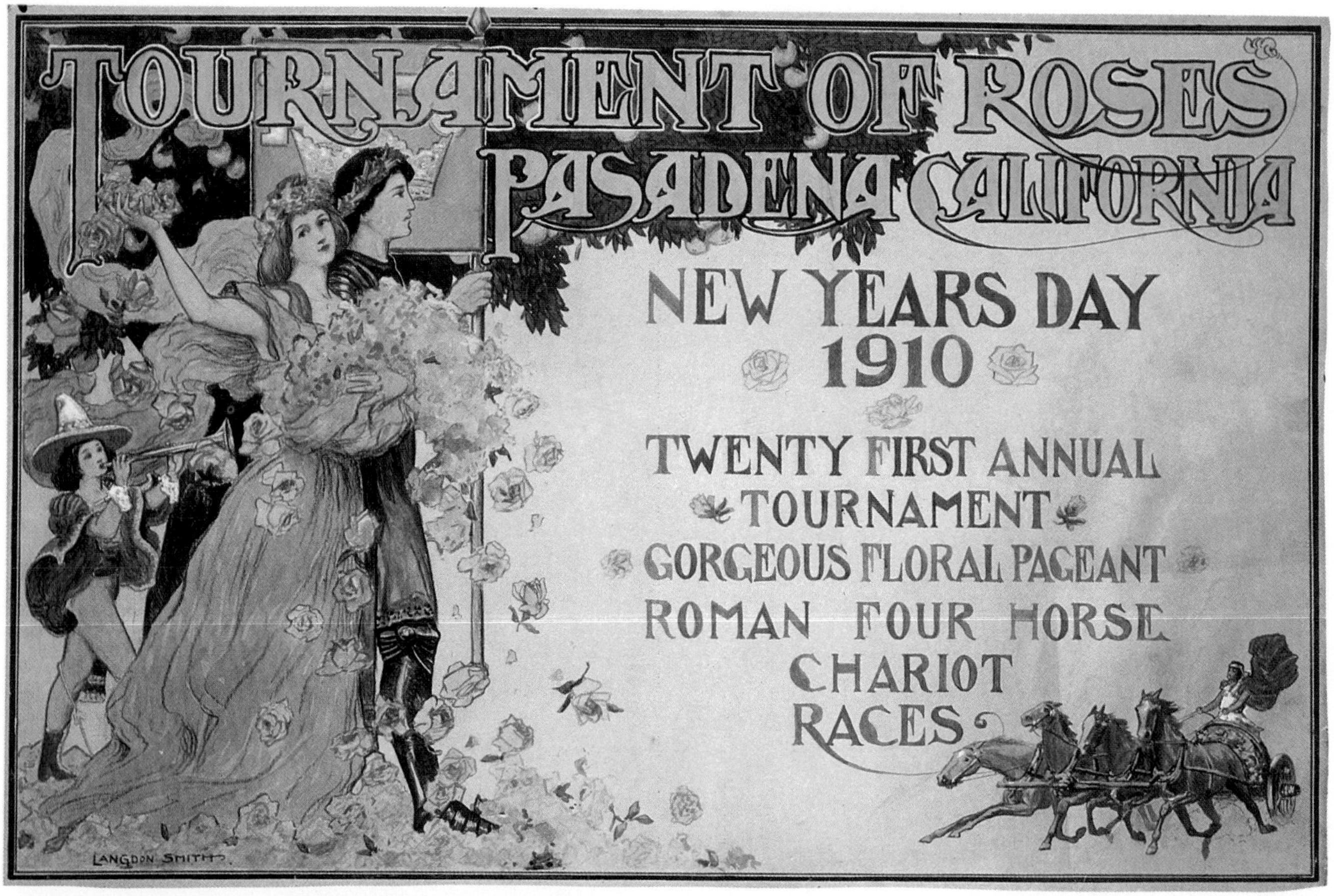
TOURNAMENT OF ROSES
PASADENA CALIFORNIA
NEW YEARS DAY
1910
TWENTY FIRST ANNUAL
TOURNAMENT
GORGEOUS FLORAL PAGEANT
ROMAN FOUR HORSE
CHARIOT
RACES
LANGDON SMITH

TOURNAMENT of ROSES
and
FOOTBALL
CLASSIC
PASADENA
CALIFORNIA
1926
New Year's Number
PASADENA STAR-NEWS

Tournament of Roses
Pasadena, California.
Pasadena
Star-News
New Year's
Number
1918

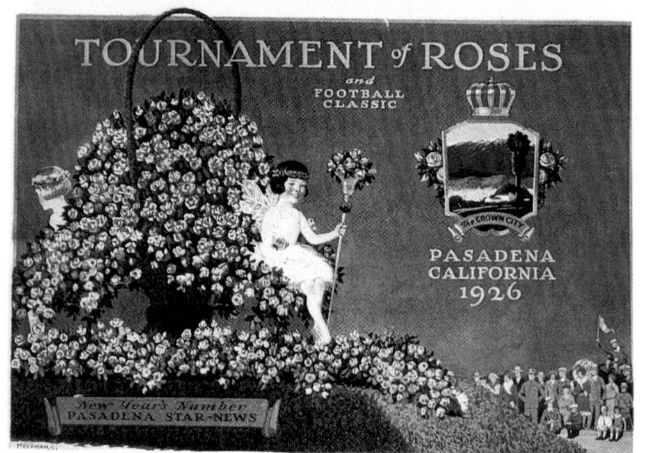

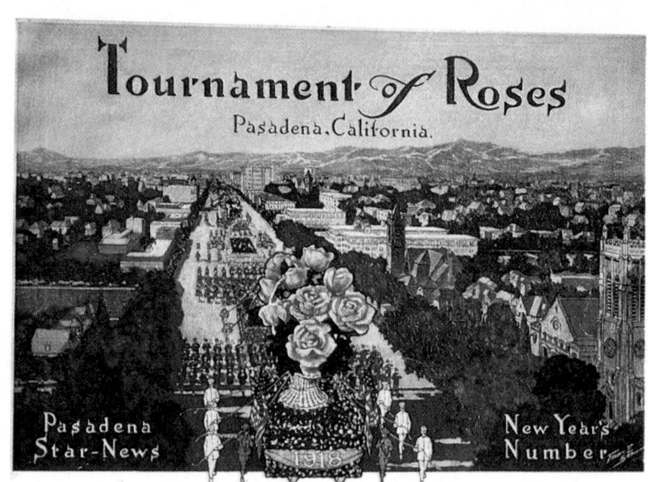

Colorful posters and covers of annual pictorials promoted the Tournament of Roses as a floral pageant and a major sporting event. They furthered the purpose of the parade itself, which was to attract seasonal tourists and permanent residents to Pasadena. Courtesy, Pasadena Historical Society

Early pictorials like this one promoted the Mt. Lowe Railway. Many of them were written by George Wharton James, Pasadena author and authority on Southwest Indian culture, who worked for a time as publicity agent for Thaddeus Lowe.

Left: *One of the trolley cars that served Pasadena stopped on Raymond Avenue just beyond the arched bridge linking the two buildings of the Hotel Green. Trolley service took Pasadenans to Los Angeles as well as to various beach towns, as the sign on this car proclaims. The painting is by Harlan Hiney. Courtesy, Charles Seims. Copyright, 1976*

Above: *In their "Sunday-best" these tourists eagerly anticipate their railway ride in the clouds as they are about to experience the leading tourist attraction of turn-of-the-century Southern California. The Mt. Lowe Railway, with its well-appointed hotels and attractions, drew over three million visitors between 1893 and 1937.*

Right: *Pasadena City Hall has been a favorite subject of artists and photographers since its completion in 1927. This unusual view by artist Frank Leighton shows the fountain and the dome behind the arcade of the eastern entrance. Courtesy, Office of the Mayor, City of Pasadena*

Opposite, above: *Pasadena's beautiful setting at the foot of the San Gabriel mountains, its tree-lined streets, and its notable civic buildings gave it an early reputation as a fine residential city. This panorama shows the business district and Civic Center in the foreground, surrounded by the green treetops of Pasadena's residential neighborhoods. Courtesy, Pasadena Historical Society*

Opposite, below: *South Marengo Avenue with its lovely homes and large pepper trees was a must on the tourist circuit in early Pasadena. Here the street is depicted in a circa 1920 postcard. Courtesy, City of Pasadena*

This aerial perspective shows Bertram Goodhue's plan for the Caltech campus. Using the original Throop Hall as an anchor, Goodhue proposed a magnificent domed library building to the west, flanked by symmetrically arranged wings linked by arcades. Reflecting pools stretching west toward Wilson Avenue enhanced the visual effect. Although the domed library was never realized, the west campus developed basically according to Goodhue's plan. Courtesy, California Institute of Technology

ral arrangements, including wisteria hanging from the chandelier, awaited him. That evening a reception and banquet with 135 male guests lasted into the early morning hours and created a minor scandal when it was discovered that the waiters had drunk most of the wine. One story has it that the president, in deference to Pasadena's reputation for temperance, turned over his wineglass, signalling others to do the same. Apparently the waiters felt the wine should not be wasted, and so proceeded to drink it up themselves. Needless to say, the service deteriorated as the evening wore on.

The following morning the president toured the city, passing under a monumental floral arch on Marengo near Green Street. But as Page reports in his book, the arch was raining orange juice, for the words "Welcome to our guests" had been spelled out in oranges nailed across the top of the arch. On the whole, however, the visit was a great success, and Pasadenans pointed with pride to the fact that a president had found their city important enough to honor it with a visit.

The visit of the president seemed to confirm what Pasadenans already believed, that they were living in the finest, most beautiful, most healthful, most cultured, and intelligent community in the West. The collapse of the boom had momentarily weakened confidence in the future of the community, but as people looked around them at the climate, the scenic beauty, and the fine buildings that had already been erected, they took heart again and proceeded to proclaim the advantages of Pasadena to all who would listen.

One of the events highlighted in the booster literature of the 1890s was the newly established New Year's Day festival, the Tournament of Roses. Conceived by Charles F. Holder, president of the Valley Hunt Club, the first festival was held on New Year's Day in 1890, and it consisted of a parade of flower-bedecked carriages and an afternoon of games in the open field east of Los Robles Avenue and north of Colorado. Holder later wrote that it was a "combination of fete, fiesta and tournament to celebrate, in a poetic and beautiful manner, the ripening of the orange, which took place about January first, that being the one event of importance in the year in Pasadena at that time." The inspiration for the parade had come partly from Dr. F.F. Rowland, who had seen Rome's Battle of the Roses, a floral parade which was part of Rome's carnival celebrations. It was a particularly apt model because of Pasadena's Mediterranean climate.

The games consisted of foot races, an egg and spoon relay, hurdles, and a "tourney of rings," the latter giving its name to the Tournament of Roses. This Spanish jousting match—in which horsemen with lances tried to spear three rings hanging at thirty-foot distances—was suggested to Holder by old Spanish and Indian games he had seen at Pala, a mission station northeast of San Diego.

The tournament continued to be celebrated through the 1890s, evolving and growing as it has done every year since. The 1891 festival was held near Devil's Gate, with the parade beginning on Orange Grove Avenue and winding its way down into the Arroyo, where spectators picnicked and watched the games. In 1892, the organizers specified for the first time that "every man, woman and child plus horse and carriage should be decorated with flowers." Ironically, a severe winter caused a shortage of roses, so the event was called the Orange Tournament that year. In 1893, female equestrians were allowed to ride astride, a new and daring thing. For the 1894 parade, the first reviewing stands were built. In 1895, the Valley Hunt Club declared that the tournament had become too much of a burden on the organization, and it was then that the Tournament of Roses Association was formed. Track events, horse and bicycle races made up the afternoon games during the 1890s. By the end of the century, the tournament was becoming a major tourist attraction. When New Year's Day dawned in 1900, 50,000 people were on hand to watch the parade and the games.

The early settlers had enjoyed the simple pleasures of riding, hunting, and hiking in the mountains, but with the arrival of the tourists, new diversions became a part of Pasadena life. Tennis was introduced to Pasadena in the 1880s. The ho-

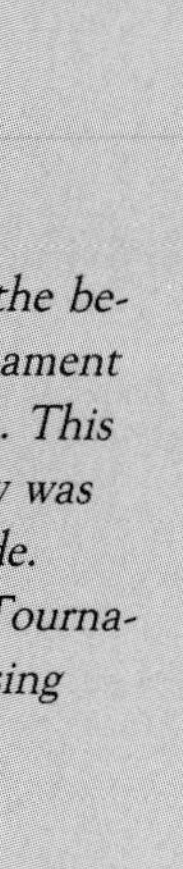

Right: *1890 marked the beginning of the Tournament of Roses in Pasadena. This flower-bedecked entry was part of an early parade. Courtesy, Pasadena Tournament of Roses Licensing*

Left: *This elaborate float appeared in the 1897 Rose Parade. Courtesy, Pasadena Tournament of Roses Licensing*

Left: *This floral contraption pedaled by Messrs. Boynton, Bliss, Stevens, and Goodale, decked out in eighteenth-century costume, enlivened the 1897 Rose Parade. Courtesy, Pasadena Tournament of Roses Licensing*

Below: *Lovely ladies riding in flower-bedecked carriages have always been features of the Rose Parade. This 1897 entry of the Tuesday Evening Club was drawn by elegant white horses. Courtesy, Pasadena Tournament of Roses Licensing*

This early clubhouse of the Valley Hunt Club was located on Grand Avenue, the scene of the annual formation of the Rose Parade on New Year's Day. From here the parade proceeded east on Colorado Boulevard to Tournament Park at Wilson and California, now part of the Caltech campus. Courtesy, Western History Collection, Natural History Museum of Los Angeles County

tels, particularly the Raymond and La Pintoresca, had tennis courts on their grounds and some families, notably the Daggetts on Columbia Hill and the Channings on North Orange Grove, had their own private courts. The Daggetts organized the Columbia Hill Tennis Club, which became a focal point for the social life of the younger people in the community and also produced several nationally-ranked tennis players.

The 1890s also saw the beginnings of golf in Pasadena. Pasadena's first golf course was a make-shift affair located north of the Painter Hotel on Raymond near Montana Street. Laid out in 1892 by early settler McDougall Snowball and his Scottish compatriot, J.L. McFarland, the course was nine holes bounded roughly by Dakota Street (now Howard) and Mountain View Cemetery. Fairways were dust, putting greens were dust, and after a game, "the players looked as if they had had dust shot at them with a spray-gun," according to an article in the *Pasadena Star-News.* Cups were tomato cans embedded in the ground. A similarly primitive course was laid out on Campbell-Johnston's San Rafael Ranch in 1894 by an Englishman, E.H. Stafford. In 1898, a proper nine-hole course was constructed east of Wilson Lake on the old Lake Vineyard Ranch. This course became the home of the Pasadena Country Club and was in use until the founding of the Midwick Country Club in Alhambra in 1912, when the old course was subdivided for residences.

Probably the major tourist attraction of the 1890s, however, was the Mt. Lowe Railway. In his

an average grade of 59 percent, passing each other in the middle of the slope. The weight of the descending car provided part of the power propelling the ascending car. At the top was a small hotel, the Chalet, and at the base stood a pavilion, the Hotel Rubio.

Lowe soon extended his railroad three miles up to Crystal Springs, elevation 5,000 feet, where he built the large rustic Alpine Tavern, which became a favorite retreat for tourists and locals alike. Herbert F. Brown remembered that "special deluxe cars took guests on this unique trip from Los Angeles to Alpine Tavern for $2.50. You could remain overnight at the Tavern or you could dine and dance and come down on the one o'clock special which ran to Los Angeles." Below Alpine Tavern, on Echo Mountain, Lowe built the elegant Echo Mountain House and an observatory to promote scientific research. Lowe also installed a searchlight on Echo Mountain which swept the valley with its powerful beam, occasionally frightening horses and causing panicky runaways in the

Above: *Perhaps the most celebrated personality in early Pasadena was Professor Thaddeus Sobieski Constantine Lowe (1832-1913). He doggedly developed and then lost in 1896 the Mt. Lowe Railroad and several hotels along the route. Courtesy, Pasadena Public Library*

Right: *A proud and enterprising Thaddeus S.C. Lowe (with cane, seated) poses for the camera on North Lake Avenue in his work car after inspecting the construction work in Rubio Canyon on the Echo Mountain incline railway. Professor Lowe left an enduring legacy in the Mt. Lowe Railway and in significant gas and refrigeration inventions. Courtesy, The Huntington Library*

Above: *One of the "white chariots" of the Mt. Lowe Railway carries passengers, shaded by parasols from the intense California sun, up to Echo Mountain House. The hotel, completed in 1894 and designed by British architect T.W. Parkes, accommodated tourists with seventy bedrooms, a large dining room, and various social rooms and shops. Courtesy, The Huntington Library*

Opposite: *Thaddeus Lowe and his family are pictured here in a horse-drawn sleigh at Alpine Tavern. Lowe's investment in his mountain railway and resort hotels brought millions of visitors to the Pasadena area, but proved a financial disaster for him. In 1896, the year this picture was taken, he was forced to sell out, losing much of his personal fortune. Courtesy, The Huntington Library*

valley below.

All of this investment, however, proved disastrous for Lowe. He was finally forced to sell out in 1896 and so lost control of his dream railway, besides losing much of his personal fortune. Nevertheless, the railway and hotels remained one of the greatest tourist attractions in Southern California, for no trip to the area was complete without a ride up the mountain to enjoy the breathtaking views and to wander in what became known as the "Alps of America."

The growth of the tourist trade brought many people of national prominence to Pasadena, especially wealthy Easterners seeking to retire in the land of eternal sunshine. Lowe was only one of several Eastern millionaires who discovered Pasadena in the 1890s. Another was Andrew McNally of the Chicago publishing company, Rand-McNally. McNally built his Queen Anne-style mansion in Altadena, just across the road from the house of his millionaire friend, Colonel Green, whose fortune was built on such elixirs as "Green's August Flower" and "Bosche's German Syrup." Nearby was the home of another friend, Alfred C. Armstrong, whose fortune had come from railroad and drug interests as well as from the inheritance of his wife, a member of the Du Pont family.

Down in Pasadena, the millionaires were beginning to buy up property and build their mansions on or near Orange Grove Avenue, the most fashionable street in town. Joining Thaddeus Lowe,

Professor Thaddeus S.C. Lowe's home was located on the west side of Orange Grove near Bellefontaine Street. It was one of the earlier mansions on the street that became known as "Millionaires' Row." The 24,000-square-foot house was crowned with Lowe's own personal observatory. Courtesy, The Huntington Library

whose 24,000-square-foot mansion on Orange Grove had started the whole town talking, was Hulett C. Merritt, a member of the Minnesota family that had developed the great Mesabi iron range and subsequently founded U.S. Steel. Another resident on Orange Grove was Henry Calvin Durand, who had made his fortune in the wholesale grocery business in Chicago. He built a fairytale castle with spires and turrets on the street in the 1890s. Demand was so great for Orange Grove property that of the original settlers, only three still resided on the street in 1900.

One of the most prominent residents on Orange Grove Avenue was Amos G. Throop, who had come to Pasadena in 1886 after retiring from a long career as a prominent politician and civic leader in Chicago. "Father" Throop, as he was affectionately called in Pasadena, was as concerned with the improvement of Pasadena as he had been with Chicago.

Throop became active in community affairs, served on the city Board of Directors, and was mayor of Pasadena from 1890 to 1892. He founded the Universalist Church in 1886 and gave more than $30,000 to finance the building of the church at Raymond and Chestnut. He was remembered by the Universalist congregation when their new church was dedicated in 1923 as Throop Memorial Universalist Church. More important for the history of Pasadena, though, was Throop's interest in education and his founding of Throop University in 1891.

Father Throop solicited the cooperation of Professor M.M. Parker, whose Pasadena Academy combined with Throop University at the founding. The new institution opened in November 1891 in the Wooster Block on the corner of Fair Oaks and Green Street (still standing as part of the Hotel Green). The next year, the school moved to a new building at Fair Oaks and Chestnut Street and the name was changed to Throop Polytechnic Institute. This new name reflected more closely the philosophy behind the founding of the school, based on Chicago educator John Dewey's slogan,

Below: *Throop Institute, the forerunner of Caltech, got its start in rented quarters in the Wooster Block at Raymond and Green streets in 1891. A few years later, the college moved to new quarters, pictured here, at Raymond Avenue and Chestnut Street. Begun as a four-year college, the school evolved into a manual arts training school for all grades, then into an engineering college, before becoming the scientific research institution we know today. Courtesy, Western History Collection, Natural History Museum of Los Angeles County*

Right: *Amos G. Throop, known affectionately as "Father" Throop for his benefactions to Pasadena, lived only eight years after his arrival in 1886. In that short time he founded Throop University (later to become Caltech), and the Universalist Church. He also obtained crucial support for the Pasadena Public Library, ensuring its survival. Courtesy, Pasadena Public Library*

Above: *Pasadena's ornately Moorish opera house, built on South Raymond Avenue in 1888, was a financial failure. Thaddeus Lowe rescued the building, putting his offices in it and selling tickets there to his mountain railway, but the building was eventually demolished after the turn of the century. Courtesy, Security Pacific National Bank Photograph Collection, Los Angeles Public Library*

Opposite: *This view of Pasadena from Raymond Hill around 1900 shows the two buildings of the Hotel Green linked by a covered bridge across Raymond Avenue and a few industrial buildings near the railroad tracks to the east. The scattered houses and absence of large buildings reflect the rural, small-town atmosphere of nineteenth-century Pasadena. Courtesy, Western History Collection, Natural History Museum of Los Angeles County*

"Learn to do by doing." The aim of the school, influenced also by the ideas of William Morris and John Ruskin, was to instill in its students, both men and women, a knowledge and respect for manual skills and crafts. To this end, the institute offered not only the standard academic courses in the classics, English, science, and philosophy, but also courses in "sloyd" (Swedish for crafts), woodworking, machine shop, cooking, sewing, and weaving. Art, music, and physical education were also part of the curriculum. This was revolutionary in an era when education was still based on classic academic subjects. Father Throop wanted those students who might become owners or managers of businesses or factories to respect the skills of their workers and to take pride in quality work. For those seeking a more practical training, Throop offered business courses such as typewriting and stenography. By 1895, Throop Polytechnic had 300 students housed in two substantial brick buildings at Fair Oaks and Chestnut.

Father Throop, however, did not live to see the growing success of his institute. On March 22, 1894, he died, occasioning "the most impressive demonstration of popular sorrow that ever occurred in Pasadena" (according to Reid) at his funeral a few days later. Flags were at half-mast, businesses closed, and thousands crowded into and around the church. Many speakers paid tribute to Father Throop, including Governor Henry H. Markham, a Pasadenan who served as governor of California from 1891 to 1895.

Pasadena's other important cultural institution, the library, experienced significant growth in the years following the boom. In 1887, the library was able to sell its lot on Colorado Street for $10,000, creating a tidy sum to build a new building. Charles Legge offered the Library Association a lot at Raymond Avenue and Walnut Street free, if a building costing not less than $25,000 were erected there by January 1, 1888. A number of citizens pledged sums to cover the additional cost. A grand stone building, designed by architect Harry Ridgway, was begun, but the contractor failed, causing a delay. In the meantime, the land boom collapsed, making many subscribers unable to make good on their pledges. Various means were tried to raise additional funds, including a loan from a local bank signed by prominent guarantors, and an Art Loan Exhibition, but finally the only way to save the library was to have the city take it over. This was done, and an $8,500 bond issue was voted to finish the building. The library

opened on Sepember 9, 1890, with 3,000 volumes, quite a gain from the 329 volumes on the shelves at the first opening in 1884. During the 1890s, circulation grew apace; in 1896 it was an astounding 6,500 a month and by 1898 there were nearly 13,000 volumes in the library. Pasadena was well on its way to becoming a well-read community, at least in terms of circulation statistics.

The opera house was another early cultural achievement, which, unfortunately, did not survive for very long. Located on South Raymond Avenue and built in a lavish Moorish style, the opera house was conceived in the flush of the boom years, but its very lavishness and size made it too expensive to operate in the post-boom community. Thaddeus Lowe finally purchased it and used the first story space for his offices. A few performances were held there by traveling companies, but most Pasadenans still traveled to Los Angeles for their entertainment.

Despite its growth and increasing sophistication, Pasadena remained a largely rural community, even in the 1890s. Records of the San Rafael Ranch show that many Pasadenans kept cows on their property, boarding them at the ranch when they were calving or dry of milk. Most householders also kept a few chickens. Although electricity had come to the town for streetlighting purposes it was not in widespread use. Until 1889, Pasadenans had to go to the post office to pick up their mail. When deliveries were instituted, resident artist Charles Walter Stetson reported: "We have now lettercarriers! They are mounted, with fine horses and they deliver letters promptly."

By the turn of the century, however, Pasadena had begun to shed its rural ways, although the image of country peacefulness was still an important factor in attracting tourists and new residents. The population in 1900 of less than 10,000 was lower than it had been during the boom of the 1880s, but the stage was set for solid growth and prosperity. The small village of prosperous orange growers had become a major town in Southern California, distinguished by an unusually high level of wealth and culture.

Chapter IV

By 1910, Busch Gardens had become a major tourist attraction and "automobiling" was a favorite pastime in Pasadena. Pasadena's prominence as a winter resort drew presidents and financiers, business tycoons, and statesmen. The man on the far left in the first car may be President William Howard Taft, who visited Pasadena in 1911. Courtesy, The Huntington Library

The Roots Of Greatness

"I selected Pasadena as the winter home
of my family because I consider it
a veritable paradise,
it has no equal in the world,
regarding healthful climate,
scenery, vegetation, flowers, shrubberies,
fruit and general comfort of living....
Pasadena is undoubtedly destined to become...
a most popular American winter residence."

–Adolphus Busch, 1911

The comments of St. Louis beer millionaire Adolphus Busch reflect the typical views published in the 1911 New Year's Day issue of the *Pasadena Daily News* under the title "Why I Live in Pasadena." During the first two decades of the twentieth century, Pasadena experienced phenomenal growth in population and wealth, claiming by 1920 to be the wealthiest city per capita in the nation. Orange Grove Avenue became known as "Millionaire's Row," and luxury hotels catering to wealthy Easterners proliferated. Sophisticated and wealthy patrons fostered the arts, and Pasadena became an important center for distinctive architecture, painting and sculpture, music, literature, and science. Altogether, wrote resident Charles F. Holder in 1908, Pasadena was "made up of the cream of the culture, education and refinement of Eastern cities."

Although the natural attributes of Pasadena might have been enough to attract outstanding citizens, the activities of the Pasadena Board of Trade were a major factor in the city's development. Formed in 1888 in the aftermath of the boom, the board was, according to its president D.W. Coolidge in 1905:

. . . a Pasadena Promotion Board. The sole purpose . . . is to advertise Pasadena and to promote and encourage everything that will make our beloved city more beautiful, more healthful morally and physically, and more and more the home of the highest type of American and foreign citizenship. We do not bid for factories but lay special stress on our superior location, climate, civic improvement, churches and schools as making the most desirable place of abode.

The board's successful efforts coupled with the strong pattern of migration into Southern California resulted in the tripling of Pasadena's population from just under 10,000 in 1900 to 30,000 in 1907. By 1920, the population had more than quadrupled—to 45,000 people. During the same period, Los Angeles grew even faster, from 170,000 in 1900 to a city of half a million in 1910 and nearly a million in 1920.

Initially, in the 1880s, many of Pasadena's migrants had come from the East, especially Boston. Later, however, residents of Midwestern cities, especially Chicago, predominated. Not only the wealthy responded to the advertising by the Board of Trade. Middle-class people streamed into Southern California, drawn by the promises of health and easier life in the mild climate, and they came to Pasadena as well. The city's reputation as a haven for the wealthy, however, caused the boosters some concern. In 1906, it was estimated that only 10 percent of the population were "laborers and artisans." Since middle-class and working-class people were needed to support the comfortable lives of the rich and to provide a year-round, stable population, booster literature in this period began to make direct appeals to the workingman, promising good opportunities in Pasadena for sober, hard-working individuals.

The southwestern part of the city remained the province of the wealthy, but the rapidly expanding neighborhoods to the north and east provided housing for middle-class retired people, small businessmen, and working people. These neighborhoods, which cover most of the total land area of Pasadena, still retain much of the atmosphere of that period; the tree-lined streets are a progression of modest cottages and bungalows, interspersed occasionally with larger, more substantial dwellings. While the mansions of the wealthy and the grand hotels commanded the most attention, a contemporary writer noted, "there is no less charm . . . in viewing the miles upon miles of flower-embowered cottages or bungalows, which indicate even more plainly than anything else that while wealthy people are coming to Pasadena from all over the country, the city is still preeminently . . . middle-class."

The overwhelming majority of these migrants were white, but other ethnic groups contributed to the population boom. Blacks began arriving in large numbers after the turn of the century, most of them to staff Pasadena's mansions and hotels.

Blacks had come to the area as early as the

1850s, when Robert Owen cut wood in El Prieto Canyon to sell in Los Angeles, but the earliest black settler in Pasadena was Joseph Holmes, who bought a vineyard in 1883. Although Hispanics and Chinese had preceded them and the Japanese had come shortly afterward, blacks later became the most populous minority in Pasadena. Many of them worked as domestic servants or chauffeurs for the occupants of the grand houses along Orange Grove Avenue and elsewhere. By 1900, Pasadena had about 250 black residents, and by 1915, nearly 2,000 blacks lived in the city.

Early social life in the black community centered around the churches. The first meetings of the Methodist congregation were held in 1885 in the Holmes residence, and in 1892 the first church built by a black congregation was erected at Fair Oaks and Villa by the African Methodist Episcopal (AME) congregation. Friendship Baptist Church was organized in 1893; the congregation's first church building was located near the present Ambassador Auditorium.

The black community was concentrated on

One of Pasadena's pioneer black families, the William Nelson Jackson family, came to California from Arkansas around the turn of the century because of Mr. Jackson's poor health. Jackson and his wife Caroline brought four girls and two boys; a third son came from Arkansas later with his family. The family lived on Congress Street and later on Fairmont Avenue, near the present Huntington Hospital. Courtesy, Pasadena Historical Society

South Vernon Avenue, just a short distance from the Orange Grove houses where many black residents worked. In some cases, employers supplied housing, but many blacks could afford to own property, and so bought their own houses. Perhaps the wealthiest black in town in the early 1900s was Reuben Scott, who owned a transfer business, picking up trunks at the railroad station and delivering them to residential areas.

In the early years, blacks had the general respect of the community at large and had access to most institutions and public accommodations. That there was little discrimination can probably be attributed to the fact that Pasadena, unlike much of Southern California, was settled by people from the Midwest and New England; many of them had been veterans of the Union Army and a number of them had been prominent abolitionists. But as the memories of the abolition movement and the Civil War faded, and a wave of new white migrants came to Pasadena in the early years of this century, the atmosphere of tolerance was replaced by incidents of racism and the beginnings of segregation in public accommodations and schools. At the same time, blacks expanded their political organizations to protest against new segregation policies.

The first major racial incident occurred in 1909 when the AME congregation began building a church on North Vernon Avenue. Attempts to burn the church down forced parishioners to stand guard at night with rifles. There were also threats against the proposed Metropolitan Baptist Church building on Waverly, following the burning of two houses on Cypress Avenue owned by blacks. Later that year a house on Sunset Avenue occupied by a black man was burned in a fire of mysterious origin.

The issue of segregation of Pasadena's only public swimming pool, Brookside Plunge, arose in 1914, only a week after its opening on July 4. Pasadena's black citizens protested that they were not being allowed to use the new pool. After some discussion, the city decided to open it to blacks and other minorities on Wednesdays. White women and girls were also restricted to one day a week, and black women had no privileges at all. Led by William Prince and others, black Pasadenans formed the Negro Tax Payers' and Voters' Association and hired lawyers from Los Angeles to press their case. Although they cited California's laws prohibiting discrimination in public facilities, they failed to move the City Commission. The segregation of Brookside Plunge remained a major source of resentment in the black community until the 1940s, when it was finally opened on an equal basis.

In 1915 Pasadena's black citizens began a drive to get jobs with the City of Pasadena, applying for policeman and fireman positions. At the time, blacks were employed only in menial jobs in the Street Department, and as janitors in City Hall. Another sign of rising black consciousness was a float entered by the black community in the 1916 Rose Parade. The float, depicting the Dove of Peace in 2,000 white carnations, was awarded a major prize. A little over a year later, two black women who were charged twenty-five cents admission to a Pasadena theater which admitted whites for less, sued the theater, won their case in Superior Court, and were awarded $100 in damages. The increasing political action by blacks led to the founding in 1919 of Pasadena's chapter of the National Association for the Advancement of Colored People (NAACP).

A relatively small but important minority group in Pasadena around the turn of the century was the Chinese. A considerable number of Chinese had lived in the San Gabriel Valley well before the founding of Pasadena. At the old ranches such as the Sphinx Ranch, Fair Oaks Ranch, and the Sierra Madre Villa Hotel, house servants and field hands were Chinese.

After the founding of Pasadena, one of the first businesses established was Yuen Kee's laundry, which apparently did the laundry for the whole village. Chinese entertainments were popular for churches and bazaars; a Chinese orchestra played at the library's first Art Loan Exhibition in 1884; and itinerant Chinese peddlers sold vegetables and

Chinese wares to householders and to tourists at the Raymond Hotel. By the early 1900s, many of the cooks in the great houses along Orange Grove were Chinese.

Despite often amiable relationships, anti-Chinese feeling, fed by anti-Chinese sentiment in California, persisted in Pasadena. The 1885 riot directed against one of Pasadena's Chinese laundries was not the only example of anti-Chinese feeling in Pasadena. Members of the Chinese-American Vegetable Cooperative suffered a great loss in 1918 when their warehouse on South Arroyo Parkway was destroyed by fire. Many of the peddlers lived on the premises and seventeen horses were stabled there. The fire, attributed to arsonists, destroyed personal possessions, all the produce, and killed most of the horses.

Also important in the early history of the community were the Hispanics, whose numbers were swelled in that early part of the century by migration from Mexico, especially around the time of the Mexican Revolution in 1910. A considerable Hispanic population lived in the San Gabriel Valley before the 1873 land purchase by the San Gabriel Orange Grove Association and the subsequent settlement of Pasadena. Of Spanish or mixed Spanish and Indian ancestry, the Hispanics lived near the mission, in small settlements, or on ranches scattered throughout the valley.

An important figure in the early days of Pasadena was Arturo Bandini, a sheep rancher of Spanish ancestry, who led the early hunts and taught Spanish to some of the settlers. Bandini married Helen Elliott, daughter of Dr. Thomas Elliott, and their son, Ralph Bandini, was one of the founders in 1915 of the Hispanic Society, a statewide organization dedicated to preserving the history of Spanish California.

The Hispanic community in early Pasadena was concentrated south of California Street. A focal point of the community was a Catholic mission church, Our Lady of Guadalupe, built on California at Raymond in 1911. The Pasadena Settlement House (later called the Edna P. Alter Memorial Association) was established by Associated Charities in 1911 to serve the neighborhood. Operating out of small buildings on California Street and Raymond Avenue and organized along the lines of Jane Addams' Hull House in Chicago, the association provided help to indigent families, educational programs, a day nursery, and a small maternity hospital set up in a former garage. (Non-whites were not admitted to Pasadena Hospital for treatment.)

Like Hull House, where work centered on European immigrant communities in Chicago, the goal of the association was Americanization, and to this end it offered English classes and other programs designed to teach American customs. Women were taught housekeeping, cooking, and baking, so that they might better care for their families, but also so that they might be employed as domestics.

In east Pasadena, east of Lamanda Park and Eaton Wash, another Hispanic community, Titleyville or *Chihuahuaita,* founded to provide labor for the railroad, stood in marked contrast to Pasadena's industrial district. According to an early newspaper account, the houses there were "neat and comfortable, there are little yards and in most of them flowers are growing. There is a small mission church here, [which] serves on weekdays for school purposes and on Sunday for church services. It is undenominational and is well attended by all."

In about 1915 separate schools were set up for Spanish-speaking children, one on Raymond Avenue, called the Raymond Avenue school, the other in Titleyville, which later became Fremont School. At Garfield School on California Street, where Anglo children also attended, Hispanic children were taught in separate classes and steered toward manual work. According to a newspaper account of 1912, "the Garfield school is unique in that it has representatives of all classes—those of wealthy parentage from millionaires' row, as well as the humble Mexicans." Most of the Hispanic children came from families whose parents worked in the fields or did heavy labor for the railroad or construction projects. In 1916 at the behest of

Almost every form of conveyance—buggies, bicycles, automobiles, and streetcars—can be found in this photograph of Pasadena's commercial center, taken in about 1910. The simple lines of the newly-built Slavin Block on the northeast corner of Colorado and Fair Oaks contrast with its elaborate Victorian neighbors, built in the 1800s boom. Courtesy, The Huntington Library

Anglo citizens, the Arroyo Seco school was opened on South Grand Avenue for their children, altering the social and ethnic mix at Garfield.

The rapid growth of the school population paralleled the increase in the general population in the early 1900s, straining city government and utilities. Since incorporation Pasadena had been governed by a Board of Trustees, citizen-volunteers who had functioned well within the limits of their prescribed responsibilities. In 1901 Pasadena got a new charter, enabling it to increase revenues and gain greater control over its water supply, which was approaching a crisis situation. The charter provided for a mayor-council form of government, vesting important powers in the mayor, a salaried official.

Pasadena's first mayor elected under the new system was Martin H. Weight, who won despite fears that he might interpret the liquor ordinance too liberally. Although Weight was mayor for only two years, his administration is remembered for its establishment of Pasadena's first parks, Central Park and Library Park (now Memorial Park), and the completion of Pasadena's first City Hall building in 1903. A stolid Mission Revival style structure located at the northeast corner of Fair Oaks and Union, the new City Hall was "a disappointment in location, convenience and architecture," according to historian John W. Wood. Moreover, it soon proved inadequate for the needs of the rapidly growing city.

Weight was defeated in the 1903 election by William H. Vedder, a "retired capitalist," who was an extremely popular figure in the community. Vedder's most important accomplishment was to obtain the approval of the voters to form a municipal water department by combining Pasadena's two water companies, the Lake Vineyard Water Company, which served the neighborhoods east of Fair Oaks, and the Pasadena Water Company on the west side of town. Aggravated by the city's rapid growth, the water situation had become a major issue by the time of Vedder's election.

Pasadena's water supply was limited to the waters of the Arroyo Seco and the reserves of the Raymond Basin, which were tapped by wells. For the small colony of orange growers, these sources had been perfectly adequate, once an efficient piping system had been installed. But after little more than a decade, the early cast-iron mains began to

By the mid-1920s, Pasadena had developed a park system of over 1,000 acres. This early view shows Pasadena's first park, Central Park, from the roof of the Hotel Green. Courtesy, Western History Collection, Natural History Museum of Los Angeles County

deteriorate, and pollution of the unlined ditches and uncovered reservoirs caused further problems. Increased consumer demand at the time of the boom, and a dry winter in 1887-1888 caused the water supply to dry up completely in the late summer of 1888.

Both water companies undertook extensive repairs and improvements to their systems, but by the late 1890s the water question again became acute. In 1896, extensive fires in the mountains destroyed most of the vegetation that protected the watershed of the Arroyo Seco. A well-known hydraulic engineer, J.B. Lippincott, hired in 1898 to assess the water needs and resources of the city, determined that Pasadena would need to tap outside sources in order to accommodate future growth.

Finally, in 1903, the voters approved acquisition of the two water companies by the city and the funding of a project to obtain water from the San Gabriel River at Whittier Narrow. But Mayor William Waterhouse, who succeeded Vedder in 1904, declared the election invalid on technical grounds, putting the water question back where it had started and delaying the formation of the department for another eight years. Annexations of North Pasadena in 1904 and East Pasadena in 1906 had more than doubled the city's area, further straining the water supply.

Thomas Earley, who ran successfully against Waterhouse in 1906 by campaigning on the water question, failed to accomplish his goal during his four years in office. It was left to Mayor William Thum, who took office in 1911, to finally achieve the passage of the bond issue that paid for the acquisition of the private water companies and their merger into the Pasadena Water Department. Thum, who had gained his wealth as the inventor and manufacturer of a sticky flypaper sold under the brand name of "Tanglefoot," was a civic-minded philanthropist known for his active interest in public affairs. Under his guidance, the two original water companies and the North Pasadena Water Company were purchased for a total of $1,211,209.16, and the municipal system was officially established on November 1, 1912. Until the 1930s Pasadena continued to get its water from local wells and streams, principally the Arroyo Seco; no water was ever developed from the Whittier Narrows source.

The first accomplishment of Pasadena city government to attract national attention in this period was the city's unusual sewage disposal system. With no available outlet to a river or the sea, the City of Pasadena purchased 300 acres of farmland in present-day Alhambra for $37,500 in the 1890s to develop a working farm, watered and fertilized by sewage. Using deep irrigation and deep cultivating methods, the process was claimed to be sanitary and odorless. Walnuts, pumpkins, hay and grain, corn, and alfalfa were raised, and the land was made to produce constantly throughout the year.

For years the sewer farm was a profitable enterprise; the 1904-1905 auditor's report shows $10,500 in receipts, against $8,000 in disbursements. Walnuts were the biggest source of income, and the walnut grove was said to be the largest in the nation in the early part of the century. By 1908 the farm, which had grown to over 500 acres, also raised food for the horses of the street and fire departments; pigs kept on the farm consumed table scraps collected and trucked in from Pasadena. The farm proved to be a profitable investment in other ways; by 1914 the land was valued at half a million dollars, and with the increasing urbanization of Southern California, parcels sold off at later dates financed such major city projects as the building of the Municipal Golf Course in Brookside Park in the 1920s and the Pasadena Civic Auditorium in the early 1930s.

In the early years of the century Pasadena pioneered in municipal lighting, and its battle with the giant Edison Electric Company (later Southern California Edison) received national attention. The Edison Company began selling electricity in Pasadena for streetlighting and other purposes in 1904, but the initial year's service was so unsatisfactory that Mayor Waterhouse refused to pay Edison's bill. Soon afterward the City Board decided

A testament to Pasadena's strong awareness of its history is the Pasadena Pioneer Society, organized in 1908 at this meeting at "Wynyate," home of Jennie Collier and Margaret Collier Graham. Membership was open to those who had come to Pasadena before 1884 and their descendants. Courtesy, Pasadena Public Library

to start a municipal streetlighting system of its own. Pasadenans approved a bond issue to finance streetlighting and by 1907, Pasadena was able to terminate its contract with Edison. City electricity proved to be cheaper than Edison's, and in 1909, the voters approved extending the utility, ably managed by lighting engineer C. Wellington Koiner, to serve residential and commercial customers. Thus began a decade-long struggle between the competing municipal and private systems.

Though the city's rates were initially cheaper than Edison's, Edison soon undercut the price, subsidizing its Pasadena losses with higher rates in neighboring cities and starting an all-out rate war. Pasadenans, however, remained loyal to the city system, even though they were paying more. The struggle was made more bitter by the fact that

For many years Busch Gardens equaled the Tournament of Roses as a widely known Pasadena tourist attraction. It had its origin in 1903 and consisted of approximately thirty acres of sunken gardens, rolling lawns, and winding paths. Statues of fairy-tale figures and miniature buildings were a conspicuous feature of the gardens. Several miles of walks and roadways served the thousands of tourists who visited the park until its closure in the late 1930s. Courtesy, Pasadena Public Library

many Edison officials and influential stockholders lived in Pasadena, and they tried to bring their political influence to bear on the city. Edison employed salesmen to solicit business for the company among residential customers. The city responded with volunteers who talked to their friends and neighbors and to new residents about the advantages of the municipal power system.

A major turn of events in the rate war was the passage of the Unjust Competition Act by the state legislature in 1914. Introduced by Senator William J. Carr, formerly Pasadena's city attorney, the new law made it illegal for Edison to charge discriminatory prices among various cities. Rate regulation proved favorable for Pasadena; by 1920, the city utility had 12,000 customers, while Edison served only 4,000. Later that year, Edison sold its Pasadena business to the city, giving the municipal utility a monopoly on Pasadena's power supply.

Besides providing for water, electricity, and sewage disposal, the city was also responsible for streets and parks. In 1906, architect Alfred Heineman urged the City Board to institute a street tree planting program to enhance the beauty of Pasadena, arguing that tree-lined streets would improve everyone's property values. The earliest settlers had recognized the importance of mature shade trees in the Southern California climate and had planted pepper trees along Orange Grove and Marengo avenues and walnut trees along West Colorado Street. By 1909 the city had established a tree nursery and began to designate official street trees.

This effort at civic beautification was followed by efforts to acquire public park land, particularly in the Arroyo Seco. The great wooded gorge on the western edge of the city had long been a park-like refuge from city life. Unfortunately, the Arroyo had also long served as a dump. Dead horses and cows as well as garbage were routinely dumped over the banks, and since 1902 the city had operated an incinerator in the northwestern part of the Arroyo near the present site of the Jet Propulsion Laboratory.

Arroyo land was held by a number of owners. Most prominent of these was Adolphus Busch, whose property on Orange Grove Avenue stretched down into the Arroyo bed. In 1905,

Mrs. Adolphus Busch survived her husband by fifteen years, continuing to live in the Orange Grove mansion until her death in 1928. Mindful of the prejudice against her husband because of his German heritage, Mrs. Busch arranged for American war veterans to collect admission fees to Busch Gardens. Courtesy, Pasadena Historical Society

When President Theodore Roosevelt visited Pasadena in 1903, feelings over the Panama Canal ran high, as evidenced by this sign at the Raymond Hotel. Roosevelt's itinerary included a speech at Wilson School, a visit to Throop Institute, a call on Mrs. James A. Garfield, widow of the assassinated president, and a stop at the Pasadena library. Courtesy, Security Pacific National Bank Photograph Collection/ Los Angeles Public Library

Busch began developing his "backyard," a former horse pasture, into one of California's most celebrated gardens. In the hands of Busch's Scottish landscape gardener, Robert J. Fraser, and a staff of twenty to thirty trained nurserymen, the Arroyo slopes were terraced, picturesque stone walls were built, fountains and pools were put in, trees and flower beds were planted. Winding paths led down the slopes past a quaint mill and Hansel and Gretel cottages, where terra-cotta fairy-tale figures decorated the lawns. Developed over the course of several years, Busch Gardens became a prime tourist attraction. First opened to the public in 1906, by 1909 it was open daily during the winter tourist season.

As early as 1887, leading citizens proposed making the Arroyo a public park. When conservationist President Theodore Roosevelt visited Pasadena in 1903, he gave impetus to the idea, saying to Mayor Vedder: "What a splendid natural park you have right here! O, Mr. Mayor, don't let them spoil that! Keep it just as it is!" It was not until 1911, however, under Mayor Thum, that the city began to acquire Arroyo land. The city bought the first parcel of thirty acres for $4,500. By 1912, the city held or had options on 200 acres. A syndicate of wealthy citizens bought up most of the remaining options and held them until the city could purchase the parcels.

A plan for the Arroyo was formulated in 1917 and 1918 with the help of Emil T. Mische, a well-known landscape architect brought to Pasadena through the efforts of the Pasadena Garden Club. Mische and the Arroyo Park Committee, headed by architect Myron Hunt, recommended that the Lower Arroyo be preserved, restricted to walking and bridle paths and planted only with native plants. The Upper Arroyo was termed more suitable for recreational development.

The city had begun developing a park in the Upper Arroyo in 1913 with a playground, picnic tables, plantings, and sports facilities. In 1914,

Mrs. E.W. Brooks had donated funds to build a municipal "plunge," and the park was renamed Brookside Park in her honor. Tennis courts and a baseball diamond were added shortly afterwards, and plans were made for an outdoor "Greek" theater, which was finally built in 1924.

Throughout the century's early decades Pasadena's schools struggled to keep pace with the growth of the city. The schools were forced to resort to half-day sessions and the use of basements and tents for classrooms. In 1901, Pasadena's first public kindergarten opened. During this period, Pasadena became one of the first cities in the nation to create an "intermediate school" (later called junior high school).

Pasadena High School was built in 1904 at

Pasadena's Brookside Plunge, built in 1914, was enlarged for the 1932 Olympics, when diving and water polo trials were held there. Not until the 1940s was this important recreational facility open to all of Pasadena's citizens on an equal basis. Courtesy, Security Pacific National Bank Photograph Collection/Los Angeles Public Library

Left: *Pasadena's first high school building was completed in 1904 at Walnut Street and Los Robles Avenue. When a much larger school was built on Colorado Street near Hill Avenue in 1912, this building became John Muir Junior High School. Courtesy, Pasadena Historical Society*

Left, below: *The Horace Mann Building was one of three buildings on the Pasadena High School campus located on the old Rose Villa Ranch on East Colorado Street. Completely remodeled and stripped of their classical Beaux Arts decoration in the late 1930s, these buildings still stand, forming the central quadrangle of the Pasadena City College campus. Courtesy, Pasadena Historical Society*

Walnut and Los Robles, the first separate high school in the city. It later became John Muir Junior High School when in 1912, Pasadena built another Pasadena High School located "out in the country" on the old Rose Villa Ranch, known for its half-mile long blooming rose hedge. The high school's three new buildings were sited in an open quadrangle facing Colorado Street near Hill. Planned as a community center, the new school had an assembly hall, lecture rooms, and sports facilities intended to serve the entire community.

By 1920 Pasadena schools had an enrollment of 10,000 pupils, compared to fewer than 4,000 in 1900. In 1915, adult education was started, with evening high school classes in Spanish, automobile repairing, and domestic science. There were also "Americanization" classes to aid the foreign-born.

The Pasadena Public Library grew rapidly after the turn of the century. The imposing building on North Raymond Avenue, which pre-dated the first City Hall building by over a decade and was often mistaken for a church, was visible evidence of the importance of the library to the community. In 1898, when Miss Nellie Russ took charge as librarian, the library had 14,000 volumes, which in health-conscious Pasadena were regularly disinfected with formaldehyde to prevent the spread of disease.

Miss Russ began at once to make Pasadena's library a leading cultural institution. The library housed not only books, but also many collections of artifacts and paintings, objects which today would more properly belong to a museum. In those days, however, the library did serve as a museum, and it was particularly rich in natural history collections. The library for some time also had a "California table." Miss Russ developed this collection, buying many items from her small budget that later proved to be important, even priceless, works related to California history. By the time she resigned her position in 1919, her California collection had become the third largest of its kind in the state, and was considered by many the best in any California public library.

Pasadena was known as a city of churches, and by 1910, over fifty churches were serving the community. The Methodists claimed the greatest numbers, having one of the largest congregations in the country, while the Presbyterians were Pasadena's wealthiest congregation. The three Friends Meetings numbered among their members many prominent early citizens. The Catholic church, St. Andrews, founded in 1886, also served a growing congregation. Certainly the largest and most striking building belonged to the Christian Scientists. Completed in 1909, the majestic domed First Church of Christ Scientist dominated the residen-

Above: *During her tenure as librarian, Nellie Russ purchased Spanish manuscripts, rare letters, magazines, and books on California history for the Pasadena Public Library. What had begun as a few books for tourists interested in California became a major California history collection. Courtesy, Pasadena Historical Society*

Left: *Pasadena's massive stone library building, completed in 1890, was a monument to the cultural aspirations of the early townspeople. The library has remained one of Pasadena's primary cultural institutions, although this building, damaged by the 1933 earthquake, was pulled down in the 1950s. Courtesy, The Huntington Library*

tial neighborhood where it stood at Green Street and Oakland Avenue. The Nazarenes, led by their founder, Phineas Bresee, a former Pasadena Methodist minister, moved their Pacific Bible College to the old Hugus ranch in northeast Pasadena in 1910. Known later as Pasadena College, the school offered religious instruction and later a standard liberal arts curriculum on its Pasadena campus before moving to San Diego in the 1970s.

Musical life in Pasadena began in earnest with the establishment in 1904 of the Coleman Chamber Music Association. The founder, Alice Coleman, was a gifted pianist, who had studied in Boston and considered pursuing a concert career. The annual series of chamber concerts which she organized has come to be recognized as the oldest chamber music association in the nation. Launching the series was not easy; Alice Coleman recalled telephoning friends and acquaintances in that first year to explain to them what chamber music was. Suitable halls were unavailable, so the concerts were held at Clune's Theatre, the Hotel Green, the high school auditorium, and even in Alice Coleman's home after her marriage to Ernest Batchelder. Not until 1928 did the association find a semi-permanent home at the Pasadena Playhouse.

In 1921, the association established a Composer's Fellowship to aid Southern California composers. The first recipient was Arthur Farwell, and the second Roy Harris, both of whom are recognized as distinguished American composers. The Coleman continues to sponsor concerts by leading chamber music groups from this country and abroad, and its prestigious annual competition for young artists has greatly advanced the careers of the winners.

In 1911, Alice Coleman noted that Pasadena had a growing audience for music and a flourishing musical life. But she envisioned an even greater role for Pasadena. "Why should we not make of Pasadena a veritable little home of the best in music and kindred arts? . . . Let us cease to lament our distance from the music centers of the

Right: *Literary societies, amateur theater groups, and musical organizations were part of the social life of early Pasadena, as was typical of small towns across America. Here a musical quartet of young women poses with instruments. Courtesy, Pasadena Historical Society*

Opposite: *Ernest Batchelder and his wife, Alice Coleman Batchelder, were among Pasadena's leading artists and supporters of the arts. Ernest taught design at Throop, created unique art tiles, juried the Civic Center design competition, served on the Planning Commission, and as president of the Playhouse Association. Alice, a trained concert pianist, founded the Coleman Chamber Music Association and was one of Pasadena's leading musicians. Courtesy, Robert Winter*

Formerly the Shakespeare Club, the building for the Stickney Memorial School of Fine Arts, located at Fair Oaks and Lincoln avenues, was donated to the Pasadena Music and Art Association by Miss Susan Stickney. Many of Pasadena's most noted artists, such as Guy Rose, Jean Mannheim, and Alson Clark, taught at the school, which also sponsored a Beaux Arts atelier for architects. Courtesy, Pasadena Historical Society

east and stand shoulder to shoulder in making of Pasadena a worthy center of art."

One who took up her challenge was George Ellery Hale, internationally known astronomer, who had come from Chicago in 1903 to establish an observatory on Mt. Wilson. Hale, who was from a wealthy Chicago family, became a leader in Pasadena's intellectual and cultural life. In 1912, he founded the Pasadena Music and Art Association, an organization that began to bring well-known concert artists and the Los Angeles Philharmonic to Pasadena. The association had as members of its board some of the most influential men and women of the city, including Henry Huntington, James Culbertson, James Scherer (president of Throop), Charles F. Holder, C.B. Scoville, George S. Patton, Bishop Joseph Johnson, and Arthur Fleming. Hale was able to persuade Miss Susan Stickney to donate the Shakespeare Club building on North Fair Oaks to the association, founding the Stickney Memorial School of Fine Arts, where many important Southern California artists were active. The association began to acquire paintings and pieces of sculpture in anticipation of the establishment of a permanent art museum.

Literary figures who lived in Pasadena after the turn of the century included Upton Sinclair, Robinson Jeffers, and George Wharton James. Jeffers, who came to Pasadena with his family at the age of sixteen, graduated from Occidental College and soon settled in Carmel, where he did most of his writing. Upton Sinclair came to Pasadena in 1915, staying and writing for about two decades. The Sinclairs lived first on North Hudson Avenue, and later moved to Sunset Avenue, where they owned several lots, onto which Mary, Sinclair's wife, kept moving old houses and attaching them to each other, forming in the end a large but rather strange-looking dwelling. Publication of some of Sinclair's books was subsidized by Kate Crane Gartz, a Chicago heiress who lived in Altadena. Sinclair was known in Pasadena less for his literary achievements than for his excellent tennis playing, which he indulged in regularly on the courts of the exclusive Valley Hunt Club, partnering Pasadena businessmen.

A usually neglected writer, but one who has well over fifty books to his credit, is George Wharton James. James, who came to Pasadena in the 1890s and worked as a publicist for the Mt. Lowe Railway, wrote a number of volumes on Indians of the Southwest, and especially on Indian basketry, on which he was an acknowledged expert. He also wrote on the California missions, on travel in Southern California, on psychological subjects, and on Craftsman design. Given his interests, it is not surprising that James was a rival of Charles F.

George Wharton James arrived in Pasadena in the early 1890s, a defrocked Methodist minister, his reputation sullied by a scandalous divorce. He soon went to work for Thaddeus Lowe as a publicity agent for the Mt. Lowe Railway. James went on to become a leading cultural figure and promoter of Craftsman ideals. Courtesy, Southwest Museum

Astronomer George Ellery Hale was the moving force behind the development of Throop Institute into a major scientific research institution, the California Institute of Technology. Hale is shown here working with a spectroheliograph, an instrument he developed to study the sun. Courtesy, California Institute of Technology

Lummis, his better-known counterpart in Los Angeles. In Pasadena, James was known for Thursday evening salons at his home on North Raymond Avenue and for his founding of the local Browning Club, a society devoted to the study of the works of the poet Robert Browning.

Another largely forgotten writer of the period, Charles F. Holder, wrote not only about Pasadena, but about wildlife, marine animals, hunting, and fishing. Elizabeth Grinnell was a well-known author who wrote about bird life in Southen California. Ernest Batchelder wrote on education, aesthetics and design; Una Nixon Hopkins and Helen Lukens Gaut spread knowledge of Pasadena's unique architecture in articles in major national magazines. Helen Elliott Bandini, daughter of original settler Dr. Thomas Elliott, wrote on early Pasadena and California history. Elizabeth Boynton Harbert, feminist and social activist from Chicago, wrote articles and books on women's issues. Writers who were temporary residents included Gertrude Potter Daniels of Chicago; novelist and short story writer George Peck, creator of the Peck's Bad Boy series; Noah Brooks, best known for his works on Abraham Lincoln and his editorship of Mark Twain's works; and Francis Leupp, an authority on American Indians.

Despite the material prosperity and vital cultural life of Pasadena in this period, its history would undoubtedly have developed differently if George Ellery Hale had not established Mt. Wilson Observatory at the top of Mt. Wilson near Pasadena. As early as the 1880s, Mt. Wilson had been recognized as enjoying an unusually stable atmosphere, ideal for astronomical "seeing." An early collaboration between Harvard University and the University of Southern California to found an observatory on the mountain foundered for financial reasons after the collapse of the Southern California land boom in 1888, but Hale, a young MIT student at the time, was impressed by Harvard professor E.C. Pickering's enthusiastic accounts of the fine atmospheric conditions at Pasadena.

In 1902, Hale was appointed to the committee on astronomy for the newly-established Carnegie Foundation. Remembering Pickering's accounts, Hale made an expedition to Southern California in 1903 to view the site and immediately proposed to Carnegie the installation of both a solar observatory and a sixty-inch stellar telescope.

The following year the Carnegie Institution awarded Hale $150,000 for each of the next two years. Work had already begun on the mountain, and an instrument shop was set up in a building on West Union Street in Pasadena to fabricate the necessary equipment. In anticipation of the construction of the sixty-inch telescope, the shop was moved to a new building on Santa Barbara Street in 1905, where land had been donated by the city. Walter S. Adams, a colleague of Hale's and later director of the observatory, recalled that Santa Barbara Street in those days was a dirt country road "with only occasional small farmhouses and barns scattered here and there."

If conditions were primitive in Pasadena, they were even more primitive on Mt. Wilson. Transportation up the mountain was by burro, and these beasts proved to be wily and unpredictable, preferring the trip down to the trip up and stopping to graze on the slopes whenever they had the chance. The limitations of this mode of transport meant that no building materials or equipment could measure more than eight feet long. The animals, however, proved their worth when one professor discovered that their very fine hair could be used to make cross-hairs for the guiding telescope. Astronomers and workmen lived in tents or at Martin's or Strain's mountain resort camps nearby, while an old building, known as the Casino, was repaired and made ready for use. Other buildings, such as the legendary Monastery, a dormitory for professors and students, soon followed. From that first summer of 1904, the new observatory was visited by important scientists, culminating in the meeting of the International Solar Union in Pasadena in 1910.

While Hale was busy with activities on Mt. Wilson, he also took an interest in the future of Pasadena's chief educational institution, Throop Polytechnic Institute. Primarily a coeducational manual training school for all ages from first grade through college, the institute added a College of Science and Engineering in 1905. Hale saw in the school the opportunity to create an "MIT of the West," an institution of international stature on a par with the growing Mt. Wilson Observatory. Named to the Throop Board of Trustees in 1907, Hale convinced his fellow trustees to appoint a new president, James A.B. Scherer, whom Hale had met in 1907 while sailing to Europe. Although no scientist, Scherer was an accomplished orator and a proven fundraiser, just the person needed to head a new and growing institution.

Throop's location at North Fair Oaks and Chestnut at the edge of the expanding business district limited the size of its campus. Hale per-

The erection of this small telescope on Mt. Wilson marks the beginning of the Mt. Wilson Observatory established by George Ellery Hale. Pictured here with Hale (third from left) are some Pasadena promoters of the telescope: H.J. Holmes (second from left), who was Pasadena's first mayor; and William R. Staats (fourth from left), a successful real estate promoter. Courtesy, The Huntington Library

suaded Arthur Fleming, whose lumber interests in the Pacific Northwest had made him a millionaire, to donate funds to purchase twenty-two acres of orange groves at Wilson and California and to build a building. Myron Hunt and Elmer Grey, local architects who had practiced together since 1904, were hired to draw up a campus plan and to design the first building, Pasadena Hall (later called Throop Hall), which was dedicated in 1910.

No sooner had Throop opened its doors as Throop Institute, an engineering and science college for men only, than news came that the California state legislature was considering establishing a "California Institute of Technology" in Southern California. Pressure from Northern Californians, who wanted no rival state institution in the south, finally forced the legislature to abandon the plan, but the resultant publicity for Throop and

"Automobiling" was a favorite pastime in Pasadena in the early 1900s. Here Charles Gibbs Adams and his wife Mary drive down Colorado Street in their horseless carriage. By 1915 Pasadena claimed more autos per capita than any other city in the world. Courtesy, Pasadena Public Library

President Scherer brought in $250,000 in new endowment funds, and enhanced the prestige of the institute.

Assuming yet another name, Throop College of Technology in 1913, Throop began to develop its various departments by attracting famous scientists. First to come, on a part-time basis, was Arthur Amos Noyes, distinguished chemist at MIT and former classmate of Hale's. Then came physicist Robert Millikan of the University of Chicago, who at first spent only three months each year in Pasadena. Gifts from Arthur Fleming of one million dollars, from Dr. Norman Bridge (a Chicago physican who had retired to Pasadena for health reasons) of $250,000 for a physics laboratory, from Robert R. Blacker of $50,000, and others, put the college on a solid financial footing. In 1919 Noyes resigned from MIT and came to Throop full-time; and in 1920, the college formally adopted the name, California Institute of Technology.

By 1920, President Scherer's health was failing and he submitted his resignation. Tapped for president of the institute was Robert Millikan, who was wooed ardently by George Hale, and tempted by Norman Bridge's offer of a new physics laboratory and by Arthur Fleming's promise to turn over his entire fortune to the institute if Millikan would accept the post. Millikan came to Pasadena and formally took charge of the institute in the fall of 1921. With Millikan's assumption of the presidency, the modern history of the California Institute of Technology began.

As Pasadena and its institutions grew during the first two decades of the century, the beginnings of a major change in the Southern California way of life were taking place. "Automobiling" was becoming a popular pastime, and Pasadena's Board of Trade aggressively promoted the development and paving of roads in the Los Angeles area, opening the vast and picturesque countryside to the driver. According to a 1906 article about Pasadena, "the automobiles are nearly as numerous as residences, and the little city boasts of the largest garage on

Opposite: *The graceful curves of the Colorado Street Bridge, built in 1913, resulted from difficulties in finding solid footing in the Arroyo bed. Engineer John Drake Mercereau conceived the idea of curving the bridge, thereby creating not just a bridge, but "a work of art," as one of his contemporaries called it. Courtesy, Western History Collection, Natural History Museum of Los Angeles County*

Above: *Crossing the Arroyo Seco was an arduous task before the Colorado Street Bridge was built. Horses and wagons descended the steep eastern slope (road in foreground), crossed the stream over Scoville Bridge, and then climbed up the west bank through Eagle Rock pass. A second road leads off to the right toward Linda Vista. Courtesy, Western History Collection, Natural History Museum of Los Angeles County*

the coast." The Huntington Hotel's two-story garage provided space for 150 autos with forty sleeping rooms for chauffeurs above. In one month alone, the newspaper reported that eighteen railroad cars loaded with fifty-four tourist autos had arrived in town. In 1915, Pasadena claimed more autos per capita than any other city in the world, 5,000 in a city of 40,000 people; and by 1916, the police department was reporting an average of one automobile stolen per week in the city.

The completion of the Colorado Street Bridge in 1913, and the subsequent designation of Colorado Street as a link in the transcontinental highway known as the National Old Trails Route made Pasadena a through-route for automobile traffic, both for the transcontinental traveler and the Southern Californian traveling between the San Gabriel and San Fernando valleys. Rising 160 feet above the channel of the Arroyo Seco, the new bridge greatly simplified the crossing of the Arroyo. Previously the traveler had had to descend to the bottom of the Arroyo and cross the stream over the small Scoville Bridge, before climbing arduously up the other side. The new bridge not only shortened and eased the trip, it was a marvel of modern engineering, the longest and highest bridge in the Southwest. Its curved concrete span of enormous arches prompted one contemporary to claim it as "one of the few bridges that can properly be classified as a work of art." Ornamental lights and floodlights, installed some years later, illuminated its graceful lines at night.

Ceremonies to open the Colorado Street Bridge were held at Carmelita on December 13, 1913. Afterward a procession of cars decorated with banners and pennants and led by Chamber of Commerce President Edwin Sorver drove across the 1,467-foot long span, where celebrants could enjoy the beautiful views of the Arroyo and the mountains. Built in eighteen months, the bridge had cost $200,000, with half the cost being borne by the City of Pasadena, the other half by Los Ange-

Pasadenans pulled together to raise money and to gather clothing, medical supplies, and food during World War I. This photograph shows Pasadena City Hall decorated with patriotic flags, bunting, and slogans exhorting citizens to help the war effort. Courtesy, Pasadena Historical Society

les County.

A few months after the opening of the new bridge the Automobile Club of Southern California posted signs at Colorado and Fair Oaks, directing the traveler to New York or Los Angeles along the National Old Trails Route (later Route 66). By 1916, twenty to thirty cars a day were arriving in California over the new route. Like the railroad only a few decades earlier, the transcontinental automobile route affected the development of all the towns through which it passed; in Pasadena, Colorado Street developed from a residential street into an automobile-oriented commercial strip.

Although thousands of miles distant, the outbreak of World War I in August 1914 had consequences in Pasadena. The war gave a great boost to Pasadena's tourist trade, as wealthy Easterners could no longer frequent their favorite resorts in Europe. And, Pasadenans and visitors alike organized relief efforts, beginning in late 1914 with the founding of a local chapter of the American Red Cross. Dr. James Scherer and Mrs. James A. Garfield were among the founders. The local chapter distinguished itself by being the first to organize and equip a Red Cross Ambulance Corps. The Pasadena chapter sent thousands of surgical dressings, hospital supplies, and refugee garments to Europe and in three years collected almost $200,000 for war relief. Other relief groups in Pasadena aided the Belgians, Italians, Syrians, and Armenians.

In drives for Liberty Loans and War Savings Stamps, Pasadenans subscribed over nine million dollars. Education in food conservation and thrift extended down to the smallest children, who were encouraged to perform small household tasks for money; in ten weeks Pasadena schoolchildren earned and saved $5,500 for the war effort. A fabricated ship, "The Good Ship Thrift," built over the body of an automobile, toured the town campaigning for membership and enrolling over 2,100 citizens. Once the United States entered the war, the Navy League (later the Army and Navy League) under the chairmanship of Mrs. Myron Hunt, set up a knitting program, with 4,000 knitters knitting 61,000 garments in little over a year.

The most visible part of the war effort near Pasadena was an Army balloon training camp, established in June 1917 at Arcadia on the site of Lucky Baldwin's race track. Leased from Mrs. Anita Baldwin for a dollar a year, the camp contained spartan military barracks, a canteen and clubhouse, and a large swimming pool, which was a former reservoir. The soldiers were being trained in making observations of enemy movements from tethered balloons at 3,000 to 4,000 feet. In their free time, they were entertained at clubhouses in a converted bungalow on Colorado Boulevard and in the Chamber of Commerce building in Pasadena, where they could read, play pool, listen to music, and socialize with local people.

Throop College also mobilized to make a contribution to the war effort. Under the auspices of the newly-formed National Research Council, the first attempt to organize scientists to contribute to a national war effort, Throop faculty conducted research in aeronautics, submarine detection, supersound, and nitrate supply. Military training was made compulsory on the campus, which had the first ROTC unit in Southern California. Throop was also slated to become an officer training camp; the orange groves that covered the campus were cleared for rows of tents to house the trainees. In the end, the project was never realized, although Throop did train some enlisted men in the last month of the war.

Pasadena's increasing prosperity during and after the war helped it become what the Board of Trade had long claimed it to be, an ideal residential city. Well-built houses, both large and small, bordered its tree-lined streets. Good schools and many churches sustained a stable middle-class community, which supported artists, writers, musicians, and architects. As a winter resort, Pasadena offered an unparalleled natural environment as well as sophisticated hotels and amusements for the wealthy. As the fame of the resort spread, more and more people began to choose Pasadena as a permanent residence, creating an ever-growing year-round community.

THE ARROYO CULTURE AND CRAFTSMAN PASADENA

By the turn of the century, Pasadena's reputation as a fine residential city had been firmly established. The wealthy Easterners who settled in their winter residences comprised a community of sophisticated tastes, leisure time, and money that was unique in Southern California. It was only natural that artists, writers, designers, and architects should be attracted to Pasadena, where they could also expect to find wealthy patrons. While their patrons lived above, on the bluff along Orange Grove Avenue, the artists congregated below, on the slopes of the Arroyo Seco, forming a colony which has been termed the "Arroyo culture."

Many of Pasadena's artists were landscape painters who found their inspiration in the wild park of the Arroyo Seco. Perhaps the most well-known was Benjamin Chambers Brown, who came to Pasadena in 1895. Trained as a photographer as well as in painting, Brown supported himself by teaching art and tinting photographs until he sold a painting of the Altadena poppy fields in about 1900, launching his career. Although known primarily for his accomplished landscapes, Brown also gained recognition as a printmaker in later years.

A contemporary of Brown's was Franz Bischoff, an Austrian immigrant. Initially, he made his living as a china decorator, but in 1908, when he built his house on the Arroyo in South Pasadena, he began to paint landscapes, many of which are characterized by a bold sense of color. Another notable landscape and portrait painter was German-born Jean Mannheim, who built his studio on the banks of the Arroyo in 1908. Known for impressionistic landscapes, Mannheim continued to paint figure compositions and genres, unlike most of his contemporaries.

Farther down the Arroyo in Highland Park was the studio of William Lees Judson, the first head of the University of Southern California School of Fine Arts, and founder of the Arroyo Guild, an association of artists, architects, and craftsmen. On the west side of the Arroyo, in Linda Vista, Elmer and Marion Wachtel lived and painted landscapes, he in oils, she in watercolors. Their paintings are distinguished by subtle colors and a decorative quality different from the impressionistic style of most of their Southern California counterparts. Another interesting figure was Guy Rose, son of L.J. Rose of Sunny Slope Ranch. Rose grew up at Sunny Slope but spent many years in France, where he lived at Giverny as a disciple of Monet's, and became an accomplished impressionist painter. In 1914, he returned to Pasadena, becoming director of the Stickney Memorial School of Fine Arts.

Alexander Stirling Calder, who lived with his family in the Scoville water tower overlooking the Arroyo, was a sculptor with a national reputation. His most important legacy to Pasadena was a series of relief sculptures decorating the entrance of Throop Hall at Caltech. The sculptures (which were taken down and stored when the building was demolished after the 1971 earthquake) depict allegorical figures symbolizing nature, art, energy, science, imagination, and law. Calder left Pasadena to become director of sculpture for the Panama-Pacific Exposition in San Francisco in 1915; but his family, particularly his son, Alexander, the inventor of the mobile and known as Sandy to his childhood friends, is still remembered in Pasadena. Myron Hunt's son, Hubbard, recalls Sandy making authentic-looking suits of armour for himself and playmates from metal scraps, a sign of Calder's early skill in metal work.

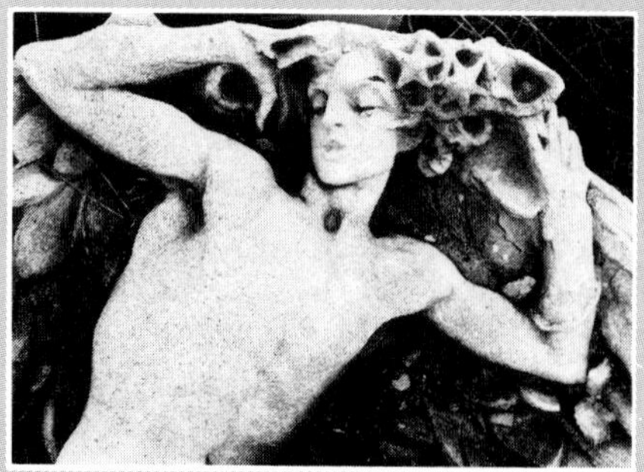

This figure, representing Inspiration, is by Alexander Stirling Calder and graces Throop Hall at Caltech. Photo by Geraint Smith

After the turn of the century, Pasadena became a major West Coast center for the burgeoning American Arts and Crafts movement, the focus of Pasadena's Arroyo culture. The Arts and Crafts movement originated in England in the late nineteenth century in response to a growing disillusionment with the industrial revolution, its shoddy products and inhuman working conditions. William Morris and others sought a return to the medieval guild system, which would unite the artist with the process of production and which would foster craftsmanship in the making of objects for everyday use.

The American popularizer of the Craftsman ideal was a German immigrant, Gustav Stickley. Stickley's magazine, *The Craftsman,* and his New York company, which manufactured "Craftsman" (often called "Mission") furniture, helped spread the Craftsman aesthetic in America. In Pasadena, the Craftsman movement took root in the early years of the century, and it remained the dominant taste in architecture and design until World War I.

One of the leading members of the Arroyo culture was Ernest Batchelder, a New Englander who had studied in Birmingham, England at the School of Arts and Crafts. Batchelder absorbed the teachings of William Morris, and came to Pasadena in 1904 to teach design at Throop

The Arts and Crafts movement looked to nature and the Middle Ages for inspiration. These tiles, designed and manufactured by Ernest Batchelder, depict a castle, a knight on horseback, and a parrot perched on a branch. Photos by Geraint Smith.

Polytechnic Institute. About 1909, Batchelder began to produce the unique decorative tiles associated with his name. Batchelder's tiles of this period make use of medieval motifs, landscapes, and botanical and animal forms (a favorite was the peacock), executed in relief, colored in muted earth tones and left unglazed or given a soft matte glaze. These tiles, decorated and undecorated, found their way into many of the Craftsman houses built in this period in Pasadena and throughout Southern California, usually as fireplace surrounds.

The most enduring legacy of the Arts and Crafts movement in Pasadena was the Craftsman bungalow, which became known during this period for its innovation and high quality. Articles in national and local periodicals about Pasadena extolled the outstanding architecture and garden settings of the city. Peter B. Wight, Chicago architect and critic, praised the Pasadena bungalow in 1918 for its simple design and lack of ornamental details. Moreover, Wight noted that Pasadena and Southern California had "a larger proportion of educated architects . . . than in any other community which has come under my observation" and they "are *more generally artists* than . . . in other parts of the country." This relatively large number of architects, working in close proximity to each other, resulted in an "unconscious interchange of ideas," contributing to an "evolution in artistic design," the development of a rational architecture. A few architects were the "pathfinders;" the followers were "great numbers of carpenters and builders whose education has not been interfered with or dwarfed by schools of architecture." Clients had the leisure to incorporate their personal desires and needs into the design of a house. Thus, wrote Wight, "it has been a true evolution from the social conditions of society no less than from the building materials most easily obtainable."

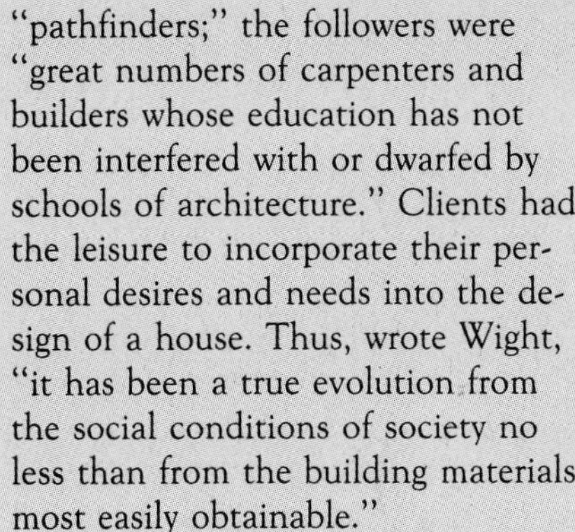

Wight credited Charles Sumner Greene of Pasadena with many of the artistic innovations of bungalow design—especially bold timberwork, broad porches, the integration of the house with its surroundings, and the attention to interior design and furniture. Greene and his brother Henry Mather Greene had many imitators, soon making the Craftsman bungalow the prevailing type of Pasadena domestic architecture.

Pathfinders of this new California architecture, besides the Greene brothers, were Frederick Louis Roehrig (whose 1899 Fleming house on South Orange Grove exhibited Craftsman characteristics); Louis B. Easton, whose small bungalows are as rustic and natural as the Greenes' are refined; Sylvanus Marston; and Alfred and Arthur Heineman, all three of whom pioneered in the develop-

Probably the first Craftsman-style house in Pasadena was this Swiss chalet, designed by Frederick Roehrig for Arthur Fleming on Orange Grove Avenue in 1899. Courtesy, California Historical Society/Ticor Title Insurance (Los Angeles)

The interior of the California Craftsman bungalow focuses on the hearth. The Volney-Craig house features rustic inglenook seats of redwood. Photo by Brian Thomas

ment of the bungalow court.

While the "pathfinders" generally designed for the rich or sophisticated, other architects and builders produced the vast majority of Pasadena's bungalows. Writing in 1908, Charles F. Holder noted that Pasadena suffered from its reputation of being only a home for the wealthy. Although Pasadena had a great number of ostentatious mansions, it had a greater number of small but strikingly artistic homes and bungalows, which were "the mecca of visiting architects." Articles on Pasadena houses in many national magazines such as *Ladies Home Journal,* and in "bungalow books" (catalogues for bungalow plans), extended the city's architectural influence beyond Pasadena.

The design of these bungalows was a peculiarly regional one, based on local materials, but at times reminiscent of Swiss, Scandinavian, English cottage, or Japanese prototypes. The California houses were almost always clad in stained shakes or shingles. Most bungalows, constructed of California redwood, rested on a foundation of boulders gathered from the nearby Arroyo Seco (although by 1906, the supply was depleted, and stones were being brought in from washes east of town). Roofs of the one-story houses were shallow-pitched, almost horizontal gables, with broad overhanging eaves supported by exposed and extended rafters. Sturdy square posts and tie beams supported the porch roofs, and beam ends often protruded below the gable, emphasizing the structural honesty of the design. Bands of vertical casement windows allowed light into the interior. Chimneys were prominent on the exterior and were typically of Arroyo stone.

The focal point of the interior was the hearth, sometimes flanked by built-in seats to make a cozy inglenook fireplace. Handcrafted andirons and fireplace implements were set off by the earth-tone tiles of the hearth and fireplace surround. Woodwork was simple but extensive: beamed ceilings, wainscoting, plate rails, built-in buffets, window seats, and benches of oak or redwood lent warmth to the interior. Both furniture and woodwork were finished in a soft matte finish; American Indian and Oriental rugs were the preferred floor coverings.

The integration of the house with the outdoors was an important aspect of the design. French doors often led out onto the porch, and windows were arranged to take advantage of garden views. The house was set in an informal "natural or English" garden, creating "the environment of a home, not a mere house." Often, a vine-covered pergola extended out from the porch and even across the driveway to form a porte-cochere. The entire design emphasized harmony with nature, the low ground-hugging lines and the integration of the house with trees and plants creating a kind of California Prairie style. Care was taken to preserve the natural environment when building. In the best designs, the house was planned to conform to the site, saving the fine old oaks, and taking advantage of uneven sloping sites, rather than leveling and clearing.

The bungalow floor plan was also innovative. Entrance halls were generally done away with, and the guest entered into a spacious living room, which opened directly into a dining room and perhaps a study. This open plan created space that could accommodate large groups. The addition of a courtyard or pergola-covered terrace and expansive porches made even larger areas available for entertaining.

Bowen Court on Villa Street was designed by Alfred and Arthur Heineman. Courtesy, Gamble House Library

Another feature of the bungalow plan was the sleeping porch. Nearly every house had one, and many of the larger ones had three or four, in order to accommodate the whole family. Separate tenthouses with canvas walls, originally designed for invalids, also served as sleeping porches. Medical experts of the time advocated living, or at least sleeping, out-of-doors, for everyone, not just respiratory sufferers.

An extension of the bungalow idea was the bungalow court, which first appeared in Pasadena around 1910. Individual dwellings were grouped on one lot, with the bungalows built along both sides of a central grassy court, typically bisected by a walkway giving access to all the units. Pasadena's first bungalow court, St. Francis Court on Colorado Street, was designed by Sylvanus Marston.

Initially the courts were planned for the tourist. But the bungalow courts were not just for tourists; they were, in fact, a new idea for apartments. The court combined the economies and sociability of apartment living with the porches, gardens, and privacy of the single-family dwelling. As in larger bungalows, the living rooms always had a fireplace and often built-in bookcases or benches which concealed a disappearing bed. Kitchen tables folded up against the wall to maximize the space. Bowen Court on Villa Street even had a two-story community summer house, rustic and open to the air, to be shared by all residents.

The tremendous building boom of the first fifteen years of the century slowed during World War I, coinciding with a change in taste in architectural style. While the bungalow remained a permanent feature of the architectural landscape in the 1920s, it appeared no longer as a rustic Craftsman bungalow. Instead it took American Colonial, Spanish Colonial, European cottage, or even Pueblo forms, providing for the common man smaller versions of the then-fashionable European-style villas of the rich.

"A MOST POPULAR WINTER RESIDENCE"

During the early years of the century, millionaires continued to gather along Orange Grove Avenue, where palatial mansions were fast replacing the simple homes of the early settlers. Described as "the great picture street of Pasadena," Orange Grove was a panorama of flowers and magnificent homes. Many early settlers on the west side of the street had built their homes on the bluff of the Arroyo, on what is now Grand Avenue, and when Grand was cut through in the 1880s, a second boulevard of mansions developed along it. Known as the West Side, the neighborhood was touted as the "Fifth Avenue district of Pasadena."

"Casa Propia," a graceful Victorian Italianate structure of the 1880s built by the Edwin F. Hurlbut of Oak Park, Illinois, was the first large mansion to be built on the street. Among the most palatial residences from the late nineteenth century was that of Henry C. Durand, a Chicago merchant and wholesale grocer, who built a turreted and crenellated Gothic stone mansion at the corner of Orange Grove and Arlington. Another stone mansion was that of Adolphus Busch, the St. Louis beer millionaire who developed his "back yard" into one of the major gardens of Southern California, known as Busch Gardens.

Carmelita, which had been purchased by the Simeon G. Reeds of Portland, Oregon, remained one of the showplaces of Orange Grove, principally for its gardens planted by Jeanne Carr. Upon Mrs. Reed's death early in the century, concerned

Right: *Architect Frederick Roehrig designed this mansion in the popular Mission style for W.C. Stuart in 1897. Courtesy, Western History Collection, Natural History Museum of Los Angeles County*

Above, left: *When Dr. and Mrs. Adalbert Fenyes moved to Pasadena in the 1890s they had this exotic "Algerian style" mansion built for them on Orange Grove Avenue. After the turn of the century, the Fenyes family built a new mansion on North Orange Grove Avenue, that is now the home of the Pasadena Historical Society. Courtesy, Western History Collection, Natural History Museum of Los Angeles County*

Top, right: *St. Louis beer millionaire Adolphus Busch purchased this stone mansion on Orange Grove Avenue around the turn of the century and began to develop his land into the famed Busch Gardens. Busch died in 1913, and Mrs. Busch maintained the house until her death in 1928. The house remained in the family until the 1940s, when it was sold and demolished. Courtesy, Western History Collection, Natural History Museum of Los Angeles County*

Above, right: *Built in 1895 for Henry C. Durand, millionaire Chicago grocer, this mansion was sold later to the Barnum family. Mrs. Barnum's first husband, J.W. Robinson, founded Robinson's department stores. The property was purchased sometime after 1914 by William Wrigley and the house was demolished to make way for Wrigley's pergola and rose garden. Courtesy, Western History Collection, Natural History Museum of Los Angeles County*

One of the few mansions remaining on "Millionaires' Row" is the Wrigley House, designed for the Chicago chewing gum magnate by Pasadena builder George L. Stimson in 1919. Photo by Linda Jones Simmons

citizens proposed making the site into a public park. The land was eventually given to the city by the pledges of a group of public-spirited citizens in the 1920s.

Another showplace of Orange Grove was the home of Robert and Clara Burdette. In 1899, Robert Burdette, preacher, humorist, and author, married Clara Baker, a widow, who had inherited a considerable fortune and the Orange Grove mansion. Mrs. Burdette became a prominent clubwoman, founding the Women's Civic League in Pasadena, as well as the National Federation of Women's Clubs. The Burdette mansion, "Sunnycrest," was famous for its view of the Arroyo and the mountains.

Probably the wealthiest man to live on Orange Grove at this time was Lamon Vandenburg Harkness of New York City, who owed his fortune to the success of the Standard Oil Company. Harkness had his winter residence at the corner of Orange Grove and Columbia Street. More prominent but not so rich was Mrs. James A. Garfield, the assassinated president's widow, who moved to Pasadena and lived for a time on the avenue, before building her own house just off Orange Grove on Buena Vista Street in South Pasadena.

Other prominent residents on the street were Arthur H. Fleming, the chief financial supporter of Caltech, whose Swiss chalet-style home, built in 1899 by architect Frederick Roehrig, was an early example of the rustic Craftsman style, and John S. Cravens, whose third house on the street, a brick and stone French manor, is now the headquarters of the local Red Cross chapter. Fleming's money had come from lumber while Cravens' had come chiefly from his wife's connections to the Liggett-Myers tobacco fortune. Chicago chewing gum millionaire William J. Wrigley purchased his mansion on Orange Grove from G.L. Stimson.

an early Pasadena builder. The Fenyes house, a handsome "Algerian" style residence, was another showplace on Orange Grove. Dr. Adalbert Fenyes was a well-known entomologist, and his wife, Eva, was an artist and patron of the arts. The family later built a mansion on the site of the William Channing house on North Orange Grove, now the home of the Pasadena Historical Society.

Grand Avenue boasted personages of no less importance. On the street resided Joseph Johnson, Bishop of the Episcopal Church and one of the most prominent clergymen in California; Mrs. George M. Pullman, widow of the Chicago sleeping-car magnate, who rented the house of ex-Senator George H. Barker of New Jersey at the south end of Grand Avenue; and J.S. Torrance, developer of Torrance. Mrs. Pullman reportedly "brought her own blooded horses and some dozen handsome equipages which were often seen upon the avenues."

The development of Oak Knoll, beginning in 1905, created a new neighborhood for the wealthy to rival Orange Grove and the West Side. Comprising 300 acres of the former Allendale, Oak Knoll, and Richardson ranches, plus the golf course of the Pasadena Country Club, Oak Knoll was a park-like area of gentle slopes and wooded canyons dotted by majestic oak trees. The brainchild of William R. Staats, a successful real estate investor, the Oak Knoll Company developed the tract with the help of capital from Henry Huntington and A. Kingsley Macomber, a local physician. Huntington, successful transport executive and heir to millions from his railroad magnate uncle, Collis, had purchased the Shorb property in 1903 and had begun to transform it into the estate now known as the Huntington Library and Art Gallery.

Situated just north of the Old Mill, the slopes of Oak Knoll boasted olive trees and palms planted by the San Gabriel Mission fathers. Wide winding streets bordered by shade trees were laid out, and care was taken to retain most of the native oaks. Many of the wealthy bought large tracts of land in Oak Knoll. The tract was intimately associated with the Huntington family; one of the early houses in the neighborhood was built by Gilbert E. Perkins, Huntington's son-in-law. The first house in Oak Knoll, a Mission Revival style mansion, belonged to the Lunkenheimer family of Cincinnati, whose fortune was amassed in the manufacture of brass fittings. Robert R. Blacker, a lumber magnate from Michigan, built his extraordinary home on a five-acre estate, a masterpiece of California Craftsman architecture designed by Pasadena's leading Craftsman architects Charles and Henry Greene.

Other exclusive neighborhoods developed in this period were the gated communities of Ford Place and Prospect Park, the tiny Westmoreland Place, and "Little Switzerland." Ford Place, located just north of the Maryland Hotel, was laid out in 1904 and comprised only four square blocks of substantial residences, secluded behind red sandstone gateposts. The most notable house on Ford Place was designed for Edmund Blinn of Chicago by George Washington Maher, one of Frank Lloyd Wright's Prairie School compatriots. Maher's use of the wisteria vine motif in the leaded glass windows, carved wooden staircase, and art glass and ceramic fireplace surround makes the Blinn house one of Pasadena's most significant landmarks.

The stone and clinker brick gates of Prospect Park on North Orange Grove formed the entrance to a curving street along the Arroyo of Craftsman chalets and Mission Revival residences, later filled in with Spanish and Tudor-style houses and Pasadena's only Frank Lloyd Wright house, *La Miniatura.* Just to the south was tiny Westmoreland Place,

One of several residential districts that developed in the first decade of the twentieth century was Prospect Park, shown here in about 1910. Courtesy, Pasadena Historical Society

Visitors to Pasadena could rent this nine-room "bungalow" in the Hotel Maryland's famous "Bungalowland." Courtesy, Pasadena Historical Society

a street of only five houses, some of them Greene and Greene designs, of which one, the Gamble House, now open as a museum, is a public monument to their work. South of Westmoreland Place and curving around the bluff of the Arroyo was the famous "Little Switzerland," so named because of its rustic chalets. Many had been designed by Greene and Greene and included Charles Greene's own house. Rustic retaining walls and brick sidewalks mark this distinctive Pasadena neighborhood.

The expansion of Pasadena's residential sections was paralleled by the growth of the hotels. Several new hotels joined the Greene and the Raymond (which was rebuilt in 1901 after the disastrous 1895 fire). Most notable of these were the Maryland, built in 1903, and the Wentworth (now the Huntington-Sheraton), built in 1906 on twenty-five acres set aside in Oak Knoll. During this period, Pasadena hotels hosted many celebrities: presidents, senators, foreign aristocrats, leaders in the arts and science, as well as business tycoons.

The Wentworth, designed by architect Charles Whittlesey in the then-popular Mission Revival style, had a broad U-shaped plan and commanded the slope on which it stood, just above the Old Mill. Its financial underpinnings, however, were shaky, and the hotel was forced to close within a few months of its February 1907 opening. Only partially finished, the Wentworth stood empty until 1911, when Henry Huntington bought it. Huntington chose architect Myron Hunt and landscape gardener William Hertrich, who had designed the buildings and grounds of his new estate, to work on the newly-acquired hotel. Hunt redesigned the interior and much of the exterior, adding two floors to the building and moving the main entrance from the north side to a porte-cochere on the east in recognition of the growing importance of the automobile. Hertrich designed the landscaping for the expansive grounds, particularly the Horseshoe Garden on the south side of the hotel and the Japanese Garden on the west. The hotel reopened in 1914 as the Huntington Hotel, with a grand reception for over 2,000 people. Selected to manage it was Daniel Moore Linnard, then also manager of the Hotel Maryland, and Pasadena's most successful hotelman. At one time or other, Linnard or his son-in-law, Stephen Royce, either owned or managed all the major hotels—the Green, the Raymond, the Maryland, the Huntington, and the Vista del Arroyo.

The Maryland was located on Colorado Street between Euclid and Los Robles in a residential neighborhood just east of the business district. Under Linnard's stewardship, the Maryland became the center of Pasadena's social and civic life, as it was the only hotel to remain open throughout the year. Linnard also pioneered a new form of hotel accommodation, the bungalow, at the Maryland. Bungalows (many of them actually substantial two-story houses) dotted the grounds north of the hotel, providing exclusive private accommodations for families. Often built to the specifications of the tenant, the bungalows were leased for a specified number of years with full hotel services, reverting to the hotel after the lease expired. "Bungalowland" at the Maryland was successfully imitated at both the Vista del Arroyo and Huntington Hotels, creating an even more deluxe accommodation for Pasadena's wealthy guests.

Symbol of the Maryland was its white-columned vine-covered pergola which stretched across the front from Euclid Avenue east to the middle of the block. Designed by Myron Hunt, the pergola was one of the most photographed and admired sights in Pasadena. A later pergola at the Vista del Arroyo sought to capitalize on this distinctive architectural feature, which became a favorite motif of Pasadena architects and builders. The shops in the hotel behind the picturesque pergola were among the most elegant in town; they formed the nucleus of a new fashionable shopping district which grew up around the hotel.

Pasadena's third great hotel fire virtually destroyed the Maryland in April 1914. Starting in the basement and fed by exploding gas pipes, the fire spread so rapidly that guests were forced to hurl their belongings, including large trunks, out the windows. At first it was feared that "Bungalowland" might also go up in smoke, but the Los Angeles Fire Department sent a contingent to Pasadena, and the bungalows were saved. As the guests, many in their nightclothes or in evening dress, stood outside in the eerie darkness lit only by the blaze of the huge building, the hotel staff, led by D.M. Linnard, hurriedly began preparations to reopen the Huntington Hotel, which had

Opened in 1903, the Hotel Maryland was the first large hotel to serve the Pasadena community the whole year round. Courtesy, Pasadena Public Library

just closed after its first season.

Myron Hunt, a resident at the Maryland since his wife's death two years earlier, began work on plans for the new hotel at four in the morning on the night of the fire. Within a few days, the new design was ready. Work commenced almost immediately, and the new Maryland, strongly reminiscent of the original but with many improvements including fireproof construction, opened on Thanksgiving Day, 1914.

Each hotel offered its own special attractions. The Raymond, reached by a picturesque flower-bordered road, boasted a golf course and grounds landscaped by Theodore Payne, an expert on native plants and flowers. The Green, in the center of town, appealed to those who enjoyed an urban atmosphere, with shopping and transportation right at the doorstep. The Maryland, with its bungalows, formed a unique home-hotel combination appealing to the very wealthy who could afford to rent entire houses for months on end. The Huntington was situated on a large acreage on the outskirts of town, and became a resort for the growing class of automobile and sports enthusiasts. It offered a golf course with the picturesque Old Mill as its clubhouse, and tennis courts designed by May Sutton Bundy, a Pasadena girl who in 1905 became the first American to win Wimbledon. The Vista del Arroyo, not fully developed until the 1920s, offered a panoramic site on the Arroyo bank overlooking the Colorado Street Bridge. Its elegance eventually surpassed the older hotels, as it gradually became the scene of Pasadena's most sparkling social life.

Distractions during the "season," which began as early as November and extended to mid-April, included equestrian sports such as riding, polo, and hunting; cycling, and automobile excursions. The mountains retained their attractions, mule or horseback rides to rustic mountain camps and trips on the Mt. Lowe Railway remained popular. At the annual spring horse show at Tournament Park, the major event of the spring social season, the Paris dresses and Tiffany jewels of the women rivaled the thoroughbreds for attention. By the early decades of the twentieth century, a glittering social life, an ideal natural environment, plus the favor of some of America's most famous and wealthiest individuals had all conspired to make of Pasadena "a most popular American winter residence."

An important social event of 1920 was the wedding of Margaret Mortenson to banker Ernest Crawford May at the Mortenson home on Orange Grove Avenue. Courtesy, Pasadena Historical Society

Chapter V

The City Beautiful movement became reality in Pasadena with the completion of the Civic Center, a major achievement of the 1920s. This view from the library toward City Hall down the broad Garfield Avenue axis, eventually terminating in the Civic Auditorium, illustrates the principles of the City Beautiful tradition of broad boulevards terminated by monumental buildings. Courtesy, Pasadena Historical Society

Pasadena's Golden Age: "The City Beautiful"

"To make

a city attractive

is to make it

prosperous."

–Willis Polk, 1921

Pasadena's development into an attractive residential city culminated in the 1920s, when its full promise was finally achieved. The cultural reawakening across the United States in the period just prior to World War I had resulted in a proliferation of new magazines, clubs, little theaters, experimental schools, and art galleries. Pasadenans had founded musical organizations, an art school, many clubs, and a little theater which during the following decade reached their full flowering, supported by an urban, cosmopolitan middle class. Moreover, Pasadena's already distinctive architecture developed in the 1920s into a unique California Mediterranean style, a blend of Spanish and Italian motifs. The building of the Civic Center, the construction of major commercial buildings, the development of the Caltech campus, and the proliferation of white-walled, red-tile-roofed villas set in luxuriant gardens gave Pasadena an elegant character which still remained primarily suburban and informal.

Between 1920 and 1930 Pasadena grew from a population of 45,000 to 76,000. Although accounts of the period concentrate primarily on the wealthy and famous, Pasadena remained predominantly middle class. Besides the hotels with their large staffs and the many retail establishments serving both tourists and residents, by 1929 Pasadena had over 150 industrial plants, some of which may have been attracted to the city by a Chamber of Commerce campaign in the early 1920s. Offering low electricity rates and the promise of a stable work force as enticements, the chamber's campaign specified only clean industries, such as textiles, clothing, food products, printers, potters, and machine tools for Pasadena. The growth of the construction industry contributed to employment in Pasadena, bringing architects, contractors, builders, carpenters, plumbers, plasterers, and painters to the city. A number of small companies and individual craftsmen supplied the extra touches needed by the building trades; interior decoration, cast stone work, ornamental tiles, wrought iron railings and light fixtures, stenciling, leaded glass, even adobe construction and furniture designed to fit the new architecture. Most of these small businesses and industries were owned by and employed Pasadenans, and at the height of their prosperity, many extended their trade beyond Pasadena's borders to Los Angeles and other Southern California communities.

Symptomatic of a trend taking place in similar middle-class cities across the nation in the 1920s was the reorganization of Pasadena's city government and the establishment of a city manager system in 1921. In 1913 Pasadena had changed its government from the mayor-council system to the commission system. Five elected, salaried commissioners, each charged with administering designated city departments, governed the city. As a legislative body, the commission was empowered to pass ordinances, some of which were subject to referendum by the voters.

Despite the greater efficiency promised by the commission system, some Pasadenans began agitating as early as 1914 for another change, to the city manager system. Advocates of the city manager plan saw in the commission system opportunities for political abuse; they were also the advocates of civic beautification, concerned with preserving Pasadena's residential character and opposed to the building of a rapid transit line to Los Angeles, which some commissioners favored and which opponents felt would create too rapid growth. Under five equally powerful commissioners, it was difficult to resolve disputes; it was said that Pasadena's commissioners "fought among themselves like cats and dogs."

The city manager plan was appealing for many reasons. Based on the organization of a private corporation, it applied business methods to government, promising to increase efficiency and to improve accountability. It separated administrative responsibilities from direct political influence, and it unified all the branches of city government by concentrating authority and responsibility in the manager. The city manager system was spreading rapidly throughout the country in this period; ninety-eight municipalities had adopted it by 1918. On adopting the system in 1921, Pasadena chose as its first city manager C. Wellington Koiner, who had risen to prominence as director of the financially successful Municipal Light Department. Koiner had a clear sense of dedication to public service and had proven managerial abilities. He was widely known and respected, and within a short time was elected president of the International City Managers' Association.

In Pasadena Koiner took charge at once, and with the support of the newly-elected board of directors (whose chairman retained the honorary title of mayor) embarked on a series of projects that would have lasting effects on the city. Both Koiner and the members of the board were visionaries, men used to doing things "in a big way." The most far-reaching project of the new city government was the establishment of a planning commission, which hired a team of experts from Chicago to prepare Pasadena's first city plan.

Some Pasadenans had been working for years for a city plan. The City Beautiful concept, which had been introduced at Chicago's Columbian Exposition in 1893, made Americans aware of the possibilities of city planning. The "Great White City" of Beaux Arts buildings, with pools, fountains, open plazas, uniform cornice lines, and vistas, created a sense of order hitherto unknown in American cities and spread a taste for the City Beautiful throughout America.

Long proud of their residential neighborhoods, Pasadenans turned their attention early in the century to the beautification of the public and commercial sections of the city. Women's organizations were in the forefront of the movement. The Outdoor Art Association called for a plan in 1902 to determine the placing of public buildings, the arrangement of streets, the location of parks and monuments, the planting of street trees, and the preservation of natural beauty and historic places. The Shakespeare Club, one of Pasadena's oldest and most prestigious women's clubs, sponsored lectures by experts, explaining the advantages of city plans and the work of Daniel Burnham, who had played a major role in the 1893 fair.

By 1908, when a new post office building was proposed, calls for a city plan and civic center became louder. Prominent clubwoman Clara Burdette saw the post office as an opportunity to create a civic center. The Board of Trade invited city planner Charles Mulford Robinson to Pasadena in 1908, but nothing came of the project. Even Daniel Burnham visited Pasadena, but the city was not yet ready to hire such a renowned expert.

Nevertheless, interest in creating a plan for Pasadena continued to grow and in 1914, a City Beautiful Association was formed, with representatives from twenty-eight different organizations, including the Parent-Teacher Association, the Women's Civic League, the Pasadena Realty Board, the Tournament of Roses Association, and the Chamber of Commerce. Recognizing Pasadena's dependence on tourism, these groups were especially inspired by the hope that 1915, the year of the California-Panama Exposition in San Diego and the Panama-Pacific Exposition in San Francisco, would bring even more tourists to California. Moreover, the European war had greatly increased tourist bookings at Pasadena's hotels for the coming season, and Pasadenans knew that their city would have to compete with the charms of Europe to convince these newcomers to return to Pasadena once the war was over.

At first, City Beautiful efforts were concentrated on cleanup, especially of streets, empty lots, and the Arroyo Seco. Businesses were persuaded to remove billboards and put up flower boxes on downtown buildings. Then George Damon, a member of the Throop faculty who had some city planning experience, especially in the area of transportation, put forward a plan to create a union terminal for all the railroads at Colorado and Broadway (now Arroyo Parkway), on the site of the Southern Pacific station. North of the terminal, Damon planned the City Hall facing onto a plaza surrounded by the library, an auditorium, and a "social center" for use by clubs and other organizations. The railway station would function as a gateway for visitors, who, as they exited the station would see a beautiful civic center set against the mountains, with major traffic arteries providing quick access to the rest of the city. Although never implemented, Damon's plan was widely discussed. It was published in 1915 by the Women's Civic League and a model was exhibited in the Board of Trade offices.

The proposed civic center would solve several problems. The old City Hall was by now inadequate. The library, too, was antiquated and needed more space to house its growing collections. Pasadena's expanding cultural life demanded a suitable auditorium for concerts and plays and a museum for art exhibits. The business community wanted an exhibition hall that could be used for trade fairs and conventions. A civic center was an obvious solution, but it was a huge project for a town of only 45,000 people.

Finally in 1921, George Hale turned his attention to Pasadena's need for a civic center. Hale, an internationally recognized scientist with cosmopolitan tastes, had enormous energy, and he could be highly persuasive. He had garnered the support of industrialists like Charles Yerkes and Andrew Carnegie for his scientific projects. He persuaded Arthur Fleming to donate most of his fortune to Caltech and Henry Huntington to create a major research institution, the Huntington Library and Art Gallery. His Mt. Wilson Observatory was the leading observatory in the world, and it continued to grow, expanding from the sixty-inch telescope to the 100-inch, finally culminating in the project for the great 200-inch telescope at Palomar.

Hale wanted to create in Pasadena an "Athens of the West," a city which would have a full complement of the best in cultural and scientific institutions. He dreamed of a major medical school and hospital and a school of architecture and design at Caltech. He envisioned a Pasadena art institute, modeled on the Art Institute of Chicago. As for Pasadena itself, Hale dreamed of a City Beautiful plan which would be a fitting setting for the institutions he was establishing.

Hale went before the City Board in January 1922 to present his ideas. Following the endorsement of the board and of Mayor Hiram Wads-

Henry E. Huntington and his wife, Arabella, left behind a significant cultural legacy to Southern California in the major research institution known as the Huntington Library and Art Gallery. Huntington's Pacific Electric system also provided transportation for most of Southern California until the 1950s. Courtesy, The Huntington Library

worth, Hale presented his proposal to prepare a city plan with a civic center to a group of influential Pasadenans at a dinner at the Hotel Green. To gain the support of businessmen, Hale repeated the words of San Francisco architect Willis Polk: "To make a city attractive is to make it prosperous."

In April a Planning Commission was established by city ordinance. In May, the Chicago firm of Bennett, Parsons and Frost, architects, planners, and successors to Daniel Burnham, were retained to make a plan for Pasadena. Over the next few months, the planners visited Pasadena several times, even taking an airplane flight over the city, as well as descending into the Arroyo to explore a "through route without any intersections to the big city."

The Bennett plan had several components. Central to it was the Civic Center, which Bennett located on two axes, Garfield and Holly, to take advantage of three buildings aleady in place, the 1915 Post Office, the YWCA, designed by Julia Morgan, California's first woman architect, and the YMCA. Bennett proposed two major automobile entrances to the city, one at the head of the Colorado Street Bridge, the other at Lamanda Park on the east. Bennett's recognition of the growing importance of the automobile also led him to propose widening and cutting through Green and Walnut streets to create more east-west arteries in the city center, and landscaped medians to beautify major auto routes.

In his report to the City Board, Bennett emphasized the garden nature of Pasadena and its residential character. The purpose of his plan was to enhance these qualities. Bennett's analysis of Pasadena's primitive zoning led him to recommend changes that would limit population growth. He foresaw that it could result in congestion, which would destroy Pasadena's unique character. Bennett recommended planning for a stable population of 120,000, which he predicted would be achieved in about fifty years. (In 1980, Pasadena's population was about 118,500.)

The Bennett plan linked the western entrance of the city to the Civic Center by a broad boulevard, Holly Street, to be lined by double rows of trees. Driving into Pasadena over the Colorado Street Bridge, the visitor would see panoramic views of the Arroyo Seco and Pasadena spread out before the majestic San Gabriel Mountains. Passing a memorial flagstaff at Colorado and Orange Grove and turning north toward Holly, the motorist would view an art museum set in the gardens of Carmelita. Far ahead would be a monumental City Hall, which would draw the visitor's eye while proceeding eastward through the city. Arriving at the City Hall plaza, the visitor would view the Public Library to the north, and the Civic Auditorium to the south. Looking west, the view would be of a hilltop park along the San Rafael heights.

Only the core of the Bennett plan, the Civic Center, was adopted by the board. On June 7, 1923, the voters approved a $3.5 million bond issue to build three Civic Center buildings: a library, a city hall, and a civic auditorium. The vote was overwhelmingly in favor, with over 8,000 votes for and only 2,300 against. No organized opposition had surfaced during the campaign. Edwin Sorver, president of the Chamber of Commerce, was chairman of the Boosting Committee, although he had earlier been lukewarm to the plan. The business community had been promised an exhibition hall on the auditorium grounds, satisfying their need for a convention center.

George Ellery Hale's idea for an architectural competition for the Civic Center buildings had aroused great enthusiasm among the voters. Hale wanted a national—even an international—competition, but the Planning Commission chose to limit it to California architects. The ten firms invited to submit plans were the leading California architects of the day. Each firm was to submit drawings for all three buildings, and the competitors were advised that the architecture of the Renaissance or later periods in Mediterranean countries could serve as "fruitful sources of inspiration."

The jury, with Hale as chairman, announced its decision on February 28, 1924. The jury had

The winning entry in the architectural competition for Pasadena City Hall was this design featuring a Mission-style campanario *by architects Bakewell and Brown of San Francisco. The jury liked the plan of the building, centered around a garden patio, but they asked the architects to design a dome to replace "that horrible belfry." Courtesy, Urban Conservation, City of Pasadena*

Opposite, above: *A real estate boom hit Southern California in the early 1920s and Pasadena was no exception. Many a bank clerk and shop assistant decided to try selling real estate. Here members of the Pasadena Realty Board display signs boosting Pasadena. Courtesy, Pasadena Public Library*

selected one design from each of three firms. Bergstrom, Bennett, and Haskell's design for the auditorium was chosen because of its excellent seating arrangement, colorful tiles on the north-facing facade, and exterior terraces and stairways. Myron Hunt's firm was selected for the library, which had a beautiful entry patio, good provision for expansion, and a charming facade. The jury liked Bakewell & Brown's design for the City Hall best because of its unusual arrangement around a garden courtyard, combining the best in modern office design with a plan ideally suited to Pasadena's climate. They objected, however, to the "belfry tower" at the front of the building; the architects produced several alternative designs before the present dome was accepted.

Construction of the library began first, and it was completed in February 1927. Work on City Hall began in January 1926, and the building was officially opened on December 26, 1927. The building of the auditorium was delayed for lack of funds, and it was not completed until 1932. Monies from the ever-profitable Light Department and funds raised from the sale of a portion of the sewer farm were used to build the auditorium.

The development of the Civic Center stimulated property values and encouraged new building in the area, most of which conformed to the style of the principal buildings. The YMCA building was remodeled to be compatible with the Civic Center and the YWCA across the street. The American Legion building, the First Baptist Church, and the Hall of Justice completed the Civic Center on the

west. The Southern California Gas Company, several small-scale commercial buildings on Colorado and Garfield, and the Post Office addition in 1939, all enhanced the setting of the City Hall. The civic and government uses of the Civic Center buildings created a focus for community activities in a park-like setting. The area around the Civic Center and the Maryland Hotel was Pasadena's exclusive shopping district in the 1920s. Silver and jewelry shops, milliners, haberdashers, banks, interior decorators, art and antique galleries catering to the carriage trade prospered. Perhaps the most outstanding shop was Grace Nicholson's gallery of Oriental art across Los Robles from the Maryland Hotel. Housed in a fanciful Chinese temple modeled on Chinese prototypes and roofed in decorative green tile, the gallery was guarded at its entrance by Ming dogs.

The new Civic Center district drew business away from the traditional downtown at Colorado and Fair Oaks. In an attempt to revitalize the older commercial center, the western end of Colo-

Right: *The development of Pasadena's Civic Center in the 1920s reinforced the movement eastward of the business district, which centered on Colorado Street near the Civic Center. This view up Garfield Avenue from Colorado shows new buildings in the California Mediterranean and Classical Revival styles designed to complement City Hall and the library. Courtesy, Pasadena Historical Society*

This photograph of the intersection of Colorado Street and Raymond Avenue from the mid-1920s clearly shows the beginnings of the street-widening that was completed in 1929. Several buildings west of Raymond have already been set back the required fourteen feet. Farther down the block, however, the buildings remain in their original locations. The Union Trust and Savings Bank, on the far right, retains its 1904 look; in 1929 it was set back and remodeled with a new Art Deco facade by architects Bennett and Haskell. Courtesy, Security Pacific National Bank Photograph Collection/Los Angeles Public Library

rado Boulevard was widened in 1929. The fourteen feet cut off the building fronts on each side of the street allowed for the design of up-to-date facades, many of which were done in the California Mediterranean style, tying the street more closely to the Civic Center.

At about the same time, one of Pasadena's most renowned institutions was also building a new home near the Civic Center. The new Pasadena Community Playhouse theater, situated on a palm-studded site on South El Molino, was taking shape to plans by Elmer Grey. Modeled on Spanish Colonial forms, the new playhouse had a large patio with a Baroque fountain fronting on the street. The main auditorium, as well as many interior and exterior elements, was designed by artist Alson Clark, whose painting of a Spanish galleon on the curtain still dominates the main stage.

The playhouse became one of the most active and successful little theaters in America. It had been founded by an enterprising young actor-director named Gilmor Brown in 1918 with the support of the local chapter of the Drama League. Originally located in the old Savoy Theater on North Fair Oaks, the playhouse in its heyday presented twenty-four plays annually, ranging from Shakespeare to Ibsen, Molière to Noel Coward. The playhouse's greatest triumph came with the world premiere of Eugene O'Neill's *Lazarus Laughed* in 1928.

A small paid staff of about a dozen operated on an annual budget of approximately $100,000, most of it raised through box office sales. Members of the Playhouse Association provided additional financial support. One of the playhouse's greatest benefactors was Fannie Morrison, who essentially paid for the new theater by her generous gifts in 1929 and 1930. She also paid for the construction of the school building behind the main theater in 1938.

The playhouse was largely a volunteer organization. Casts, although they generally featured professional actors, were all volunteer, giving talented amateurs from the community a chance to participate. Sets and backstage work, costumes and ticket sales were also handled by volunteers under the supervision of paid staff. A smaller theater, the Workshop, trained players for the main stage; and the Playbox, an experimental theater in Gilmor Brown's backyard on South Fair Oaks, did avant-garde productions for a small subscription audience. The Playhouse School, founded in 1928, produced some of America's best-known actors.

The success of the playhouse was largely due to the energy, charisma, and genius of Gilmor Brown. Not surprisingly, Brown was named the recipient of Pasadena's first Noble Award in 1925, a civic honor reserved for the person making the "most valuable contribution to civic advancement" in the preceding year. Charles Prickett, the group's business manager from its earliest days, kept the playhouse on solid financial footing.

Pasadena's cultural life was further enriched by the founding of the Pasadena Art Institute in 1924. Spearheaded by Ernest Batchelder and George Hale, the Art Institute set up its first museum in the Reed house at Carmelita. Unfortunately, the Art Institute failed to gain enough support to build a suitable building during the most prosperous years of the 1920s, although the Carmelita site was designated for that purpose. It was not until the 1940s that the institute found a temporary home in Grace Nicholson's Oriental art gallery on North Los Robles Avenue.

A major political crisis hit Pasadena in 1925, in the midst of the building program for the Civic Center. After four years of the city manager system, some members of the public began to raise their voices against what they saw as arrogance, elitism, and reckless expenditure. They criticized the long delays in producing the final design for City Hall, the miscalculation of land purchase and construction costs necessitating an additional bond issue of $750,000, and the raising of the city manager's salary to $12,000 a year, half of which was borne by the Light Department, which Koiner continued to superintend. The cost of various other improvements such as streets and sewers had begun to be felt by the taxpayers. Opposition focused on the city manager, who was accused of

Above: *Students at the Playhouse School were taught every aspect of theater work, from directing and acting to set and costume design, lighting and business management. Here a class is being instructed in the use of color in set design. Courtesy, Pasadena Public Library*

Opposite, top: *Many famous actors began their careers at the Pasadena Playhouse. Here screen actor Victor Mature (second from right) is shown in a 1930s Playhouse production. Courtesy, Pasadena Public Library*

Right: *Gilmor Brown was the founder and guiding force of the Pasadena Playhouse. Here Brown (on right) works with a group of young actors rehearsing a scene. Courtesy, Pasadena Public Library*

Below: *Cast members pose in front of the Pasadena Community Playhouse on South El Molino Avenue. Designed and built in the Spanish Colonial Revival style of the 1920s, the new theater provided a permanent home for the community theater group founded and led by Gilmor Brown. Courtesy, Pasadena Public Library*

Left: *Increasing numbers of blacks migrated to Pasadena after the turn of the century and during the 1920s. Politically active, well-educated, and cultured, Pasadena's growing black community produced many notable individuals and organizations, such as the Morris Orchestra, shown here. Courtesy, Pasadena Historical Society*

Left, below: *California's Spanish heritage has been continuously romanticized since the earliest days of Anglo settlement. Here a Pasadena group, Fred Walker's Spanish Troubadours, poses in about 1930 on the steps of the newly-completed City Hall, itself an architectural expression of the Spanish past. Courtesy, Pasadena Historical Society*

Opposite, above: *The 1926 Rose Parade is pictured here as it passed the corner of Colorado Street and Madison Avenue. Courtesy, The Huntington Library*

Opposite, below: *Crowds and cars filled the streets at Colorado and Fair Oaks following the 1926 Rose Parade. A sign on a lamppost at right pointed the way to the "stadium." Courtesy, The Huntington Library*

dominating the board. Board members, who were elected at large, all came from the wealthier sections of town, which also led to the charge that the board was unrepresentative.

Led by O.D. Hunt, former acting mayor of Tulsa, Oklahoma, the opposition attained a majority on the board in the 1925 election. A dispute soon developed between Koiner and the new board over the disciplining of some city employees, and Koiner resigned. Koiner defended his action, maintaining that the interference of the board in personnel matters violated the city manager concept, "making the manager nothing more nor less than an office boy or clerk to the board." His resignation sparked national debate, for it was seen as a significant confrontation between the new city manager system and old-style city politics.

Hunt's bid for the city manager post failed after he announced his intention to revert to the spoils system in making appointments at City Hall. In the end, Robert V. Orbison, manager of South Pasadena, was appointed city manager, and in the November 1926 election, voters reaffirmed their support of the city manager plan over the mayor-council system.

Despite political controversies, the momentum established in the early twenties and fed by a prosperous economy carried Pasadena through the decade. Pasadena's reputation continued to be enhanced by the annual Tournament of Roses. By 1922, the parade had grown from a few carriages

decorated with garden flowers to 100 motor-driven floats, numerous equestrians, marching bands, and a Rose Queen. The first radio broadcast describing the floats came over KPSN from the Pasadena Star-News building on Colorado Boulevard in 1926.

The tournament's afternoon sporting events had changed over the years. In 1904, informal field sports had been supplanted by spectacular chariot races held at Tournament Park at Wilson and California, where the parade terminated. A football game had been a feature of the tournament in 1902, but it was not until 1916 that football became a permanent part of the festivities. A wave of enthusiasm for college football across the nation helped put Pasadena on the map as the home of an important contest. The 1916 game between Washington State and Brown, however, was not a great success. It rained, and the Tournament of Roses Association lost $11,000, which caused the organization temporary financial difficulties. The next year's game recovered the loss, and it soon became clear that the bleachers at Tournament Park, with a capacity of only 25,000, were inadequate for the football crowd.

By the early 1920s the association was able to finance the building of the Rose Bowl by selling 210, $100-box seats guaranteed for ten years and an additional 5,000 seats for five years. In a complicated agreement, the city swapped land in the Arroyo for Tournament Park, and the association built the bowl, deeding it to the city with the provision to lease it back each year for the New Year's festivities. The new stadium, completed in 1922, seated 57,000 persons, more than double the capacity of Tournament Park. For the 1931 game, the bowl was enlarged to accommodate 86,000.

Myron Hunt, the architect for the bowl, came up with an open horseshoe design in the shape of an ellipse, which accommodated a football field and a 220-yard track. Borrowing an idea from the ancients, who had placed their stadiums in natural depressions, Hunt cut and filled the flat site, putting half the mass below grade, thus minimizing the visual impact of the bowl on the surrounding park and reducing the climb for the spectators. Each riser was six-hundredths of a foot higher than the previous one, creating a dramatic bowl-like form and improving the views from each seat—a refinement copied from the Yale Bowl. The earth-banked sides of the bowl were planted with rosebushes to blend with the surrounding park.

Not everyone liked the location of the new stadium in the Arroyo. Stuart French, chairman of the Planning Commission and a leader in the building of the Civic Center, charged that "it now stands in the center of the area like a huge anthill . . . It will forever intercept vistas and will prevent a natural 'flow of landscape.'"

North of the bowl the new Municipal Golf Course at Brookside was completed in 1928. It filled a long-standing need in Pasadena, where the only golf courses available belonged to the hotels or private clubs. In the early years, most of these private courses had been open to the public for a fee, but later policy was more restrictive, creating the need for a public course. A clubhouse, designed free of charge by Myron Hunt and Harold C. Chambers, was paid for through the $45,000 bequest of Emma Dickinson, a former Methodist missionary.

Efforts continued in the 1920s to acquire even more land in the Arroyo. Although by 1917 the city owned or held options on 70 percent of the land, key parcels still remained. One was the Dontanville property, which included an auto tourist camp north of Brookside Park and property near the Rose Bowl. The city acquired these and other parcels through condemnation proceedings for $128,000 in 1924, making nearly all the Arroyo between Columbia Street and Devil's Gate city property, except the Dontanville home site on Lester (now Rosemont Avenue), Busch Gardens, a small poultry ranch near the stadium, and several lots near Howard Street. One of the city's last acquisitions was an eleven-acre strip of wooded land, covered with fine specimens of oak, laurel, and sycamore, situated south of La Loma Road on the west bottom and side of the Arroyo. The land was held by the Campbell-Johnston family who offered it to the city on very good terms ($10,500) in 1927. To protect the watershed the city continued to acquire land in the Upper Arroyo above Devil's Gate.

Other parks purchased or developed by the city in this period included Washington Park, acquired from the Serrurier family, and La Pintoresca Park, site of the old La Pintoresca Hotel. Both parks were landscaped by Theodore Payne and Ralph Cornell, two of Southern California's most noted landscape architects. Defender's Parkway at the eastern entrance to the Colorado Street Bridge was landscaped through generous donations from neighborhood residents, a project spearheaded by Arthur Fleming. Fleming also led the drive to acquire Carmelita Park for the city; a group of public-spirited citizens provided the initial down payment and pledged to pay the balance over a period of years. By 1930, Pasadena boasted over 1,000 acres of parkland.

In order to support its expanding population Pasadena took major steps in the 1920s to increase the water supply by exploiting outside water resources. In the mid-1920s, the city began development of the Pine Canyon Dam (renamed Morris Dam) located in the San Gabriel Canyon. The dam was completed in 1934, but in the meantime Pasadena initiated the organization of the Metropolitan Water District, an association of eleven cities formed in 1928 to finance the building of

Pasadena's police force had to deal with increasing traffic problems and bootlegging during the 1920s. Enforcement of prohibition was unpopular in Pasadena where bootleggers found a ready market among the town's affluent, cosmopolitan population. Courtesy, Pasadena Historical Society

Parker Dam and the Colorado River Aqueduct, thus securing for Pasadena a virtually unlimited supply of water for the foreseeable future.

Like the water department, the police department grew in size and sophistication in the 1920s in response to an increase in the major crimes of the day—bootlegging and traffic violations. The 1922 City Manager's Report stated that arrests had increased 64 percent over the previous year, owing to "a vigorous campaign prosecuted against bootlegging." The report noted that many upstanding citizens chose to disregard the Volstead Act, believing it to be an infringement of their rights. In fact, it was well-known in Pasadena that no jury would convict persons charged with selling liquor. Too many people were themselves buying it from the bootleggers. Yet, police raids on bootleggers continued, and hundreds of gallons of liquor were seized annually. The police had the benefit of a new radio communications system, which also helped in apprehending the increasing number of traffic violators. Traffic arrests rose from 3,000 in 1922 to 11,000 a decade later.

Pasadena's model sewer farm had become an embarrassment by the 1920s, forcing the city to build a modern sewage processing plant. Still, Pasadena's sewage continued to be recycled profitably; the processed sludge was sold as "Nitroganic" fertilizer in bags emblazoned with the city seal. Table scraps were still sold for hog feed, and

Opposite, above: *Introduced by wealthy Easterners, lawn bowling became an established sport in Pasadena in the 1920s. These greens, perhaps located in the Arroyo, are no longer, but the Pasadena Lawn Bowling Club still uses greens built in the 1920s in Central Park. Courtesy, The Huntington Library*

Opposite, below: *During the 1920s much of Pasadena's social life revolved around events at the Midwick Country Club, located in Alhambra. Here high society of the Los Angeles area met to play golf or tennis, to swim, and to celebrate holidays or special events. Midwick also had polo fields, like the one shown here, which hosted regional and national tournaments. Courtesy, The Huntington Library*

Above: *Guests relax with tea on the lawn of the Hotel Raymond. On the far right is Walter Raymond, owner and manager of the hotel. Fourth from the right is Mrs. George Pullman, wife of the Chicago sleeping car magnate and a frequent visitor to Pasadena. Courtesy, Pasadena Historical Society*

Above: *The Hotel Huntington was a favorite resort for automobile, golf, and tennis enthusiasts in the 1920s. Its large front lawn boasted an obstacle golf course to provide diversion for guests. Courtesy, Security Pacific National Bank Photograph Collection/Los Angeles Public Library*

Opposite: *During the 1920s the Vista del Arroyo Hotel developed into Pasadena's most fashionable hotel. Its landmark tower, built in 1930, commanded the western entrance to the city. Its bungalows, perched on the Arroyo bluffs, resembled a Mediterranean village with stairs and walkways traversing the slopes. Courtesy, The Huntington Library*

tin cans, bottles, and paper were collected separately to be recycled.

As Pasadena grew and prospered so did the tourist industry and the grand hotels. D.M. Linnard, who now owned or managed four Pasadena hotels—the Huntington, the Green, the Maryland, and the Vista del Arroyo as well as the Fairmont in San Francisco—concentrated on developing the Vista in the early 1920s. New buildings and bungalows were built on the Vista grounds, making it a hotel to rival the Huntington or the Maryland. With the opening of the Flintridge Riding Academy, the establishment of a riding school at the Hotel Raymond, and the development of bridle paths in the Arroyo, riding became an even more popular sport with the guests. Entertainment was provided for the guests at all the hotels, including concerts, pageants, fashion shows, bridge tournaments, and inter-hotel golf tournaments. Easter Sunday at the Huntington featured John McGroarty's Easter Pageant set in Spanish California. Saturday night dance music and the regular Sunday evening concerts were broadcast weekly from the Maryland on Pasadena's radio station, KPSN. Linnard also led guests on tours of the Orient after the close of the winter season.

In 1926, the Huntington, Vista, and Green remained open for the summer for the first time. A swimming pool was built at the Huntington, and all the hotels began to solicit convention business to fill their off-season.

Of the local country clubs, the Midwick, a few miles away, was the most outstanding, offering four polo fields, an eighteen-hole golf course, tennis, swimming, whippet racing, and a brilliant social life. The Pasadena Athletic and Country Club, located in a multi-story building on Green Street, offered squash and handball courts, a swimming pool and gymnasium, dining rooms, reading rooms, and dormitory rooms. The club played an important role in fostering athletic achievement among young people, especially women. In 1925, the Amateur Athletic Union recognized the club for its sponsorship of a national women's track and field meet at Tournament Park. In 1926, the club sponsored the National Women's Basketball championship, national women's swimming relay and water polo meets, and the Pacific Coast track and field championship meet for women.

Expansion of the public schools continued in the 1920s, with new buildings for Washington Elementary and Junior High schools, McKinley School, Daniel Webster School, a Pasadena Vocational School (now Muir High School), and others. In 1922, Pasadena High School was rated the best in California for its physical plant by the University of California's Building Survey Committee. A new emphasis on physical education led to regular physical education programs. Junior high schools became integral parts of the Pasadena school system in the 1920s, and in 1924, a junior college was established on the Pasadena High School campus. This led in 1928 to a reorganization on the 6-4-4 plan, offering six years of elementary school, four years of junior high school, and four years of high school-college. In effect until 1954, this plan was carried out under the leadership of Dr. John A. Sexson. It integrated college courses into the public school system, and brought Pasadena national recognition for innovative education.

Pasadena's private schools supplemented the excellent public school system. The Polytechnic School, descended from the old Throop Polytechnic Institute, offered grammar school education to the very highest standards. The Orton School, a classical school for girls, and the Classical School for Boys, founded by Stephen Cutter Clark, prepared students in classical subjects for entrance to the top colleges and universities in the East. Westridge School, founded in 1914 by Mary Ranney, was an exclusive girls' preparatory school.

By the end of the decade, Pasadena had developed into the quintessential American suburb, a residential community dominated by the wealthy and middle classes. Pasadena differed, however, from similar suburbs around the country, in that it supported its own thriving cultural life and was not a mere bedroom satellite of Los Angeles. Its educational and cultural institutions attracted educators, scientists, artists, and writers who contributed much to the community. Working-class people and servants who lived in Pasadena were employed largely in the service industries needed to maintain the leisured life of the rich or in the booming construction industry. Pasadena had escaped the industrialization and commercialization so much a part of the prosperous 1920s in the rest of the nation. Most local businesses were geared to serve a growing number of residents and tourists who were escaping the climate and industrialized cities of the East and Midwest. These newcomers, in turn, contributed to the prosperity of the city, and like a self-fulfilling prophecy, the early boosters' claim of Pasadena as the ideal residential city was largely realized.

PASADENA'S ARCHITECTS OF THE 1920S

Like the developers of the Craftsman style of the previous decades, Pasadena's architects in the 1920s were "more generally artists" than in other parts of the country. Wealthy clients allowed them to fully indulge their artistic sense, and skilled builders and craftsmen made realization of their designs possible. Their contribution to architecture was, like the Craftsman style, a regional phenomenon, called "Californian" in its day and now referred to as California Mediterranean. The new style borrowed from Spanish and Italian forbears and also made use of California traditions, elements from the Anglo architecture of Monterey, the Spanish Baroque of colonial Mexico, the adobe of the Southwest, and the hacienda or ranch house of early California settlers.

The new style, whether based on American or European forms, looked to vernacular country architecture to create informal, livable homes suitable to the climate. Pueblos, Norman and Tudor country houses, Georgian and American Colonial models also furnished inspiration for the architects who made Pasadena their home.

The two centers of the California Mediterranean style were Pasadena and Santa Barbara. Of the ten or so outstanding Southern California architects of the day, eight of them were generally based in Pasadena: Reginald Johnson, Myron Hunt, Wallace Neff, Roland Coate, Garrett Van Pelt, Sylvanus Marston, Donald McMurray, and Gordon Kaufmann. Architectural critics John Burchard and Arthur Bush-Brown, writing in 1961, called the California Mediterranean style the best American domestic architecture of its time:

The houses were charming and much more than competent. Beginning with their cool and comfortable patios, filled with moist air and rich plants, they were consistently graceful and comfortable. Simple exterior facades were formed by broad, white stucco walls, covered by low-pitched tile roofs. Wrought-iron balconies, sequestered views, varied vistas and luxuriant foliage created a wealth of textures, color, patterns of light and shade . . . Outside of (Frank Lloyd) Wright's work . . . no other American architecture had comparable warmth.

Wallace Neff was probably the most innovative Pasadena architect working in the California Mediterra-

Architect Gordon Kaufmann's Athenaeum is one of the finest examples of the California Mediterranean style popular in the 1920s. Courtesy, Pasadena Historical Society

The Staats House on South Grand Avenue was designed by Sylvanus Marston and Garrett Van Pelt to evoke a manor house from the French countryside. Courtesy, Pasadena Historical Society

nean style. Neff loved circular forms, and his houses are famous for circular stairways and stair halls; one house for the Busch family in Oak Knoll has a semi-circular concave facade enclosing an auto forecourt. Neff later achieved the ultimate circular form in his unusual "balloon houses," balloon-shaped gunite houses designed for quick, cheap, construction in developing countries. His own "balloon house," where he lived in later years, still stands on South Los Robles Avenue in Pasadena.

Reginald Johnson excelled at the understated forms of Italian villas. A master at careful proportion and informal massing, Johnson designed elegant houses such as his own (later the Thomas Fleming) house on Lombardy Road and the Ford House on South Grand Avenue. Johnson also designed housing projects, one for Mexican workers on South Arroyo Parkway in Pasadena; and the Baldwin Hills project in Los Angeles, where he himself lived for a year to test his design.

Another innovator was Roland Coate, who is credited with introducing balconied Monterey colonial forms into domestic architecture. Coate's work is best exemplified in the simple Town Club building of 1925 on South Madison Avenue, which looked forward to the California ranch style houses so popular after World War II. Although Coate invented the style, the best example of Monterey Colonial Revival in Pasadena is the Swift House, with its double balconies overgrown with wisteria, designed by Donald McMurray.

In partnership with Johnson and Coate for a time in the 1920s was Gordon Kaufmann, an Englishman who had come to Southern California via Canada because of his wife's health. Kaufmann created some of the most elegant buildings in the California Mediterranean idiom, the most outstanding in Pasadena being the Athenaeum and a dormitory complex at Caltech. Kaufmann's buildings exhibit striking proportions and masterful detailing, with exquisite wrought iron and cast stone work and elaborately decorated walls and ceilings. For Kaufmann, the patio was truly an outdoor room, and he exploited its drama to the fullest, lavishing detail on paving, fountains, niches, plants, and tiles.

Sylvanus Marston, who came from an old Pasadena family, began his practice designing Craftsman bungalows, but, in partnership with Garrett Van Pelt, was one of the first to design a California Mediterranean house in Pasadena, the Garford House on Hillcrest in Oak Knoll. Designed in 1916, just one year after the San Diego Exposition that began the rage for the new "California" style, the house has a front door framed in the elaborate Spanish Baroque forms made so popular by the exposition, and an L-shaped plan enclosing a patio, onto which major rooms open. The Marston-Van Pelt collaboration also produced such outstanding houses as the Everett House (now the Shakespeare Club), a fine Italian villa design; the Staats House, an outstanding high-roofed stone French manor house on South Grand Avenue; and the unique Grace Nicholson Building, a Chinese palace with a walled garden set in the heart of downtown Pasadena.

The Caltech campus made its own contribution to Pasadena architecture, combining a model of campus

One of Pasadena's most striking commercial buildings, Grace Nicholson's shop on North Los Robles Avenue became the home of the Pasadena Art Institute in the 1940s. Courtesy, Pasadena Public Library

planning and a distinctive new style. At the behest of his good friend, George Hale, Bertram Goodhue, perhaps America's most well-known architect, created a campus plan for Caltech in 1916, a plan which followed to some extent an earlier plan by Hunt and Grey. In 1921, Goodhue's first building, Bridge Hall of Physics, was built, uniting in its highly original design the simple lines of the early modern movement with decorative elements contrasting with smooth stucco surfaces, which characterized the Spanish Baroque. Although Goodhue died in 1924, his New York office carried out the building of the two wings of the west campus plan in accordance with his original designs. East of Throop Hall, landscape architect Florence Yoch designed the olive walk leading to Kaufmann's Athenaeum, and Beatrix Farrand created the landscaping for Dabney Garden, a sheltered oasis on the campus.

In addition to its wealth of fine local architecture, Pasadena has the distinction of having one of Frank Lloyd Wright's most important buildings, *La Miniatura,* a house built of pre-formed concrete blocks, the first of its kind attempted by Wright. Built in 1924 for Alice Millard, a dealer in rare books, *La Miniatura* is sited on a small wooded ravine in the Prospect Park district. Its distinctive ornamental blocks, cubic massing, and vertical slit windows stand in stark contrast to the shingled Craftsman and stucco Mediterranean houses surrounding it. Wright's Pasadena work was the most successful of several such houses that he built in Los Angeles.

Another less well-known innovator, Irving Gill, also is represented by a house built in Pasadena in the 1920s, the Little Cloister on North Oakland Avenue. Gill designed the house as a duplex for Kate Crane Gartz, wealthy social activist, whose Altadena house, the Cloisters, lent its name to the project. A pioneer in tilt-slab concrete construction, Gill prefigured the International Style with his cubic forms in white plaster and his clean interiors, devoid of woodwork or ornament.

Florence Yoch's design for the Douglas Smith estate in Altadena featured this intimate corner with a tile fountain set into a white stucco wall. Courtesy, Huntington Library

An important aspect of these California houses was the garden, and during the 1920s, landscape architects played an increasing role in Pasadena garden design. Like the architects, the majority of the best landscape architects of the period were Pasadenans. Many of them were women, such as Florence Yoch and Lucille Council, who worked extensively with Myron Hunt and landscaped parts of the Caltech campus; Katherine Bashford; Helen Van Pelt; and the nationally-known Beatrix Farrand, who created her greatest masterpiece, Dumbarton Oaks in Washington, D.C., after moving to California with her husband, Max, the first director of the Huntington Library. Paul Thiene and Charles Gibbs Adams also contributed many notable landscape designs.

Water, in the form of a pool or a fountain, was an important element in these gardens. Walls often enclosed the garden, forming outdoor rooms. Walks of decomposed granite, paving tiles, brick, or pebbles set in patterns were common features. Where walls were inappropriate, hedges gave the garden privacy.

Like the earlier Craftsman style, Pasadena's California Mediterranean style influenced American architecture, although that influence was moderated by the inappropriateness of the style in the more severe climates of the rest of the country. More important was the regional influence on the modest bungalows springing up all over Southern California. Walled patios, terraces, red tile roofs, and white plaster walls accented by palm trees became an enduring image of the region in the 1920s.

Chapter VI

This night view of Colorado Street taken from the Star-News building at Christmas time in 1943 shows the palm trees which gave the street its name, "Street of a Thousand Palms." Courtesy, The Huntington Library

Depression And World War II

"Here the streets are lined with smart shops,
lighted at night with a restrained display
of neon lights...
business is mostly restricted
to retail trade and stores that
supply the wants of good living."

–WPA Guide to California, 1939

The WPA Guide article on Pasadena seems to speak of the Pasadena of 1929 rather than 1939. In truth, the surface of Pasadena looked much the same. Its homes and gardens remained much as they were in the heyday of the 1920s. There were no idle factories blighting the view, as was the case in many Eastern cities, for there had never been any factories to speak of in Pasadena. By 1939, however, two of the great hotels—the Maryland and the Raymond—were gone, and the smart shops had long since moved eastward, leaving the Fair Oaks-Colorado center to an uncertain future. Yet the image of Pasadena as a city of wealth persisted, not only in the WPA Guide but in other books and articles of the time.

At the beginning of the Depression, journalist Morrow Mayo wrote: "Pasadena is ten miles from Los Angeles as the Rolls-Royces fly. It is one of the prettiest towns in America, and probably the richest." In his article in the *American Mercury* in 1932, Mayo satirized the small-town atmosphere and leisure activities of the wealthy, characterizing the population as "plutocrats, domestic servants, and tradesmen . . . garnished with perhaps two thousand retired folk of more modest means." He depicted the town as conservative in politics and religion, and yet friendly to political liberals like Upton Sinclair, Kate Crane Gartz, Roger Baldwin, and to organized labor. Mayo praised Charles Prisk, editor of the *Pasadena Star-News,* as the man chiefly responsible for this atmosphere of tolerance: "He has done more than any man to make Pasadena a pleasant place to live in."

Pasadena's image was enhanced by Ralph Thorndike's study of 1939, which rated Pasadena as America's most desirable city, based on thirty-seven measurable factors, ranging from the infant death rate to the per capita public expenditures for libraries and museums and the number of automobiles, radios, and telephones per capita. As might be expected, most of the top-ranked cities in the New York professor's study were suburbs, cities like Montclair, New Jersey; Evanston, Illinois; and Berkeley, California. The book, entitled *Your City,* was based on 1930 statistics, and it confirmed Pasadena's image of itself.

Yet, for all its beauty and wealth, Pasadena did not remain untouched by the Depression. According to 1930 census figures, the city's labor force had as its largest group domestic servants, a class hard-hit by the loss of fortunes in the stock market crash. Domestic workers constituted the largest group of unemployed in the city, and most of them were women. Retail salespersons (many of whom were also women) were the second-largest group. The tremendous building boom of the 1920s was over, and many of the unemployed in Pasadena were members of the construction trades. The number of residential building permits issued fell from a high of over 8,000 in the 1920-1929 period to a low of 523 in 1930-1934. Although Pasadena had relatively few industrial plants, numbering 159 in 1929, only ninety-seven still survived in 1936.

Pasadena's chief industry, tourism, slackened, and by the end of the 1930s most of the great hotels had been closed, demolished, or converted to other uses. At the same time, the mansions of the wealthy, particularly on Orange Grove Avenue, were abandoned or converted to rooming houses, creating an area classified as "blighted" in a 1940 report by Stanford University professor Edwin Cottrell. In Pasadena, as elsewhere in the country, a great change had occurred. The Depression and the war following it altered forever many of the sources of wealth and much of the way Americans lived, worked, and played, forcing a community like Pasadena to search for new ways to sustain itself economically.

Before facing the consequences of the Depression, Pasadena had to face another crisis in city government. Scandal, rooted in the corruption of some city employees, forced Robert V. Orbison, the city manager, to resign, and created such dissension among the members of the Board of Directors that they were all ousted in a recall election in December 1931.

The scandal, which had been uncovered as early as 1927, involved employees in the street and engineering department, where a ring of forgers had embezzled thousands of dollars in city funds. A number of those involved went to San Quentin, but the City Board failed to fire the city manager. Not until the 1930 election did reformers get enough seats on the board to force Orbison's resignation, based on incriminating testimony from the deputy city controller. Once Orbison resigned, however, the board deadlocked over the appointment of a new city manager. C. Wellington Koiner, Pasadena's first city manager, applied for the job. He was supported by the reformers, but eventually withdrew his application to break the deadlock, leaving the board free to appoint the other candidate, John W. Charleville.

The deadlock over the city manager as well as many other issues led to harsh words and shrill accusations in the council chambers. On one occasion a policeman had to be called in to restore order. In the meantime, city government was standing still, water projects were not moving forward, and unemployment was mounting.

Finally, in October 1931, the Pasadena Association, an organization of 210 members newly-formed by Myron Hunt and his wife, Virginia Pease Hunt, voted to mount a recall campaign. They gathered the required number of signatures in a short time, and the election was set for December 28. What followed was a fierce campaign, characterized by vituperation and mudslinging on all sides. Another organization, the Better Government League, entered the fray, supporting the three reformers on the City Board, Francis J. Walker, William J. Wise, and Robert S. Allen; and three additional candidates, McClellan Reed, George E. Lee, and Arthur L. Hamilton, the latter a former city commissioner and superintendent of schools. Halbert P. Gardner, chairman of the Pasadena Association, charged that the reformers were preparing the soil for Communistic and "Red" propaganda, and that Mayor Patrick Walker, a conservative, was trying to re-institute the mayor-council form of government. Labor leader Edward B. Hillier supported the Pasadena Association because the city had refused to give Pasadena workers priority on city building projects such as City Hall, the Rose Bowl expansion, and the Hall of Justice. Other labor leaders, however, including Fred W. Jackson, editor of the *Pasadena Labor News,* supported the Better Government League candidates, as did Pasadena's black voters. League candidates promised to take stronger action on the unemployment question than any of the other candidates.

The incumbents fought back and were later accused of planting a spy in the association offices to report any suspicious campaign contributions. Voters went to the polls in record numbers despite the pouring rain on election day. Pasadena Association candidates were victorious, sweeping out the entire board and replacing them with a completely new slate. The new directors were Milton Brenner, Robert Fulton, Peter Hall, Robert Dawson, John Lutes, Albert Stewart, and Edward O. Nay. Once the new board took office, however, they had to face Pasadena's unemployment problem directly.

At a mass meeting on unemployment held in the new Civic Auditorium in the spring of 1932 and reported in the newspapers, Pasadenans from all walks of life told their stories of deprivation and even starvation. The newspaper reported that a young waitress hired to help serve a banquet at the Huntington Hotel had fainted from hunger, and it was estimated that over 1,000 heads of families were in dire need of help. At the meeting, chaired by Myron Hunt, a resolution was passed: "Pasadena shall not let its unemployed and their wives and children starve," and Pasadenans were exhorted to "give until it hurts."

The Pasadena Block-Aid Committee, chaired by Mrs. Myron Hunt, had already been formed to aid the unemployed. The Block-Aid concept relied on volunteers who canvassed every block in the city, soliciting pledges of weekly contributions from each householder. The goal was that each block support one family. With 1,500 to 1,900 blocks in Pasadena, the committee hoped to raise enough to support as many families. Pledges to employ the unemployed as domestics or gardeners were also solicited. Pasadena's Block-Aid organization served as a model for other cities, including New York.

One of Pasadena's major work projects during the Depression was La Casita del Arroyo. Built on city parkland and sponsored by the Pasadena Garden Club, La Casita was constructed of stones gathered in the Arroyo and wood salvaged from the Olympic bicycle track at the Rose Bowl. Photo by Linda Jones Simmons

The initial pledge drive, however, raised only $22,900, or enough to provide the employed with a mere four dollars a week. In addition, city employees contributed one day's salary per month, totaling $52,000 a year to aid the unemployed. But with over 5,000 unemployed, it was estimated that to help even 1,000 of these with a minimum of $40 per month, $40,000 monthly would be needed.

As the summer of 1932 wore on, according to newspaper accounts, the number of unemployed rose alarmingly, from 5,000 in May to over 8,000 in June, increasing to 16,500 in September. By October it was estimated that $225,000 a month would be needed to sustain the unemployed at a subsistence level. In 1933 more than 9,000 Pasadenans filed applications for employment at the city's Employment Bureau, which handled 7,000 to 10,000 inquiries and interviews monthly. In the midst of the crisis, the City Board rehired C. Wellington Koiner as city manager in 1933.

Myron Hunt and his Block-Aid Work Committee sought to devise work of permanent value that would use the skills of the unemployed. The first Block-Aid project was to repair the Pasadena Preventorium, a school for unhealthy or malnourished children. Block-Aid provided guides for the 1932 Olympics, and when the games were over started a joint project with the Pasadena Garden Club to build La Casita del Arroyo, a public clubhouse for meetings of civic organizations. Using stones gathered from the Arroyo and wood from the dismantled Olympic velodrome at the Rose Bowl, several unemployed men were kept busy for a few weeks. But the project provided only $2,000 to help the unemployed. A ballot measure to appropriate $200,000 in Light Department surplus funds for unemployment relief was defeated in November 1932, although the still-profitable Light Department hired extra employees to help ease the situation.

The Olympic Games, held in Los Angeles in 1932, provided a brief respite from the crisis. Pasadena's Rose Bowl was the site of the bicycle competition, and the water polo and diving trials were held in the pools at Brookside. Dorothy Poynton, a Pasadenan who had trained at the Pasadena Athletic Club, won the platform diving competition, a feat she repeated in the 1936 Olympics.

The election of Franklin Delano Roosevelt in 1933 brought federally-funded public works programs, such as the Works Progress Administration (WPA), Public Works Administration (PWA), and State Employment Relief Administration (SERA). In Pasadena, these projects put the un-

Right: *Pasadenan Dorothy Poynton trained at the Pasadena Athletic Club and won the platform diving events in the 1932 and 1936 Olympics. Here she is shown with Douglas MacArthur, who was to become an international celebrity himself in World War II. Courtesy, Pasadena Historical Society*

Below: *Movies and dance band music helped Americans forget their troubles during the Depression. Here the Pasadena Fire Department Orchestra prepares for an engagement at one of Pasadena's grand hotels. Courtesy, The Huntington Library*

employed to work on Rose Bowl and Brookside Park improvements; the undergrounding of utility lines; tree surgery; flood control in the Arroyo and in Eaton Wash; and in building and grading rock walls in the Arroyo. Work on the baseball diamond in Brookside Park improved the field for the Chicago White Sox, who had begun using Brookside as their spring training ground in 1933. As Myron Hunt noted in a report, most of the projects involved heavy labor, jobs from which women were excluded, so an equitable distribution of available funds was not achieved. Some women were employed in knitting and sewing projects, as domestics or in office work, but generally men received the bulk of the assistance.

Statewide proposals to deal with the Depression were made by Pasadena resident and novelist Upton Sinclair in his "EPIC" campaign for governor of California in 1934. EPIC (End Poverty in California) took control of the California Democratic Party and launched a campaign with the promise to take over idle land and factories and put people to work. Sinclair's failure to get the endorsement of President Roosevelt and a misleading poll showing him far behind three days before the election were important factors in his defeat by incumbent Frank Merriam. Sinclair was greatly feared by the conservative establishment, but was also attacked by the Socialists and Communists. Not long after his defeat, Sinclair moved to Monrovia, where he lived in his later years.

Traditionally, the majority of Pasadena's workers were dependent on the tourist trade. Hotels, restaurants, and retail shops were the principal employers, and as the full effects of the Depression sank in, these mainstays of the local economy began to feel the pinch. By the end of the 1930s, the Raymond Hotel, the Maryland, and the older portion of the Hotel Green had been demolished.

The Green underwent many changes during the 1930s. Part of the Green's West Annex had been converted into cooperative apartments in 1926, while the wing along Green Street continued to be run as a hotel by D.M. Linnard. The original hotel on the east side of Raymond Avenue was demolished in 1935. Its location, close to the railroad station, which had been such an asset in the age of the railroad, had become undesirable in the age of the automobile. The shift of the more elegant shops from the Fair Oaks-Raymond-Colorado area to the Civic Center, and the expansion of the industrial area south of Central Park further affected the fortunes of the Hotel Green, which could no longer compete with the newer, more up-to-date facilities at the Huntington or the Vista del Arroyo. The elegant Maryland, demolished in the late 1930s, was replaced in 1940 by a Woolworth's and a Broadway department store, indicating that once again the more fashionable retail trade had moved eastward, this time to concentrate on South Lake Avenue, which was developed after World War II. The Maryland's magnificent bungalows gradually disappeared, most of them being moved away to other locations in Pasadena.

The Raymond, already antiquated, was unable to compete with the Huntington, and the bank holding the mortgage foreclosed in 1931. Even hotel genius D.M. Linnard could not operate the Raymond at a profit in the Depression, and the hotel was finally demolished in 1934, the year of Walter Raymond's death.

The Vista del Arroyo and the Huntington remained open throughout the Depression years, and the Vista even added some new bungalows to house well-to-do retirees rather than seasonal guests. In 1943, however, the Vista was taken over by the U.S. Army and used as a military hospital; the property has remained in the hands of the federal government ever since. Stephen Royce, son-in-law of D.M. Linnard, made a special trip to Washington to plead that the Huntington be allowed to remain open as a civilian facility. The World War II years proved to be one of the Huntington's busiest periods, as civilians involved in the war effort in California patronized the hotel, which also served as the headquarters of the Army's 35th Division and of the Office of Civilian Defense for Southern California.

A WPA project that was to have a major impact on Pasadena was the completion of the Arroyo

Left: *The Arroyo Seco Parkway built in the late 1930s became the first freeway on the West Coast and linked Pasadena with Los Angeles through the Lower Arroyo Seco. Courtesy, Pasadena Public Library*

Seco Parkway and its accompanying flood control channel in the Arroyo in 1940. The first freeway on the West Coast, the parkway linked Pasadena with Los Angeles in a nonstop winding route cutting around Raymond Hill through the old Raymond Hotel golf course and following the Arroyo Seco south. The freeway set two important precedents for future California freeways: its banks were landscaped and billboards were banned. Rose Queen Sally Stanton and California Governor Culbert L. Olson officially opened the freeway in a ceremony on the slope of Raymond Hill on December 30, 1940.

Early proposals for the route suggested extending it up the Arroyo to Altadena and even beyond, putting a road up the Arroyo Seco canyon and across the mountains to connect the Antelope Valley with Los Angeles. Altadenans and the citizens of northwest Pasadena were the chief advocates of the plan. But opponents charged that the Arroyo could not be developed with a highway because of restrictions placed on the land in the original acquisition. Moreover, the 1918 plan for the Arroyo specified that no roads were to be built in the Arroyo south of the Colorado Street Bridge. Former City Commissioner A.L. Hamilton stated,

Above: *Rose Queen Sally Stanton and Governor Culbert Olson officially opened Arroyo Parkway (now the Pasadena Freeway) on December 30, 1940, by cutting a ribbon of roses. Courtesy, California Department of Transportation*

HOTEL

Above: *Henry Huntington's Pacific Electric Railway connected Pasadena with Los Angeles and other Southern California cities. Here one of the "Red Cars" winds its way along Oak Knoll Avenue. Courtesy, Pasadena Historical Society*

Opposite: *Although the more expensive shops were located farther east on Colorado Street, the old center of Pasadena at Colorado and Fair Oaks was still busy in the 1940s. Pacific Electric Red Cars still stopped here, and local bus service was also available. Courtesy, City of Pasadena*

"the highest possible use of this property is in affording natural seclusion and restfulness and outdoor charm," and the city manager and city attorney made a special trip to Sacramento to oppose the route.

Support was high citywide, however, for the building of Angeles Crest Highway, which began as early as 1929. A committee comprised of members of the Pasadena Board of Trade, the Automobile Club of Southern California, and the U.S. Forest Service was formed in 1919 and commissioned a survey of the route. The City of Pasadena, fearing pollution of its water supply, opposed the Arroyo route north of Devil's Gate, and so it was decided to take the high route, via La Canada, instead. In 1932 a celebration at Switzer's Camp, sponsored by the Pasadena Junior Chamber of Commerce, marked the opening of the first ten miles of the highway. The completion of the route to Red Box in 1934 was celebrated by the Pasadena Chamber of Commerce and the Auto Club at Charlton Flats. A connecting road into the Antelope Valley, the Angeles Forest Highway, was completed before World War II, using prison labor. By 1939, the Crest Highway had reached Chilao Flats, when construction was halted by the war. Further building to Wrightwood and the connection with State Highway 39 were finally completed in 1961.

The development of highways, heralded as signs of progress in the Depression years, brought with them unforseen effects on the environment of Pasadena and the whole Los Angeles basin. Smog was first noticed in Los Angeles in 1940, and in July 1943, the first smoggy day was recorded. Pasadenans and Altadenans particularly noticed the smog, which backed up against the mountains and lasted from noon until nightfall. The pollution was traced to a factory on Aliso Street in Los Angeles, where butadiene, a component of synthetic rubber, was being manufactured as part of the war effort. A cleanup of the plant by December was promised in August of 1943. The Pasadena Chamber of Commerce, noting Pasadena's reputation as a clean and healthful city, was particularly active in attempts to end smog, which was beginning to affect the health and reputation of the community. The chamber noted that "in Pasadena, where many lived mainly for the climate, smog was immediately intolerable."

The problem was not solved with the cleanup of one plant, however, and the increase in industrial production during and after the war increased pollution. It took some time before the complexity of the problem was realized; the role of automobile exhaust was not immediately recognized. In the 1940s, the public still believed that technology could solve the air pollution problems of the Los Angeles basin.

After the declaration of war by the United States in 1941, Southern California became an area of high activity in the war effort. Much of the aircraft industry, which underwent tremendous expansion during the war, was located in Southern

Albert Einstein spent three winters in Pasadena (1931-1933) lecturing at Caltech. Although Caltech's president, Robert Millikan, wanted the famous physicist on his faculty, Einstein chose Princeton University when he finally moved permanently to the United States. Courtesy, California Institute of Technology

California, a staging area for the war in the Pacific. As in World War I, the California Institute of Technology in Pasadena played a leading role in the war effort.

During the 1920s and 1930s, Caltech had matured from a provincial technical institute into a full-fledged, internationally-recognized research institution. Led by Robert Millikan, Caltech assembled an outstanding faculty in such fields as physics, aeronautics, biology, and seismology. Much of Caltech's growth can be attributed to Millikan's genius at fundraising. He organized the Caltech Associates, a group of donors who pledged support for the institute and in return, attended special lectures and events to keep in touch with the exciting new research going on at Caltech. With the stock market crash of 1929, Caltech's major endowment, Arthur Fleming's fortune in lumber stock, became worthless, but Millikan was not deterred. Salaries were cut by 10 percent, and Millikan used his connections in government and industry to keep the institute going.

Physics always held prime place at Caltech during the Millikan years. Millikan himself had won a Nobel Prize in physics in 1923 for experimental work he had carried out while at the University of Chicago, and he invited as visiting scholars such giants as Niels Bohr, Paul Dirac, and Arnold Sommerfeld. Caltech also produced outstanding students, such as Carl Anderson, a Nobel Prize winner who discovered the positron in 1932. Richard Tolman and J. Robert Oppenheimer, Caltech faculty members, were destined to play major roles in the development of the atomic bomb. And in 1931, Albert Einstein visited the campus, the first of three successive winters he spent in Pasadena.

Einstein's sojourns in Pasadena brought favorable publicity to Caltech. A genuine international celebrity, Einstein was in demand for dinner and speaking engagements wherever he went, and he had difficulty in turning down anyone, especially if they represented social or humanitarian causes. Millikan, on the other hand, feared Einstein's political views might offend potential donors, so he did his best to control Einstein's activities in Southern California, a situation which Einstein accepted good-humoredly.

Astronomy, based at Mt. Wilson Observatory, which operated in close cooperation with Caltech, received a major boost with the building of the largest optical telescope in the world at Palomar. The 200-inch telescope had long been a dream of

George Ellery Hale's and in 1928, a six-million-dollar grant from the Rockefeller Foundation made the dream a reality. The great glass disk for the telescope arrived in Pasadena in 1936, more than two years after it had been cast at the Corning Glass Works in New York. For years technicians worked at grinding the disk in a specially-built laboratory on the Caltech campus. The telescope dedicated to George Ellery Hale and located on Palomar Mountain near San Diego, went into operation in 1948, ten years after his death.

In 1928, under the direction of Beno Gutenberg from Goettingen, Germany, Caltech established a seismological laboratory where systematic research in seismology began to take place. During the 1930s, a young Caltech graduate in physics, Dr. Charles Richter, working with Dr. Gutenberg, developed the Richter scale, a method of measuring earthquake magnitude more precisely than had been possible before.

Pasadenans gathered to welcome the 200-inch Pyrex glass disc when it arrived on a special train from Corning, New York, in 1936. The giant disc was polished and aluminized in a Caltech laboratory before being mounted on the telescope on Mount Palomar in 1948. Named for George Ellery Hale, the telescope at Palomar was for many years the world's largest optical telescope. Courtesy, California Institute of Technology Archives

In the 1930s Caltech professor Charles F. Richter (shown here beside a seismograph in a 1983 photograph) developed a new method of measuring the magnitude of earthquakes with the help of Professor Beno Gutenberg. The new scale, known as the "Richter scale," made Richter's name a household word and garnered him much attention in the popular press. Courtesy, California Institute of Technology

Research scientists in biology were drawn to Caltech by the reputation of Thomas Hunt Morgan, who had done pioneering work in genetics. Charles C. Lauritsen, a physicist, developed an X-ray tube that was used in the treatment of cancer and other diseases.

In 1926, Millikan recruited Theodore von Kármán, a Hungarian working at the Technical Institute at Aachen, Germany, and a specialist in the developing field of aeronautics. Von Kármán

Clark Millikan, son of Caltech president Robert Millikan, became head of the Guggenheim Aeronautics Laboratory at Caltech and a founder of the Aerojet company. He followed in his father's footsteps by fostering strong ties between the scientific community and the military-industrial complex in the crucial years following World War II. Courtesy, California Institute of Technology Archives

joined the Guggenheim Aeronautics Laboratory at Caltech, where research carried out on aerodynamics eventually led to the founding of the Jet Propulsion Laboratory during World War II.

One of von Kármán's proteges, graduate student Frank Malina, proposed in 1936 to do his doctoral dissertation on problems of rocket propulsion. Working together with two other Pasadena rocket enthusiasts, Ed Forman and John W. Parsons, Malina conducted the first tests on a rocket motor in October 1936 about three miles above the Rose Bowl in the Arroyo Seco canyon. The first tests were a failure, but tests in succeeding months proved more positive, and in the spring of 1937 the group was allowed to start testing on campus at the Guggenheim Laboratory. Dubbed the "suicide squad" after their first laboratory test bathed the building in noxious fumes, the group was ejected from the Guggenheim and forced to do their experiments outdoors.

Others joined the group, and in 1938 Malina read a paper on their work, co-authored by colleague Apollo M.O. Smith, at a conference of the Institute of Aeronautical Sciences in New York. Malina and Smith's prediction that great altitudes could be attained by rocket propulsion excited journalists, who gave the project much publicity. A year later, in the atmosphere of a military build-up that would culminate in American entry in World War II, the Guggenheim Laboratory was granted $10,000 to pursue research on jet-assisted takeoff of propeller-driven airplanes. In 1940, funding was doubled to $22,000.

The additional money enabled the rocket group to move off campus, and they negotiated a lease with the City of Pasadena for seven acres in the upper Arroyo Seco. A few small corrugated metal and frame buildings were built, to be expanded when the next year's funding increased to $125,000. By the spring of 1942, the researchers were able to produce solid-fuel and later liquid-fuel jet-assisted takeoffs, which cut both takeoff time and the distance needed by one-third. By mid-1943, eighty-five people were working on the site, and Aerojet, a company formed by von Kármán, Malina, and others, began to market the engines to the U.S. Navy for use on carrier-based aircraft in the Pacific.

News of German rocket research changed the direction of the research toward guided-missile work. The Caltech group submitted a proposal in late 1943 (using the name Jet Propulsion Laboratory for the first time) to develop theoretical models, and to design and test rocket missiles. At the same time, scientists at Caltech's Kellogg Labora-

Theodore von Kármán, born in Hungary and educated in Berlin, first came to Pasadena in 1926 at the invitation of Robert Millikan, who wanted to start an aeronautics department at Caltech.

By 1929, Millikan had raised enough money for a building and a wind tunnel to lure von Kármán permanently to Caltech. Courtesy, California Institute of Technology Archives

tory were working on rockets in Eaton Canyon under the direction of Charles C. Lauritsen. The army offered the JPL group three million dollars if they would also produce prototypes for production. This staggering sum, soon increased to over five million dollars, marks the real birth of the Jet Propulsion Laboratory. At the same time, von Kármán vainly tried to obtain funds from Caltech for an independent laboratory under institute control, which would be devoted to research unhampered by military requirements.

Although the war had a generally positive effect on Pasadena's economy, it proved disastrous for one portion of Pasadena's population, those of Japanese descent. In early 1942, in the hysteria of wartime, all Japanese and Japanese-Americans on the West Coast (most of them United States citizens) were rounded up and moved to camps in the interior. The largest assembly center on the West Coast was at Santa Anita Race Track, but Pasadena's Japanese-Americans were assembled at Tulare, bringing only the few possessions they could carry. They traveled on an antiquated train for hours to reach Tulare, where rude barracks awaited them. Most of the Pasadenans were then sent on to a camp at Gila River, Arizona where conditions were little better. These 700 Pasadenans—physicians, accountants, businessmen, teachers, gardeners, and agricultural workers—represented a cross section of the larger Pasadena community.

Persons of Japanese descent had first come to Pasadena around the turn of the century. Seventeen Japanese were recorded in the 1900 census, increasing to 253 by 1910, reflecting a wave of immigration in the early part of the century. Many notable Japanese lived in Pasadena in this period, including T. Aoki, a well-known artist, and his daughter, Tsura, a Pasadena High School graduate who became a film actress; K. Ota, a photographer whose prints were exhibited internationally; Toichiro Kawai, who designed and built the Japanese-style bridge and bell tower in the gardens of the Huntington Library; Y. Shimanouchi, editor of the Japanese-American daily newspaper of Los Angeles; and F.T. Kuranaga, who owned the largest Japanese newspaper in the country (based in San Francisco) and was head of a big labor contracting business.

In Pasadena in the 1940s, there were a few people who thought the Japanese were being treated unfairly. Some, like Robert Millikan, joined a statewide organization to put pressure on the authorities to release the Japanese. On a local level, Pasadenans formed an organization called "Friends

Rocket enthusiasts Frank J. Malina (third from left), Apollo M.O. Smith (second from left), Deward S. Forman, and John W. Parsons (second from right and far right, respectively) conduct rocket tests in the Arroyo Seco in 1936. Their experiments led to the establishment of the Jet Propulsion Laboratory in the 1940s. Courtesy, Jet Propulsion Laboratory

of the American Way," and established headquarters in the abandoned Japanese Union Church on Kensington Place. This group, led by William Carr and Hugh Anderson, wrote monthly letters to all Pasadena citizens in the camps, to let them know that they had not been forgotten.

After some time, Carr and Anderson conceived of a novel idea: why not ask for the repatriation of a single person from the camps to demonstrate that innocent American citizens were being persecuted? They secured the agreement of General Bonesteel, who was in charge of the detention, to release Esther Takei, an eighteen-year-old Pasadenan, to the custody of Anderson and his family. The young woman arrived in Pasadena on September 12, 1943, and registered for the fall term at Pasadena Junior College. Despite adverse publicity and threats to the Anderson home and family, as well as attempts to bar her from school, Esther Takei attempted to lead as normal a life as possible, attending PJC and living with the Andersons in Altadena. Toward the close of the war, some of the internees were allowed to return to Pasadena, and by 1946 they had all been freed.

The end of the war brought a new burst of prosperity to Pasadena, and an early sign of it was the construction of Bullock's suburban store on South Lake Avenue in 1947. In the late 1930s, when the Arroyo Seco Parkway was nearing completion, the Chamber of Commerce had formed a committee named "Pasadena Preferred," dedicated to promoting Pasadena as a regional retail shopping center. Composed of 121 merchants who feared that the freeway would draw Pasadena shoppers to Los Angeles, Pasadena Preferred mounted an advertising campaign stressing Pasadena's specialty shops and traditionally high-quality merchandise.

The campaign received an enormous boost with the development of the shopping district on South Lake Avenue. The Bullock's store brought a new retailing concept to Southern California—the auto-oriented suburban department store. Other department stores, as well as many local shops, soon clustered around Bullock's, creating an early suburban shopping mall in concept if not in name.

In its new-found postwar prosperity and in a spirit of reconciliation, Pasadena adopted a sister city, Ludwigshafen, in Germany in 1948. An industrial city founded the same year as Pasadena, 1874, Ludwigshafen had suffered devastating bombing during the war, and shortly after being adopted by Pasadena, a tragic chemical factory explosion occurred there killing scores of people. Lacking food, clothing, and medical supplies, Ludwigshafen appealed to Pasadenans, who sent needed aid through a program called SHARES. (A second sister city, Mishima, in Japan, was

This photograph from the early 1950s shows Pioneer Bridge being built. The new bridge, which opened in 1953, was built to accommodate future freeway traffic. It was designed, however, to harmonize with the arches and curves of the landmark Colorado Street Bridge. Courtesy, Western History Collection, Natural History Museum of Los Angeles County

adopted in 1957, and in 1983, Jarvenpaa, Finland, became Pasadena's third sister city.) Pasadena also gained international recognition at the 1948 Olympic Games in London when Pasadena Athletic Club divers Victoria Draves and Dr. Sammy Lee carried off a total of three gold medals, Draves making history by winning two events.

Despite the signs of prosperity, the Pasadena Council of Women's Clubs, sensing that Pasadena was not quite what it used to be, conducted a Civic Betterment Survey in 1948 to determine how to improve the city. The survey, however, focused on details like streetlighting, health inspection of restaurants, and more visible house numbers, and failed to address the underlying economic issues that were changing Pasadena, such as the lack of an industrial base and employment opportunities for the middle class, the development of pockets of poverty, and deteriorating neighborhoods.

The end of the war had not brought about the total dismantling of military research. The army wanted to keep its new facilities in the Arroyo and applied for renewal of its lease after the war. Although City Manager Koiner stated that the Jet Propulsion Laboratory violated "the first principle of proper zoning in residential territory," the city was forced to accede when the army threatened to condemn and take the land.

The outcome of the dispute between the city and the army was propitious, for it augured a change in the direction Pasadena would take after the war. Linked by a freeway to Los Angeles and now a center for the aeronautics industry, Pasadena began to shed its image of a wealthy resort city. With most of its hotels and tourists gone, and smog beginning to damage its reputation for healthful living, Pasadena could ill-afford to reject a government-sponsored laboratory that was already one of the city's major employers. After the war, Pasadena would seek to build on its reputation as an ideal residential city, while also trying to attract business and industry to bolster the economy.

Chapter VII

New development in downtown Pasadena in the 1970s created sharp contrast between old and new. Here the elegant Civic Auditorium, part of the 1920s Civic Center plan, is seen through the arch of the Plaza Pasadena, a 1970s shopping mall. Photo by Walt Mancini

POSTWAR PASADENA: NEW DIRECTIONS

"Pasadena

is at

the

crossroads."

–*Robert H. Oliver*, 1959

At the end of the World War II Pasadena found itself facing a changed world. The city could no longer entertain the idea of re-establishing itself as a resort for the wealthy. American economic and social traditions had undergone a profound change; the prosperity of the 1920s, based on the fortunes of nineteenth-century industrial expansion, was being replaced by a new, technology-oriented prosperity, based on mass consumption. Moreover, the scientific and technological development of Southern California in the war years, primarily related to the aircraft industry, continued to expand after the war, drawing new people to the region.

Pasadena was no longer a remote, peaceful suburb of Los Angeles, but lay in the heart of a metropolitan area of burgeoning population, one of the fastest-growing metropolises in the country. Pasadena itself, which had gained only about 7,000 new residents between 1930 and 1940, jumped from a population of 82,864 in 1940 to 104,577 in 1950, an increase of about 25 percent. In the same period, Los Angeles County grew from 2,786,000 to 4,152,000, an increase of almost 50 percent. This population increase, based on the increasing industrial development of Southern California, brought with it housing shortages, increased pollution, and traffic congestion, all of which had an impact on Pasadena.

A fundamental change in Pasadena's self-image can be dated from the decision to rezone Orange Grove Avenue for apartment development in 1948. Recognizing that the mansions on "Millionaire's Row" represented a way of life that was gone forever, the city sealed the fate of the famous avenue by allowing garden apartments to replace the millionaires' mansions. Hulett Merritt, one of the first millionaires to build on the street, wrote a protest to the Planning Commission on a postcard bearing a picture of his famous home: "We wish here and now to go on record permanently for your files that we are utterly and violently opposed to any plan that would in whole or part change South Orange Grove from a strictly residential street." The South Orange Grove Association and the Southwest Protective and Improvement Association also opposed the zone change, but others, including absentee owners who cited the expense of keeping up their properties, were for it.

Although strict setback, density, and landscaping requirements attempted to maintain the quality image of Orange Grove Avenue, the new apartments could never match the beauty and craftsmanship of the buildings they replaced. Moreover, the rapid redevelopment of the street lent the once varied and unique streetscape a quality of utilitarian sameness. With the change, Pasadena acknowledged the end of an era, and began to move into a new period.

Though Pasadena was trying to cope with an increased postwar population and fundamental economic changes throughout the 1950s, the city managed to retain many of its cultural traditions. The Pasadena Playhouse had thrived throughout the Depression, producing all of Shakespeare's plays as well as many others. The Playhouse School had become known as an important training ground for aspiring young actors and by the 1950s had already sent on to stardom such actors as William Holden, Dana Andrews, Robert Young, Randolph Scott, Lee J. Cobb, John Carradine, Victor Jory, Eleanor Parker, and dancer Martha Graham. Its 300 students were housed in dormitories on El Molino Avenue, named for some of its leading sponsors, Ernest Batchelder (president of the Playhouse Association for twenty years), Dr. and Mrs. Robert Millikan, Dr. and Mrs. George Ellery Hale, and Mr. and Mrs. Clinton Clarke.

Pasadena's cultural life also received a strong boost in 1951, when Galka Scheyer, German emigré collector and art patron, donated her extensive collection of German Expressionist paintings to the Pasadena Art Institute. This gift of about 600 works, including major collections of the works of Paul Klee and Alexander Jawlensky, made Pasadena the home of an internationally recognized art collection and determined the course of the Pasadena Art Institute in encouraging and showing contemporary art.

Pasadena's excellent library system set as its

goal in the early 1950s a branch library within one mile of every resident in Pasadena. To cope with the expanding residential neighborhoods on the east and west sides of town, the Pasadena library established branches in Allendale, San Rafael, Linda Vista, and Hastings Ranch. A new building was provided for the old Lamanda Park Branch in 1967. The main library received a major addition, the Alice Coleman Batchelder Music Collection, which formed the nucleus of a growing collection of scores and recordings. The Pasadena Public Library system's circulation figures and expenditures per capita earned Pasadena the title as the "best read city in America" in 1963, according to an article in *McCall's* magazine.

The California Institute of Technology continued to expand during the 1950s, building a radio astronomy observatory in the Owens Valley and administering the Jet Propulsion Laboratory, which in 1958 became a facility of the newly formed National Aeronautics and Space Administration, changing its focus from military to space research.

Pasadena assumed importance in the field of medical research with the establishment of the Huntington Institute of Applied Medical Research at the Huntington Hospital (formerly Pasadena Hospital, renamed the Huntington Memorial Hospital in 1935 in memory of Collis P. and Howard E. Huntington).

The city's growing population gave rise to new residential developments in the 1950s. New housing going up on the outskirts of Pasadena, especially the large Hastings Ranch tract development, and the many new houses being built in Linda Vista and San Rafael, contributed to the decline of the center of Pasadena with its older commercial buildings and homes. New shopping centers in Hastings Ranch competed with downtown Pasadena; only two major new buildings, Robinson's department store and Mutual Savings and Loan, were constructed on Colorado Boulevard in the 1950s. Operation Junkyard, a program started by the city's Building Department in the early 1950s to enforce building codes, gave public recognition to the fact that some of Pasadena's older houses were not being properly maintained.

The expanding population also put strains on the school system, and to meet the need six new elementary schools, two junior high schools, and a new high school, Pasadena High School, were built in the 1950s. Pasadena's school system became the focus of unwelcome national attention in the early 1950s when Dr. Willard Goslin, the superintendent, was forced to resign. Goslin, who had been hired in 1948, was a nationally recognized educator who brought to Pasadena many innovative ideas in education. He also came at a time when the postwar "baby boom" mandated a boom-like expansion in school facilities. When Goslin attempted to get a tax measure passed to fund this expansion, he was roundly defeated at the polls.

The defeat of the school bond measure was in part a reluctance on the part of the citizenry to pay higher taxes, but it was also a revolt against the "progressive" ideas of Goslin himself, and a protest against the superintendent's attempt at redistricting the school system. Goslin had proposed redrawing district lines in a manner that would send pupils to the school nearest their homes, a measure that would have broken down de facto racial segregation in the city's schools. Goslin's defeat and the controversy over the role of the school board were preliminary skirmishes in the battle that would erupt in the 1960s and 1970s over segregation in Pasadena's schools.

One sign of fundamental change in Pasadena's economic and social structure was the purchase in 1954 of the Huntington Hotel by the Sheraton Corporation, which changed the focus of the hotel from a resort to a businessman's hotel. At the same time, new industries were moving into Pasadena, most notably Stuart Pharmaceuticals, which opened in 1958 in the eastern part of town. Avon Products had opened a plant in the same area in the late 1940s.

Concern over Pasadena's future prompted the Chamber of Commerce to commission an economic survey by the Stanford Research Institute, which was published in 1959. This report, often referred to as the Oliver report for its author, Dr. Robert Oliver, provided the first real data on Pasadena's economic situation and suggested ways to deal with it. Oliver cited the lack of available land in Pasadena, the large number of old houses and commercial buildings, and the increase in low-income families in the heart of the city as major deterrents to economic growth. The report, however, also noted Pasadena's major assets: a preponderance of high-income families in the Greater Pasadena area; Pasadena's central role in the San Gabriel Valley for banking, finance, insurance, retail trade, and health and legal services; increased employment in Pasadena's industrial establishments since 1940; and the community's educational and cultural advantages.

Seeking to build on Pasadena's assets and enhance its already strong areas of retail trade and offices, Oliver recommended forming a redevelopment agency to engage in large-scale planning and redevelopment efforts. Oliver also noted two goals in planning for Pasadena's future: the maintenance of Pasadena as a desirable residential community for persons working outside the city, principally in Los Angeles; and the increase in economic activity in the city itself to create a solid economic base for the future. The trick was to achieve both of these goals without tipping the balance too much in favor of one to the disadvantage of the other.

Despite the recommendations of the Oliver report, the 1960s were marked by vacillation in the area of redevelopment. Although the report had stressed the need for industrial development and new economic activity in the downtown core, uncertainty as to the routes of the proposed east-west Foothill Freeway and north-south Long Beach Freeway led the Community Redevelopment Agency (CRA), formed in 1960, to concentrate its first efforts on residential blight. Agency board members taken on a tour of the northwest part of the city focused on Pepper Street near Washington and Fair Oaks in a largely black neighborhood, designating it Redevelopment Area I, the Pepper project, in 1960. The CRA planned to level the neighborhood and build new apartments and a shopping center.

The Pepper project became controversial almost immediately, because of restrictions placed on property owners that prevented them from repairing or improving their buildings. These restrictions were to prevent higher property appraisals when the buildings were eventually taken by eminent domain. Neighborhood associations such as the Fair Oaks Businessmen's Association and Home Owner's Protective Endeavor (HOPE) agitated for the abolition of the CRA and revision of the city's housing code without success. A majority of the people in the project area owned their own homes and businesses, and many opposed the displacement that redevelopment would cause.

The project languished into 1964, when the passage of Proposition 14 in California suddenly stopped the flow of needed federal funds to redevelop the area. Proposition 14, which upheld the right of owners and realtors to discriminate on the basis of race in selling property, caused a freezing of all federal money for housing in California, until the courts ruled the measure unconstitutional. Later, federal funds were held up because Pasadena's housing inspection and code enforcement did not meet federal requirements. Demolition of the long-deteriorating buildings did not begin until 1966, and finally, in 1969, nine years after the designation of Pepper Street for redevelopment, ground-breaking for new housing units took place.

The delay of the project created worsening conditions for those prohibited from repairing their homes before demolition and relocation. The effect on business, however, was perhaps even more devastating. The largely minority-owned businesses on North Fair Oaks were promised space in the new business development, but by 1968, only one business remained, and most of the businesses had been unable to operate for several years. These businessmen simply gave up and retired or moved elsewhere, and the community of neighborhood businesses on North Fair Oaks has never been reestablished.

Attracting industry to Pasadena was one of the goals of redevelopment. The Chamber of Commerce established a "Pasadena Standard," a set of guidelines for attracting non-polluting industries that would not detract from Pasadena's residential quality. "Tech Square," a fifty-two-acre industrial park with a 6,000 car garage, office buildings, commercial shops, and several blocks of high-technology industries was planned by the CRA to be located between South Fair Oaks and the Long Beach Freeway, but the plans never came to fruition. Auto dealerships generated considerable sales tax revenue for the city but lack of available land made it difficult for them to expand. An auto center project, which was to concentrate auto dealerships along the future route of the 210 Freeway, was proposed as a solution, but it was also abandoned.

The top Chamber of Commerce goal in 1961 had been the elimination of smog, but by 1965, it had become the development of off-street parking downtown. Parking was seen as the key to revitalizing downtown Pasadena, and several solutions were proposed, including parking structures both north and south of Colorado between Los Robles and Marengo and a complete redesign of the Civic Center, using the Auditorium as a focal point. While these specific plans were not implemented, other factors later brought about downtown revitalization.

Despite Pasadena's problems, parts of the city were thriving in the 1960s. Muir High School had an outstanding reputation, with 80 percent of its graduates going on to college; among its students were seven National Merit Scholarship winners and fifty semi-finalists in the years 1957 to 1964. A new high school, Blair, was established in 1964 at the head of the Pasadena Freeway in converted industrial space. Pasadena's junior college, now called Pasadena City College, was, in the 1960s, one of the largest two-year community colleges in the nation, with a six-million-dollar development program for seven new buildings on the campus.

During the 1960s Caltech added fifteen new

Rapid redevelopment in downtown Pasadena in the 1960s, 1970s, and 1980s has changed the face of the city and dwarfed the landmark City Hall, seen here through construction girders for the Kaiser-Permanente office building. Photo by Geraint Smith

Five of Caltech's twenty Nobel Prize winners are (from left to right) Carl D. Anderson, who was awarded the prize in physics in 1936; Murray Gell-Mann, physics in 1969; Max Delbrück, physiology and medicine in 1969; Richard Feynman, physics in 1965; and George W. Beadle, physiology and medicine in 1958. Courtesy, California Institute of Technology

buildings on its campus, as well as a new solar observatory at Big Bear. The international reputation of the institute continued to grow, as evidenced by the increasing numbers of Nobel prizes awarded to its faculty and graduates. Prizes in physics went to Edward D. McMillan (1951), William Shockley (1956), Donald Glaser (1960), Rudolph Mossbauer (1961), Charles Townes (1964), Richard Feynman (1965), Murray Gell-Mann (1969), Leo James Rainwater (1975), Robert D. Wilson (1978), William A. Fowler (1983), and Carl Anderson (1936). Two prizes in medicine went to George Beadle in 1958 and Max Delbrueck in 1969. Howard M. Temin and William N. Lipscomb, who had earned doctorates at Caltech, were awarded the prize in medicine in 1975 and 1976, respectively. Caltech professor Roger W. Sperry won the prize in medicine in 1981 for his pioneering split-brain research. Working with epileptics who had undergone therapeutic surgery to sever the connection between the two halves of their brains, Sperry was able to localize certain mental functions in either the right side or left side of the brain. Linus Pauling, who won the Nobel Prize in chemistry in 1954, made history by being awarded the prize again in another field, the Nobel Peace Prize for 1964.

The dream of a major museum on the Carmelita grounds, a vision that went back to the Civic Center plan of the 1920s, was realized in 1969, when the new Pasadena Art Museum opened its doors at Carmelita. Although the new building was criticized for functional deficiencies and its exterior design, it became a West Coast center for contemporary art, drawing artists to Pasadena where many of them rented lofts and studios in the old commercial district around Fair Oaks.

During the 1960s and early 1970s, the museum staged major exhibits of modern masters such as Cezanne, Klee, Jawlensky, Feininger, and Duchamp, as well as contemporary artists such as Robert Motherwell, Roy Lichtenstein, Joseph Cornell, Richard Serra, Andy Warhol, and Claes Oldenburg. Group shows featured West Coast artists, a collection of New Mexican folk art, Asian stone sculptures, and a history of the Bauhaus. The most popular shows were the biennial California Design series, which exhibited the latest in California craftsmanship and design.

Pasadena's cultural life gained a number of important institutions in the 1970s. The Pacificulture Foundation opened a museum devoted to

Asian art (now Pacific-Asia Museum) in the Grace Nicholson Building, which had been vacated by the Pasadena Art Museum. The Pasadena Art Museum itself, however, faltered amid mounting debts. Despite shows of national importance, innovative art education programs, and the popular California Design exhibitions, the museum could not continue to operate. In 1974, wealthy businessman and art collector Norton Simon took control of the museum board, renaming the museum the Norton Simon Museum of Art and installing his own collection of celebrated great masters, creating a different but equally important museum for Pasadena. Art Center College of Design, which opened in 1976 on its new campus in the Linda Vista hills, brought a major educational institution devoted to commercial and industrial design to the city, further enriching Pasadena's artistic life.

Although the Pasadena Symphony Orchestra (founded in 1928) had maintained a fine local reputation and the Coleman Chamber Music Association continued its chamber music series, the focus of music in Southern California had shifted to downtown Los Angeles since the building of the Los Angeles Music Center. However, the opening in 1974 of Ambassador Auditorium on the Ambassador College campus made Pasadena once again an important musical center. Sponsored by the Ambassador Cultural Foundation, the auditorium hosts internationally renowned musicians, bringing the finest music to Pasadenans at their doorstep.

Pasadena sculptor Richmond Barthé enjoys world renown. He began painting as a small boy in Mississippi, later attending the Art Institute of Chicago where he learned sculpture. His work can now be seen in thirty-seven major museums in seventeen countries. Photo by Walt Mancini

A nationwide trend was reflected in the increased voice of minorities in decision-making in Pasadena in the 1960s and 1970s. In Pasadena, the largest and most vocal minority was the black citizenry. Black Pasadenans had already taken leading roles in many areas in the 1920s and 1930s. Dr. James T. Whittaker, Pasadena's first black doctor, founded Dunbar Hospital in Los Angeles in 1923, as encroaching segregation forced blacks out of community hospitals in the region. Mrs. Corinne Bush Hicks was elected president of the California State Federation of Colored Women's Clubs in 1924. James Phillips, early black real estate broker and lawyer, and William Harrison, contractor and real estate broker, both erected business buildings in Pasadena. In the 1930s, George Garner became the first black to play a leading role at the Pasadena Playhouse, and Mack Robinson distinguished himself by winning a medal at the 1936 Olympic Games in the 200-meter event, placing second to Jesse Owens.

Despite these accomplishments whites in Pasadena were organizing to place restrictive covenants on property, severely limiting where blacks could live in the city. By the early 1940s, 60 percent of

The Norton Simon Museum of Art offers a collection of the great masters of European art as well as specialized collections of German Expressionism and the art of India. The sculpture garden features works by Rodin and Henry Moore, among others. Courtesy, Office of the Mayor, City of Pasadena

the city was restricted, including all the property surrounding black neighborhoods.

By 1939, Pasadena blacks were no longer content to sit back on the issue of the Brookside Plunge. Led by Dr. Edna Griffin, a black physician, they filed suit against the city, a suit which was finally won in 1945. But it was a short-lived victory, for the city closed the plunge, claiming that revenues had fallen off so much that it was no longer economic to keep the facility open. After two years the Brookside Plunge was reopened, in the same year (1947) that a Pasadenan, Jackie Robinson, brother of the Olympic star Mack Robinson, became the first black to play major league baseball.

After World War II the great Southern California population boom was paralleled by a migration of blacks into the region, and by 1960 the percentage of Pasadena's black population had tripled. Blacks continued to press for jobs at City Hall, just as they had in the century's early years. Following an investigation by the California Fair Employment Practice Commission in 1963-1965, blacks were employed more frequently by the city in higher-paying, more skilled positions.

Throughout the 1950s and the 1960s, nationwide attention was focused on school segregation after the famous *Brown vs. Board of Education* ruling by the Supreme Court in 1954. Pasadena had its own dramatic lawsuit—*Spangler, et al vs. Board of Education*—filed in 1967, designed to confront the segregation issue through the courts. The suit resulted in a 1970 ruling that mandated school integration by busing in the Pasadena Unified School District.

Pasadena's Pacific-Asia Museum is the only museum in Southern California devoted to the arts of Asia. Changing exhibits, concerts, and other cultural events enliven the museum's program. Here a Chinese dancer performs at the museum. Photo by Walt Mancini

The City Board elections of 1969 saw a well-qualified black candidate, J. Turner Alexander, defeated in the city-wide runoff, although he had won his district by over 50 percent in the first district-only primary election in Pasadena. Previously, although candidates had to be residents of their districts, they were elected at large, making it almost impossible for a minority candidate to gain a seat on the board. A new rule, however, required the winner to get 60 percent or more of the votes in a district to avoid a city-wide runoff. In 1972, the 60 percent rule was changed to 50 percent and in 1981, district-only elections were instituted, abolishing the city-wide runoff.

Other major milestones for the black community in the 1970s and 1980s have been the election of Loretta Thompson-Glickman to the City Board in 1977 and her two-year term as mayor (1982-1984). Sylvia Peebles became the first black chosen for the Rose Court in the 1968 Tournament

Above: *Pictured here are Pasadena mayors Jo Heckman and Loretta Thompson-Glickman at the 1982 gavel ceremony marking Glickman's inauguration. Courtesy, Pasadena Star-News*

Opposite: *This aerial view of downtown Pasadena shows sharp contrasts between old and new. Small-scale older buildings cluster around City Hall in the Civic Center, while the blocky forms of modern buildings dot the periphery. The decade-old 210 Freeway at upper right separates the downtown from the tree-lined neighborhoods to the north. Photo by Walt Mancini*

of Roses, and Kristina Kaye Smith, a black Pasadena City College student, was named Rose Queen for 1985.

The Hispanic population of Pasadena showed a small increase in the 1930s and greater increases in the postwar period. Hispanics continued to be concentrated in their traditional neighborhoods in Lamanda Park and south of California Street. Fremont School in East Pasadena was all Hispanic, and both Garfield and Cleveland schools had relatively high proportions of Hispanic pupils throughout the 1950s and 1960s.

The settlement house on South Raymond Avenue became an important community center during the 1930s and 1940s. Under director Stephen Reyes, it offered recreational programs—handball, basketball, and folk dancing, and social activities such as Cub Scouts and Campfire Girls. It also ran programs in Lamanda Park at Fremont School and at Cleveland School in north Pasadena. Social organizations such as the Mexican Central Council and the Spanish-American Alliance held their meetings at the settlement house. Around 1950 the house and the organization were moved to West Del Mar, near Fair Oaks, to make way for an expansion of the city's garbage dump that had been located next to the building for years. In its new location, it gradually became a black community center before its closing in the late 1950s.

Right: *The mural at Villa-Parke Neighborhood Center is a local landmark on Villa Street. Life-size figures touch up the mural and clean off imaginary graffiti in this virtuosic display of* trompe l'oeil *mural art. Photo by Dan Dunkelberger*

By the 1940s the maternity hospital sponsored by the original Settlement House Association had been moved to a site near the Huntington Hospital and was renamed Women's Hospital. The Huntington had begun to operate a free clinic, the Dispensary, which provided medical care to those who could not afford to pay.

In the 1960s and 1970s, Reyes, who had become professor of Spanish at Pasadena City College, and others in the community fostered the development of a scholarship committee to support Hispanic students of high academic achievement. The committee is still a growing organization and grants several thousand dollars in scholarship money each year. In the same period, young Hispanics pressed for greater recognition in Pasadena community affairs, establishing El Centro De Accion Social, an organization that has increased the voice of the Hispanic minority in the community.

Throughout the postwar period, changes in Pasadena were of an evolutionary nature, but in the 1970s the pace of change accelerated in the downtown area. Private projects—such as the opening of the new eight-story Hilton Hotel near the Civic Auditorium in 1971, the ten-story Beverly Enterprises building on South Lake, and the ten-story Pacific Telephone Building on the site of Mather's Department Store on Colorado Boulevard—complemented public projects such as the Conference Center around the Auditorium, which opened in 1973. As part of the new center, a fountain, given by Pasadena's sister city Ludwigshafen and a plaza named for Mishima, Japan, were dedicated in 1974. A new Holiday Inn behind the Auditorium provided additional hotel facilities for conventioneers.

Efforts by the Community Redevelopment Agency (renamed the Pasadena Redevelopment Agency in 1963) to woo corporate headquarters to Pasadena were crowned with success when the Bankamericard Center opened in 1974. In the same year the first phase of the world headquarters of the Ralph M. Parsons Corporation, an international engineering and construction company,

Signs of revitalization are everywhere in Old Pasadena, Pasadena's National Register Historic District. Victorian and 1920s buildings are being refurbished, and new shops and restaurants abound. A prime example is this new restaurant, housed in a former gas station. Photo by Walt Mancini

opened on Walnut Street, the centerpiece of a four-block complex. Corporate headquarters of Avery International, makers of adhesive labels, opened on North Orange Grove west of Parsons in 1982. A major retail project to improve Colorado Boulevard was the shopping mall called the Plaza Pasadena, which opened in 1980. Other redevelopment projects of the 1970s included residential projects such as the Orange Grove and Del Mar condominiums, adding over 800 residential units in Pasadena (including the 400 completed in the Pepper project), and smaller office projects such as Plaza Centre and Cordova Garden Offices.

Although redevelopment transformed much of downtown Pasadena in the 1970s, the completion of the 210 Freeway, which cut a wide swath through the entire city, probably had the most far-reaching effects. All told, over 3,500 households were displaced by the freeway, which may account for Pasadena's small population decline in the 1960s. (Redevelopment projects had displaced nearly 1,000 households by 1979.) Freeway exits on Lake Avenue reinforced the development of the new city center at Colorado and Lake. Both North and South Lake Avenue sprouted high-rise office buildings in the late 1970s and early 1980s.

The drastic changes of the 1970s in downtown Pasadena were not endorsed by all of the community. As early as 1961, a referendum on a proposed high-rise apartment project at the corner of Colorado and Orange Grove was defeated, signaling that many citizens did not feel that high-density, urban-type development belonged in Pasadena. The demolition of the Neighborhood Church in 1974, one of the city's oldest churches, for a freeway that still has not been completed aroused the ire of many preservationists. Some of the downtown projects also engendered controversy: the location of the Plaza Pasadena cutting across the main axis of the Civic Center; the demolition of historic buildings along North Fair Oaks for Parsons expansion; proposed twenty-story twin apartment towers at Lake and twin office towers at Colorado and Los Robles; and the proposed redevelopment of Los Robles Avenue with tower office blocks.

In response to some of these concerns, the City of Pasadena established the Cultural Heritage Commission in 1976, which was charged with designating landmarks and conducting a survey to identify Pasadena's historic buildings. At the same time, a private organization, Pasadena Heritage, was formed to create awareness of Pasadena's cultural resources and to encourage their preservation.

Steps were taken to preserve Pasadena's old commercial district around Fair Oaks and Colorado with the establishment by the city in 1980 of an urban conservation zone, protecting the buildings from demolition or incompatible alterations. Known as Old Pasadena, this area is now sprinkled with offices, restaurants, and shops, displacing the artists and transients who formerly occupied the old buildings.

In response to the controversy over continuing

Tables for the Centennial fundraiser dot Civic Center Plaza in front of City Hall. Held in September 1985 with food donated by many of Pasadena's best restaurants, the party drew 1,000 contributors to the 1986 centennial celebration. Photo by Walt Mancini

high-rise development, a High-Rise Task Force appointed by the City Board of Directors recommended that Pasadena create an Urban Design Plan to manage growth in the Central Business District. Based on the recommendations of consultants Allan Jacobs and Thomas Aidala and the Urban Design Advisory Committee, composed of representative citizens, an Urban Design Plan was adopted which designated certain areas of the Central Business District as appropriate for high-rise development. The plan also recommended residential development around the two central city parks and height limits in the Civic Center and other areas.

The passage of Proposition 13 in 1978, which limited property tax increases, severely cut back the funds available for redevelopment, which had been financed by tax increment (the increase in property taxes on properties affected by redevelopment projects). This sharp financial cutback, plus the increasing questioning in the community of the effects of redevelopment and some of the procedures, led to the dissolution of the Pasadena Redevelopment Agency in 1981 and the incorporation of its staff and functions into the City Planning Department, under the direct control of

The garden of Pasadena City Hall is an oasis of flowers, greenery, and splashing water in the heart of downtown Pasadena. Its arcades and fountain evoke the Spanish heritage of the missions, translated by architects Bakewell and Brown into a new California style. Photo by Linda Jones Simmons

the City Board of Directors.

Pasadena experienced a number of firsts in the early 1980s. including the election of its first woman mayor, Jo Heckman, in 1980, and just two years later the election of its first black mayor, also a woman, Loretta Thompson-Glickman. In 1984, Pasadena hosted the soccer matches at the Rose Bowl for the Olympics and the Civic Auditorium was the scene of the successful dance series of the Olympic Arts Festival, which brought dance troupes from all over the world to perform in Pasadena.

As a community Pasadena has changed much over the years. Its development from an "aristocratic little colony" of orange growers into a major resort and then one of America's most desirable residential cities still influences life in Pasadena today. The standards of excellence and the cultural legacy of the past have become part of Pasadena's heritage, reflected in its architecture, museums, scientific and educational institutions, and general quality of life. Pasadena has always been a community conscious of its history, and with the passing of its first hundred years the city is experiencing a renewed awareness of its extraordinary heritage. The challenge facing Pasadena today is to use that heritage to best advantage for the future.

The graceful arches of the historic Colorado Street Bridge curving over the Arroyo Seco seem to glow in this view taken at sunset. The bridge is a Cultural Heritage Landmark of the City of Pasadena and is listed on the National Register of Historic Places. Photo by Geraint Smith

This circa 1928 painting by Marion Kavanaugh Wachtel depicts the Arroyo Seco, with the Colorado Street Bridge in the background. Wachtel was one of the Pasadena artists who lived near the Arroyo and were part of Pasadena's "Arroyo culture." Courtesy, De Ru's Fine Arts

This painting of the Arroyo Seco by California painter Guy Rose, a native of the San Gabriel Valley, shows the strong influence of French Impressionism, especially Monet. Rose lived and worked at Giverny, Monet's home, for several years before returning to California in 1914. Courtesy, The Fieldstone Company, Newport Beach

Set among pools and fountains, Ambassador Auditorium opened on the Ambassador College campus in 1974. It has since hosted many famous concert artists and other performers, making a significant contribution to Pasadena's cultural life. Photo by Geraint Smith

Above, left: *This bronze statue of a Union soldier by noted sculptor Theo Alice Ruggles Kitson was erected in 1906 in Library Park (now Memorial Park). It proclaimed the Republican sympathies of Pasadena's citizenry. Photo by Dan Dunkelberger*

Above, right: *All that remains of Pasadena's grand 1890 library is this arched entrance with its white marble columns. Photo by Dan Dunkelberger*

Left: *Each spring the Pasadena Junior Philharmonic Committee sponsors tours of a Showcase House redone by local interior decorators. The tours benefit the Los Angeles Philharmonic Orchestra. The 1984 Showcase House was the Tilt House on Bellefontaine, shown here. Photo by Dan Dunkelberger*

Left: *The former Wrigley mansion with its beautiful rose gardens now serves as the headquarters for the Tournament of Roses Association. Photo by Dan Dunkelberger*

Opposite: *Barney Williams, early Pasadena storekeeper, built this 1880s boom mansion, called Hillmont, at the corner of Hill Avenue and Mountain Street. Probably designed by architect Harry Ridgway, the house features a base of unusual green Tehachapi sandstone on the exterior. The interior retains the original stained glass windows and the original Victorian wallpaper. Photo by Dan Dunkelberger*

Right: *A notable example of Queen Anne style Victorian architecture, Lucky Baldwin's guest house on the grounds of the Los Angeles Arboretum has served as a set for the "Fantasy Island" television series. Courtesy, Los Angeles County Arboretum*

Bottom, left: *The recently restored Theodore P. Lukens House on North El Molino Avenue was designed by Harry Ridgway in the 1880s and is a fine example of the Queen Anne style. Photo by Leslie Heumann. Courtesy, City of Pasadena*

Above: *The adobe ranch house of Hugo and Victoria Reid still stands on the grounds of the Los Angeles County Arboretum. Photo by Dan Dunkelberger*

Right: *Pasadena's most famous house is undoubtedly the Gamble House, completed in 1908 for the Gamble family of Cincinnati. Designed by Charles and Henry Greene, the house is now a museum complete with original furnishings. Photo by Dan Dunkelberger*

Left: *One of the most remarkable buildings in Pasadena is the domed and turreted Castle Green. Once part of the Hotel Green, the building is now listed on the National Register of Historic Places and is part of the Old Pasadena Historic District. In recent years it has become a favorite film location. Photo by Geraint Smith*

Below: *The last great hotel from Pasadena's resort era still in operation, the Huntington-Sheraton Hotel is a large complex of buildings and gardens extending over several acres. Photo by Consolidated Media*

Above: *The 1894 Vandervort Block, recently restored to its original golden brick finish, is a prime example of restoration efforts in historic Old Pasadena. Photo by Geraint Smith*

Left: *Crowds gathered for a street party sponsored by Pasadena Heritage in Old Pasadena in 1978. Walking tours, entertainment, and refreshments attracted many for a look at the historic buildings in the old commercial center, now a National Register Historic District*

Above, left: *These dancers performed at the band shell in Memorial Park for Pasadena's annual Cultural Festival in 1984. Photo by Geraint Smith*

Above: *Three youngsters enjoy bicycle riding in Pasadena's Jackie Robinson Park. Photo by Geraint Smith*

Left: *Pasadena's annual Cultural Festival held in Memorial Park features a multinational food fair, folkcrafts, dances, and music from around the world. Photo by Dan Dunkelberger*

Opposite: *The Pasadena City College Band, shown here in striking formation, is traditionally the official band of the Rose Parade. Photo by Geraint Smith*

Left: *A major prize-winner in the 1986 Rose Parade was this artistic float carrying real mimes performing in the shadow of a giant floral mime figure. Photo by Geraint Smith*

Below, right: *Crowds begin to gather along the Rose Parade route as long as twenty-four hours before the start of the parade. Photo by Geraint Smith*

Below: *Located next to the mountains in the Upper Arroyo Seco, Caltech's Jet Propulsion Laboratory began as an Army research laboratory during World War II and is now a major NASA research center. Photo by Geraint Smith*

Right: *This tranquil view of the Caltech campus belies the intensive nature of the scientific work carried out here. Caltech is known as the most selective undergraduate school in the nation. Photo by Geraint Smith*

Opposite: *The Huntington Library and Art Gallery, located in nearby San Marino, draws scholars and visitors from around the world. It houses a major collection of English art, a gallery of American art, and important English and American books and manuscripts. Its extensive grounds display rare and exotic plants and include a desert garden, a Japanese garden, camellia, and rose gardens. Photo by Consolidated Media*

Above: *Pasadena's City Hall was illuminated for the festive fundraising event held in September 1985 to benefit the Pasadena Centennial. Guests rode down Holly Street in horse-drawn carriages to the Civic Center Plaza, which was decorated with tents and tables. Several of Pasadena's finest restaurants donated a wide variety of foods for the event. Photo by Geraint Smith*

Chapter VIII

This view from the tower of City Hall at sunset shows the principal axis of the Civic Center Historic District, tree-lined Holly Street, stretching westward on the right. Other historic Civic Center buildings, the YWCA and the First Baptist Church, are in the center foreground. Pasadena's Civic Center is listed on the National Register of Historic Places. Photo by Geraint Smith

Partners In Progress

Prior to the time of its incorporation in 1886, Pasadena was very much a rural community with an economy based almost entirely on agriculture. Because of the abundance of fruit trees, most of the early businesses were engaged in fruit packing and canning, and similar activities.

The coming of the railroads brought many changes. Rate wars broke out between the Southern Pacific and the Santa Fe, with fares dropping as low as one dollar from Missouri River areas to Los Angeles. The influx of new residents set off a real estate boom. In 1886 alone, several hundred homes were built in Pasadena, with sales totaling some seven million dollars.

Woodworking mills and a brickyard were opened, along with a variety of retail businesses. The community's first newspaper, the *Pasadena Chronicle,* published its first issue in August 1883. Three months later construction began on the Raymond Hotel—the first of many luxurious hotels erected to accommodate the wealthy Easterners who began flocking to Pasadena to escape the harsh winters.

During its first century Pasadena has seen many changes in its economy. Today, housing such world-renowned institutions as the California Institute of Technology and the Jet Propulsion Laboratory, the city has achieved a reputation as a high-technology center, and many high-tech companies have made it their headquarters.

Because of the highly residential nature of the community, there are virtually no heavy manufacturing facilities—although there is a steadily growing number of light, or "clean," manufacturing operations.

Pasadena is also a major retail center, as a trip along Colorado Boulevard or Lake Avenue will quickly attest. Its strategic location, close to several freeways, and its excellent array of shops attract shoppers from all over Southern California.

In recent years many new office buildings have sprung up, helping to make Pasadena a prime location for financial and other types of service industries. Many law firms, financial institutions, and insurance companies have moved to the community—joining the numerous major corporations that have chosen it as the site of their international, national, or regional headquarters.

Another major factor in the local economy, one that has done more than anything else to put Pasadena on the world map, is the Tournament of Roses Association, which annually stages the Rose Parade and the Rose Bowl football game. In 1984 an independent analysis revealed that the annual economic impact of these two events amounts to more than sixty-eight million dollars.

To attempt to calculate the number of people who have migrated to Pasadena to live and work after viewing a beautiful, sunny New Year's Day from their snowbound homes is impossible. Yet, with that relocation, they learn that the area has much more to offer than they might otherwise have suspected. At one time in its economic evolution, it may have served primarily as a bedroom community for Los Angeles workers, but today the city boasts an environment offering a solid business base combined with excellent recreational, academic, and cultural activities. Pasadena has been most aptly called "The Crown of the Valley."

The organizations whose stories are detailed on the following pages have chosen to support this important literary and civic project. They illustrate the variety of ways in which individuals and their businesses have contributed to the growth and development of Pasadena.

PASADENA CHAMBER OF COMMERCE AND CIVIC ASSOCIATION

The Pasadena Chamber of Commerce headquarters was located at 65 North Los Robles in the early 1940s, when this photograph was taken.

It was the spring of 1888. Less than two years after its incorporation, Pasadena's economic fortunes were sagging. Formation of a group to promote local business was proposed, and on March 26 the Pasadena Board of Trade was born. Its stated purpose, in part, was to: "arouse public opinion upon all matters of vital importance to Pasadena, to gather and disseminate information concerning the resources of Pasadena, . . . to aid and encourage the establishment of manufactories (sic), . . . to watch over and aid the business of the city government."

The first board of directors was comprised of J. Banbury, Enoch Knight, W.U. Masters, B.A. O'Neill, J.H. Painter, W.A. Ray, and G.A. Swartwout, with Masters serving as president and Ray as vice-president. The first secretary was E.E. Fordham, whose salary was set at twenty-five dollars per month.

Right from the start, the board of trade made its presence felt. In its first decade alone, its accomplishments included publication of a brochure extolling the advantages of Pasadena and the launching of campaigns to establish a public library, a municipal water system, a hospital, and an electric car line between Pasadena and Los Angeles.

And it was the board of trade that kept alive an event that has made Pasadena famous the world over. In 1895 the Valley Hunt Club had decided to withdraw its sponsorship of the annual Tournament of Roses Parade, which it had launched in 1890. A public subscription campaign, sponsored by the board of trade, raised $595, assuring the parade's continuance. The board chose Edwin Stearns to manage it, naming him president and grand marshal.

As the years passed the board of trade continued to grow, both in numbers and as the city's leading economic force. It was the board that chose the committee to write a city charter. It supported drives to build Arroyo Drive and the Colorado Street Bridge, as well as schools, parks, and other municipal facilities.

In 1919, shortly after its thirtieth anniversary, it merged with the newly formed chamber of commerce as the Pasadena Chamber of Commerce and Civic Association, with offices at Colorado Street and Raymond Avenue. The new group played a major role in the program to construct the Pasadena Civic Center, which was completed in 1931. In more recent years the chamber has actively supported construction of the Plaza Pasadena and has played a large part in attracting many of the outstanding firms that now call Pasadena home.

In 1953 the chamber moved to the northwest corner of Los Robles and Cordova, where it would remain until it sold the structure in 1981 to make room for a major office building. In 1985 it returned as a tenant in the newly completed structure.

From a feeble beginning in 1888 the Pasadena Chamber of Commerce and Civic Association, now some 1,500 members strong, can reflect on nearly a century of leadership that has helped build the strong business base Pasadena enjoys.

Since February 1, 1985, the chamber has occupied this building at 199 South Los Robles.

PROVIDENT INVESTMENT COUNSEL, INC.

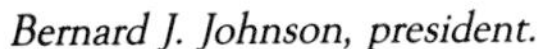
Bernard J. Johnson, president.

Robert M. Kommerstad, chairman of the board.

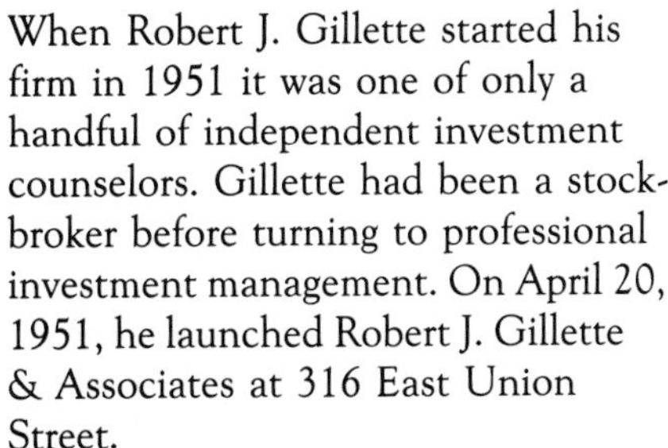

When Robert J. Gillette started his firm in 1951 it was one of only a handful of independent investment counselors. Gillette had been a stockbroker before turning to professional investment management. On April 20, 1951, he launched Robert J. Gillette & Associates at 316 East Union Street.

As the business grew, more space was needed. In the early 1960s the firm moved to East Green Street, and about a decade later relocated to the Union Bank Building on South Lake Avenue. The move to its present site, 225 South Lake, took place on July 1, 1983.

Today's top executives, president Bernard J. Johnson and chairman Robert M. Kommerstad, joined Gillette in 1957 and 1963, respectively. After a series of name changes, and following Gillette's retirement, the present name, Provident Investment Counsel, Inc., was chosen.

In the late 1960s the firm acquired its first institutional account, a college endowment fund, signaling the start of a major change in the client base. Today institutions such as pension funds and foundations comprise the vast majority of the client list, accounting for more than 95 percent of the funds managed.

That change has brought solid growth to Provident. By 1979 assets under management reached $100 million and then doubled in the next two years. By 1983 the total was one billion dollars and current assets under management reached $1.6 million, representing a sixteenfold increase in just seven years.

A full-time staff of forty oversees the firm's 300 accounts. Investments in stocks are limited to a "buy list" of sixty companies, all judged to have strong growth potential. The average holding period is two years, although one has been in the portfolio since 1971. The reason? The value has increased 17,000 percent in that period, and continues to grow steadily.

The success of Provident's investment strategies is clearly shown by its performance. The handful of independent counseling firms that existed in 1951 has grown to hundreds. Among the larger ones, Provident has consistently performed well. It was rated first in the nation in 1982, when its stock holdings increased by more than 45 percent. Three months later Provident again topped the list, with a twelve-month gain of 80.5 percent.

In addition to the day-to-day direction of their staff, Johnson and Kommerstad have various outside interests. Johnson, long active in the Pasadena Tournament of Roses Association, is now an honorary director. He is a past president of the Pasadena Bond Club and the University Club of Pasadena, and is a member of the Pasadena Rotary. Kommerstad serves on the national board of directors of Big Brothers and Big Sisters of America and is a member of the board of First Business Bank of Los Angeles.

CROWN FENCE AND SUPPLY COMPANY

Fifty years or more before the introduction of the now-famous advertising slogan, "Let your fingers do the walking," Arthur Fiedler did just that. Newly arrived in Pasadena from the Midwest and anxious to start a business, he consulted the Yellow Pages, 1922 Edition, to see how many were listed in the various categories. Noting the scarcity of fence companies, he decided that was the field for him and, shortly thereafter, Crown Fence and Iron Works was born.

Fiedler's background suited him well for his new venture. The Ohio native had worked for his home state as a civil engineer and for Chrysler Corporation as a design engineer. Following World War I, in which he served as an officer of the U.S. Army's Second Division, he formed a metal window sash company in Cleveland.

In 1921 his brother, Charles, moved to Pasadena, and soon tales of the beauty of Southern California were being sent back to Cleveland. In short order Arthur succumbed, and with his wife, Julia, and their two young children, Kern and Paula, he headed west. In April 1923, his phone book research satisfactorily completed, Arthur bought property on Broadway (now Arroyo Parkway) and began his fence manufacturing and construction business.

From the very start Crown was and is a family business. Arthur's two original partners, Joseph Cook and George Foss, were married to sisters of Julia Fiedler. Cook, who ran the plant, died in the mid-1930s, and Foss, who was in charge of the office and sales, retired in the early 1950s. In 1926 the partnership was converted to a corporation, adopting its present name, Crown Fence and Supply Company.

F. Arthur Fiedler, founder and president from 1923 to 1952.

The Depression years hit the fencing industry hard, and the small family-owned business was no exception. Many companies failed, but Fiedler was determined not only to keep going but also to see that every one of his employees continued to get a full paycheck.

By that time a third child, Richard, had been born. Yet somehow, without neglecting the care of her three children, Julia joined her hardworking husband, handling the firm's bookkeeping on a part-time basis.

The lessons learned during those lean years—hard work, determination and loyalty—continue to characterize the company, well known for its "one-for-all and all-for-one" philosophy. Turnover is extremely low, with one employee nearing the completion of a half-century at Crown Fence.

Kern Fiedler, Arthur's oldest son, began working for Crown part time at the age of thirteen. Shortly before the outbreak of World War II he joined the U.S. Army Air Corps, becoming a captain, test pilot, and flight instructor. He rejoined the business in 1946 after recuperating from serious injuries suffered in a crash while testing a new night fighter-bomber aircraft.

That same year Crown moved to its present location at 939 South Fair Oaks Avenue. The property consisted of seven lots, with a Southern Pacific track running through the middle. In 1948 the other two Fiedler children, Paula and Richard, joined the company full time, and they've never left.

Arthur Fiedler bought this land on Broadway (now Arroyo Parkway) and began his fence manufacturing and construction business in 1923. Photo circa 1924

Early security fence work at the California-Mexico border crossing. Photo circa 1920s

Kern succeeded his father as president in 1954, although Arthur maintained an active interest in the business until shortly before his death in 1959. Kern died unexpectedly in 1968, and Dick became president, a position he continues to hold.

Community service has become a tradition in the Fiedler family. Kern was an active member of Pasadena Rotary and of the Young Presidents' Organization (YPO). Following Kern's death, Dick was invited to replace him in Rotary. He joined the club in 1969 and served as its president in 1984-1985. Dick has also been actively involved in the Pasadena Chamber of Commerce, an organization to which Crown has belonged for more than fifty years.

What certainly ranks as a major highlight in the firm's history began in 1983, and, for the second time, the Yellow Pages played a significant role. A representative of the Los Angeles Olympic Organizing Committee had "let his fingers do the walking" in search of fence companies. Bids were being sought for security fencing at the sites of the various competitions in preparation for the Games of the XXIIIrd Olympiad in Los Angeles the following year.

Crown Fence was the successful bidder on several 1983 projects, gaining valuable experience that would soon stand it in good stead. By late 1983 Dick Fiedler was aware that his company, along with about twenty others, was being considered as a fence supplier for the games themselves and was hopeful Crown would get some of the work.

Eventually, the Olympic officials narrowed the field to three firms but finally chose to deal exclusively with one contractor—Crown Fence. The contract involved fifteen training sites and three Olympic villages, all the performance sites plus various television and broadcast areas for ABC Television.

Installation was completed well in advance of the July 28 Opening Ceremonies, but that was not the end of Crown's Olympic competition. When the games ended, the firm had less than three weeks to restore all the sites to their "preOlympic" condition. That meant removing fifty miles of fence, weighing over three million pounds, which included 25,000 posts, 3,000 gates, and over two million square feet of steel fence fabric.

Having cleared that hurdle, only one remained before Crown's Olympic saga would end. That was the disposal of the fencing, which was accomplished primarily via sales to the trade at base discounts.

In a classic understatement, Dick Fiedler describes the Olympic project as his company's biggest to date. It's likely to remain so until the Olympics return to Southern California. When that happens Olympic officials won't need to consult a phone directory to find the right fence company, not with the track record of Crown Fence and Supply Company.

Since its beginning Crown Fence has played a major role in fencing projects throughout the area.

LICHER DIRECT MAIL, INC.

Much of the entrepreneurial lore in America is entwined with the proverbial garage start-up—and this story is no exception. What makes this one different is that the entrepreneur is a woman, who founded her business long before the women's liberation movement was in vogue.

Besse Licher came to Pasadena from Wisconsin in October 1945 with her husband, Wayne, following his discharge as a much-decorated veteran of twenty-five combat missions with the U.S. Army Air Corps. Between missions Wayne had opportunities to exercise his cartooning skills, and a postwar job offer from Disney Studios proved irresistible.

The job turned out to be less than expected, and Wayne soon joined the advertising display department at the Broadway department store. Besse, a business school graduate with secretarial experience, was hired by the Pasadena YMCA. It was a good job, but not one to hold a true entrepreneur for very long.

A few months later, on May 6, 1946, with a used $500 addressograph machine as the primary equipment, Besse launched Licher Addressing and Embossing Service from the garage of the family home at 287 Roberts Street. She had discovered a need and was filling it—so well that within four months there was no more room in the garage. Larger quarters were found in the basement of the old Greyhound bus station at the corner of Green Street and Marengo Avenue. Besse moved in, with her one full-time employee and a boy who worked after school.

By 1952 continued growth dictated the need for even more space, and the company moved to 500 North Lake Avenue. The payroll at that time was about $300 per month. Wayne took on a new job that same year, moving to Crawford Stores as assistant advertising director. Two years later he joined his wife in the planned expansion of the family business. A few years earlier Besse had purchased an offset press to broaden the firm's service base and now, with Wayne on board, there was a full-fledged art department.

Ten years after moving to North Lake, the Lichers were again faced with a familiar problem—lack of space. They located a building at 980 Seco Street that had housed a publishing house. The couple purchased the structure in 1962 and converted it to their needs.

The business remains at that location today, though it bears little resemblance to its 1962 look. Several renovations and additions have been made over the years. The most recent, and most extensive, came in 1985 when a large, two-story addition was built on the front of the existing facility. The 5,650-square-foot structure was designed in the Craftsman

A birthday cake replica of the firm's new building, served at its open house.

style and blends well with the residential character of the neighborhood, which is near the Rose Bowl.

A Pasadena Beautiful Award for an outstanding design was given to the Lichers at the 1986 Awards Dinner.

The Lichers purchased and remodeled the residence next door to their business and now live there.

A third member of the Licher family, Wayne Jr., got an early start in the business. Working there on a part-time basis through his high school and college years, he became a full-time employee following his graduation from the University of La Verne.

The business was incorporated in 1969 as Licher Direct Mail, Inc. Wayne Sr., who continues to direct the art department, is president, and Wayne Jr. serves as vice-president in charge of production. Besse is secretary/treasurer and the chief executive officer. The company's name belies its full range of activities, which include complete printing, layout, and computer typesetting, in addition to its fully automated mailing services.

The Lichers have been very active in the Pasadena community. Wayne Sr. has been a part of such organizations as the Pasadena Chamber of Commerce, Toastmasters, the Jaycees, and the Optimist Club, where he served as president in 1970-1971.

Typically, Besse has a number of "firsts" to her credit. She was the first female president of the Pasadena Central Improvement Association and the first woman admitted to membership in the Pasadena Tournament of Roses Association. A longtime political activist, she has served as a member of the California State Republican Central Committee and as president of the Pasadena Republican Club. In her only try for public office in 1963, she came within a few votes of being the first woman elected to the Pasadena City Board of Directors.

Wayne and Besse have also given much of their time to junior baseball, no doubt inspired by their son's athletic prowess. Wayne Jr. had the distinction of playing on Pasadena's world championship team in the Babe Ruth League in 1970, the first California team to reach that goal. His father was active as an officer, coach, and manager in both the Pony League and the Babe Ruth League, while Besse directed her talents primarily to fund raising.

Literally dozens of other Pasadena groups have benefited over the years from the participation and support of the Licher family. Wayne and Besse may be midwesterners by birth, but they are Pasadenans nevertheless, in every sense of the word.

A vintage bus transporting guests to the old-fashioned open house.

HUNTINGTON MEMORIAL HOSPITAL

Fowler Memorial Building, completed in 1909, housed the hospital's original administrative offices.

It began, as so many successful projects do, because there was a need to meet. The year was 1892, and for the seriously ill Pasadenan, a bumpy train ride to Los Angeles was the price to be paid for adequate medical care.

So, on February 18 of that year, a group of community leaders met to form the nonprofit Pasadena Hospital Association. Within a few months the incorporation was completed—but another seven years were to pass before the dream would become reality.

When the first patient was admitted in 1899, there was little to suggest that the tiny sixteen-bed hospital would one day become a 606-bed facility, the third-largest private, nonprofit medical center in California. The original hospital was located on the second floor of an office building at Raymond Avenue and Green Street, leased for a period of six months.

At last Pasadena had its own hospital, to which 329 patients were admitted the first year, by 40 of the community's 75 doctors.

As the twentieth century dawned the hospital formed a nursing school, from which the first class of seven women graduated in 1902. They would be followed by thousands more during the school's 55-year history.

The hospital's first operating table was personally built by Dr. F.C.E. Mattison, a member of the founding board of directors, aided by a local plumber. The framework was gas pipe with a sheet of iron laid on top of it. A coat of enamel, applied by Dr. Mattison, completed the project.

In 1900 a committee to raise funds for a permanent building was formed, and a year later it was announced that the necessary $21,000 had been pledged and that Mrs. Caroline Walkley had donated a lot, located at Congress Street and Fairmount Avenue.

On January 4, 1902, the new 26-room hospital opened. Other buildings followed in rapid succession: a nurses' bungalow in 1903; a maternity wing in 1904; the Sprague Memorial Building in 1907; and the Eldredge M. Fowler Memorial Administration Building in 1909.

As the hospital grew, so did the community support that has been an integral part of it throughout its his-

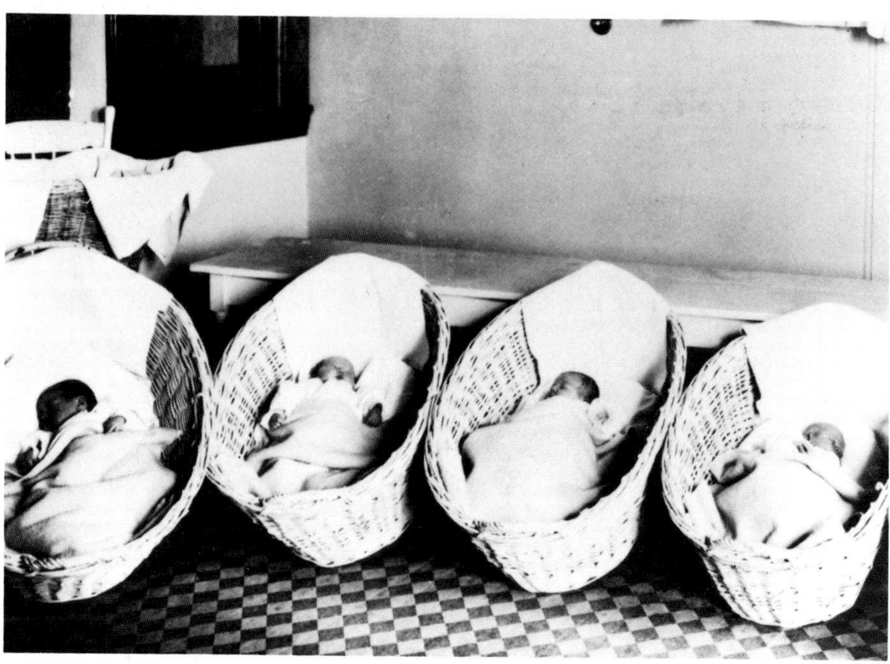

A 1907 view of the nursery.

tory. By 1921 more than $500,000 had been pledged toward the building fund. The Pasadena Dispensary had begun in 1915, supported in large measure by funds from the Pasadena Community Chest. To this day it has maintained its mission of meeting the health care needs of the community's poor, who would be otherwise unable to obtain it.

Further evidence of community support was the founding of the Women's Auxiliary in 1926, followed shortly thereafter by the Junior Auxiliary and the Clinic Auxiliary.

As the Roaring Twenties drew to a close, the once-tiny hospital had become a vital part of the community it served. Yet all was not well. Overcommitments to expansion, in order to meet the growing need for quality medical care, had placed the hospital under financial strain. Then came the stock market crash of 1929, followed by the Great Depression.

Pasadena Hospital, which had treated so many crises so well, now faced one of its own. Heavily in debt, its once-rosy future bleak, the hospital in its 1932 annual report lamented: "Each year problems of the hospital become more complex. Those unable to pay for care appear in increasing numbers. And income from paying patients has decreased markedly. How long can we continue...?"

Less than four years later that question was to be answered in a dramatic and wholly unexpected way. It was Alice G. Henninger, the hospital's superintendent, who found the answer. It lay in the will of the late Henry E. Huntington, railroad magnate and major Southern California developer. Miss Henninger noted a clause in the will, providing a $2-million gift for a hospital "in or near Los Angeles." The bequest included a stipulation that the hospital receiving the funds be named the Collis P. and Howard Huntington Memorial Hospital, in honor of the donor's uncle and son, respectively.

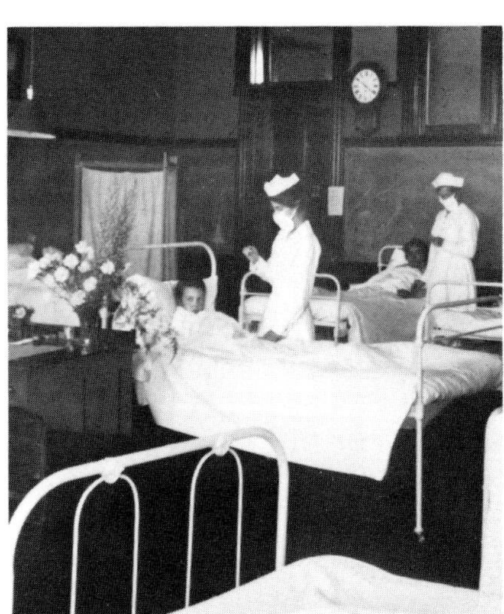

By the early 1900s the hospital's tradition of caring, quality service was already well established.

After considering other possibilities, the Huntington trustees agreed to meet with Pasadena Hospital Association officials. On February 19, 1936, Pasadena Hospital president Albert B. Ruddock announced that the hospital was "to be developed and enlarged with the addition of . . . some two million dollars . . . (and) . . . is to be designated the Collis P. and Howard Huntington Memorial Hospital."

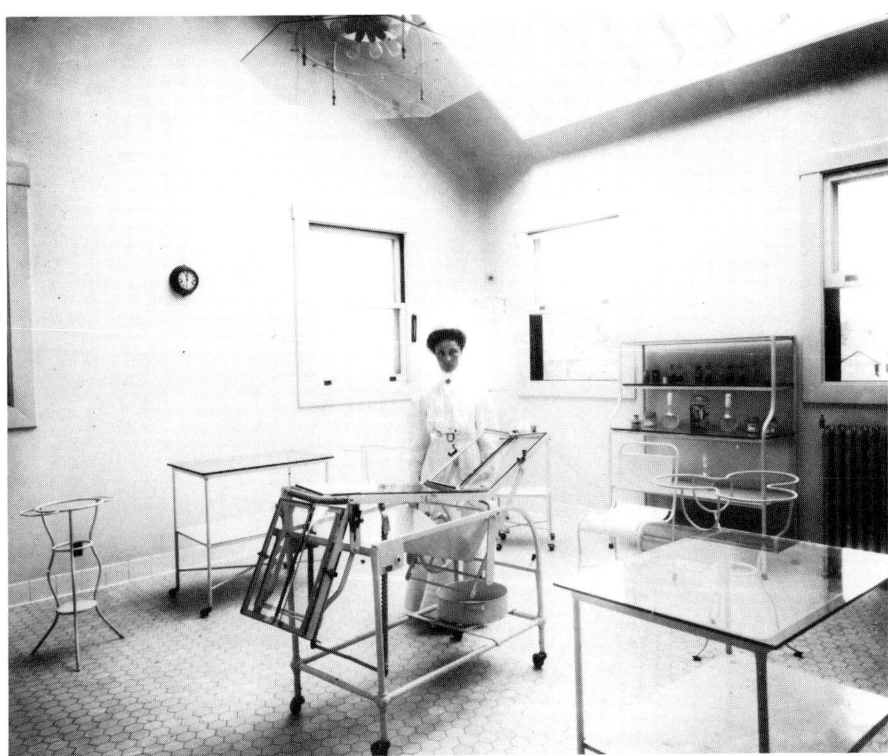

The "complete and convenient operating room" of 1907.

So, thanks to the sharp eyes of Alice Henninger, a new era began for the Pasadena Hospital Association, Ltd., dba Collis P. and Howard Huntington Memorial Hospital, or, as it would quickly become known, Huntington Memorial Hospital. The generous gift was used to pay off all indebtedness, complete badly needed renovations of older facilities, and construct new ones. A Children's Department and Physical Therapy Building opened in 1938, followed in 1940 by a major four-story fireproof hospital structure. It was all made possible by the generosity of Henry E. Huntington.

In 1941, nearing the completion of

its first half-century, the hospital admitted more than 7,500 patients, performed some 4,000 operations, and delivered 754 babies. Yet, despite all the new facilities, the superintendent's report for 1941 noted that "one of the pressing needs of the hospital at this time is space for additional beds."

As the year drew to a close a new crisis struck, one that would affect not only Pasadena and its hospital, but the nation and the world. World War II had begun, and during the next four years dozens of the hospital's staff—doctors, nurses, and others—went off to serve their country. Those left behind were severely overburdened but, aided by large numbers of volunteers, were able to keep the hospital going with no disruption in service.

Huntington's extensive pediatric program, which includes the area's only pediatric intensive care unit, provides warm, personalized care to youngsters throughout the San Gabriel Valley.

War's end brought new problems and the postwar boom taxed the hospital's facilities more than ever before. Between 1945 and 1950 occupancy exceeded 100 percent of capacity and extra beds were placed wherever space could be found. Admissions in 1950 were 12,319, nearly double the 1940 figure.

In 1951 the Jenks Convalescent Unit was completed, providing some relief from the overcrowded conditions. The following year saw the completion of the Huntington Institute of Applied Medical Research, donated by two local anonymous benefactors.

Support from the community continued as it had throughout the hospital's history, making further improvements possible. They ranged from a modern switchboard system to a new maternity facility, from new surgical recovery rooms to the piping of oxygen to every bed.

Then, in 1958, twenty-two years after the Huntington gift, came another bequest of major proportions. Former patient William H. Wingate had died at the age of ninety-five, leaving a substantial portion of his estate to the hospital. Preliminary estimates indicated a value of less than $500,000. Wingate, however, had invested many years earlier in a brand-new business in Chicago. That little company was now the multinational giant IBM, and the Wingate investment was worth five million dollars.

New hospital facilities, opened in 1940, were made possible by the generous bequest of Henry E. Huntington.

Supported by this generous windfall, progress continued through the 1960s and 1970s with the construction of the Mary Urmston Valentine Institute of Radiology, followed by the Wingate Building in 1964, the Edward Valentine Building in 1971, and the Hahn Building, honoring Herbert L. Hahn, in 1973.

Yet the hospital's growth was marked by far more than new facilities. During this era X-ray diagnostics and radiation treatment capabilities were doubled; open-heart surgery, a very innovative concept, was begun; the highly specialized Intensive Care Unit was established; emergency and cardiac care were expanded; and a new Health Sciences Library, currently housing 20,000 volumes, was opened. In the decade from 1963 to 1973 Huntington Memorial Hospital expended more funds and added more square footage than in all its previous history.

The hospital has consistently remained in the forefront of the tech-

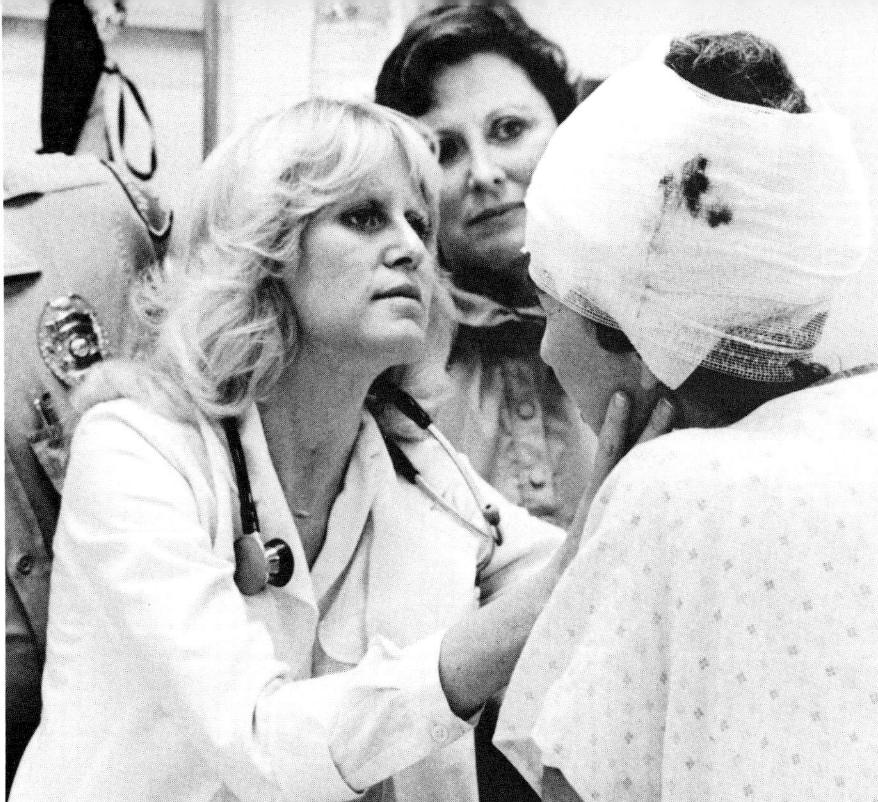

More than 40,000 people turn to Huntington every year for immediate, around-the-clock treatment of medical emergencies. Huntington is the only Level I Trauma Center in the San Gabriel Valley.

nological revolution, both in management systems and in medical care and research. In 1974 computer terminals were installed throughout the hospital, an achievement unmatched by many hospitals more than a decade later.

In 1976 the Huntington became one of the first hospitals to install a CT scanner. The following year a $250,000 Linear Accelerator for radiation therapy was installed, and another million dollars was invested in the modernization and computerization of the clinical laboratory.

The nuclear age dawned at the Huntington in 1983, with the installation of what has been described as one of the most revolutionary new tools in medical history: a $2.5-million nuclear magnetic resonance (NMR) imaging laboratory. A radiological breakthrough, promising less invasive and more precise diagnostic procedures, the NMR will keep the Huntington in its accustomed place, on the leading edge of medical technology.

Other less technical, but highly significant, milestones have been reached by the hospital in recent years. In 1978 it began a major teaching affiliation with the University of Southern California School of Medicine. In 1982 a merger was completed with LaVina Hospital, an Altadena facility with a long history of specialization in pulmonary medicine. And in 1983 the Huntington, thanks to its long-standing emphasis on quality emergency care, became the only Level I Trauma Center in the San Gabriel Valley.

Maternal and infant care also rank high on the Huntington's list of priorities and accomplishments. More than 3,400 babies were delivered at the hospital in 1985, the highest number in its history and double the rate of a decade earlier.

Because of its expertise in perinatal care and neonatal intensive care, the Huntington serves as a regional support center for distressed infants, providing the gift of life to little ones who might not otherwise survive. Perhaps nothing better typifies the philosophy of this institution, as it nears its 100th year of service to Pasadena and its environs.

As well as it has served the community, so has Huntington Memorial Hospital been served by the community. What began as a small band of concerned citizens back in 1892 has grown to a volunteer force of 900 who in 1985 alone contributed more than 146,000 hours of service.

That kind of teamwork has enabled the Pasadena Hospital Association, Ltd., dba Collis P. and Howard Huntington Memorial Hospital, to live up to its commitment to the community: "to maintain and strengthen existing services, and to ensure ongoing excellence in health care for all citizens, regardless of age or ailment."

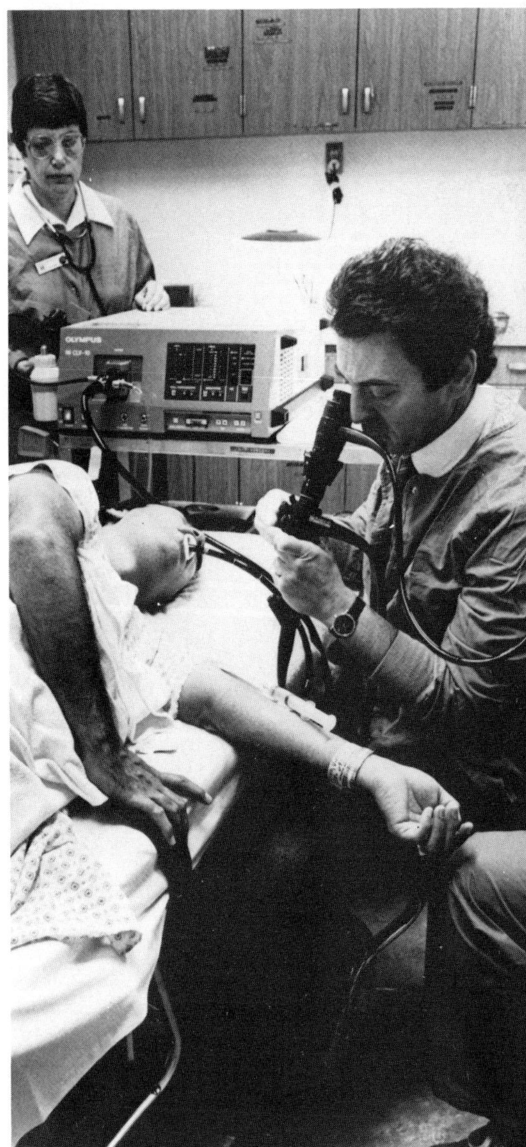

Since 1974 Huntington's day surgery program has provided patients with a convenient, less costly way to receive high-quality surgical care without staying overnight in the hospital.

MUTUAL SAVINGS AND LOAN ASSOCIATION

When Mutual Building and Loan Association was incorporated on April 22, 1925, the industry was in its infancy; there were only about 150 such institutions in all of California. Its first office was located at 2569 East Colorado Street, in what was known as Lamanda Park, now East Pasadena. The original board of directors was made up of Charles E. Barber, George D. Brown, A.N. Cole, J. Homer Hough, J.B. Keaster, L.A. Merritt, and Frank T. Olsen.

In 1930 the association was acquired by West Coast Bond and Mortgage Company, a well-established Pasadena firm. A new board of directors was named, with Hough the only member from the founding group. Selected to serve with him were H.H. Buckley, R.W. Caspers, Richard D. Aston, R.C. Merryman, George E. Higgins, and Herbert L. Hahn. Buckley was elected president; Caspers, executive vice-president and general manager; and Aston, secretary/treasurer.

The years immediately following the acquisition were difficult ones for the financial industry, devastated by the Great Depression. Nonetheless, Mutual stood the test well—honoring every withdrawal on presentation (although not legally obliged to do so) and paying interest, when due, on every account. It was a performance few financial institutions could match.

When Buckley retired in 1935, Caspers was named president of both Mutual and West Coast. The following year the growing firms moved into larger quarters at 38 South Los Robles Avenue. At that time Mutual had total resources of $850,000, and shortly thereafter passed the million-dollar mark. The $2-million and $3-million levels were reached in 1937 and 1939, respectively.

The 1940s brought more growth and many changes to Mutual. The outbreak of World War II depleted the staff as many employees, including Richard Aston, answered their country's call. Mutual itself was actively involved in the war effort—selling war bonds, organizing blood drives, and participating in other causes.

Rudolph W. Caspers served Mutual well for more than thirty years as treasurer, executive vice-president, president, and chairman of the board. He was serving as chairman at the time of his death in 1958.

In January 1942 Herbert Hahn resigned from the board and was replaced by one of his law partners at Hahn & Hahn, Louis R. Vincenti. It marked the start of a relationship that would last more than forty years.

On March 9, 1944, the institution opened the doors of its new headquarters at 315 East Colorado, and celebrated by awarding two war bonds daily. In 1945 the first branch office, in Glendale, was opened.

The war's end saw the return of Aston and other employees, as well as the start of a huge demand for housing and for mortgage loans. By December 1946 Mutual's resources were ten million dollars and the organization paid its forty-fourth consecutive semiannual dividend.

The institution changed its name in 1947 to Mutual Savings and Loan Association, as the term "building and loan" was falling into disuse. In 1949 Caspers became chairman of the board, and Aston succeeded him as president of both Mutual and West Coast. The association continued its record of growth, and marked its twenty-fifth anniversary in April 1950 by reaching the $20-million level in resources.

Richard D. Aston was escrow officer in the late 1920s and then secretary/treasurer. He succeeded Rudolph Caspers as president and then chairman, serving in the latter post until his death in 1973.

Mutual added a second branch in 1954 in Covina, and a year later hired two employees who would go on to play major roles in its future. Louis Vincenti, a thirteen-year board veteran, was named executive vice-president; and Harold R. Dettmann was hired as a teller. Twenty-eight years later the latter succeeded the former as president.

William T. Caspers, son of Rudolph W. Caspers, was already a di-

The current nine-story headquarters building, still at the same location, was completed in 1964. City Hall can be seen in the background.

rector of Mutual when his father passed away in September 1958. W.T. Caspers had been elected to the board in January 1958. His sister, Elizabeth Caspers Peters, was elected to the board in December 1958. David K. Robinson, attorney with Hahn & Hahn, filled the vacancy created by Caspers' death.

Louis Vincenti became president in 1961. Again faced with a need for more space, the board decided to build a new nine-story facility on its existing site. Temporary quarters were opened next door and construction began in 1962; the new building and a multistory garage behind it were completed two years later.

Mutual had opened two new branches during the 1960s and added eleven more between 1971 and 1975, but soaring interest rates in the late 1970s made expensive branch offices virtually unaffordable. Mutual and its holding company—Wesco Financial Corporation, which had been formed in 1959—decided to cut back and sold its branch network in 1980, retaining the main office and a satellite at the recently completed Plaza Pasadena.

Poor health forced Vincenti, who had assumed the additional duties of chairman of Mutual and Wesco following Aston's death in 1973, to retire in December 1983. He was succeeded as president by Harold Dettmann, who became only the fourth man to hold that post in nearly a half-century. Indeed, longevity has been a hallmark of the association.

Both the Caspers and Aston families have been part of Mutual since 1930. Not only are Rudy's two children on the board, but his grandson, William T. Caspers, Jr., is business development representative. The Aston family tradition is being continued by Dick's son, Robert D. Aston, who is senior vice-president.

That stability has served Mutual well. By the mid-1980s its resources had grown to over $300 million and net worth more than $60 million.

Mutual's staff prepares to greet customers on opening day of its new headquarters, at 315 East Colorado Street.

J.H. BIGGAR FURNITURE COMPANY

When John H. Biggar opened his J.H. Biggar Furniture Company in Pasadena in 1926, he was new to the community but a furniture business veteran.

Biggar came to Pasadena for the same reason many thousands of others have, lured by the Southern California climate. He had recently retired from business in Seattle, where for fourteen years he had purchased furniture for two large firms, making some sixty buying trips to Grand Rapids, Michigan, and other eastern furniture centers. It was no easy feat in those pre-airline days, but he learned the furniture business.

The new company had three employees when it opened on the morning of July 27, 1926, at 680 East Colorado Boulevard. In addition to the founder, they were his oldest son, Edson, and Edson's wife, Jane.

Sixty years later it remains the family business it was at the beginning. Between them, the founder, his three sons, and two of his grandsons, have a total of 212 years of service.

John H. Biggar, Jr., the middle son, joined the firm on a full-time basis in 1928 after graduating from college, although he had helped out on a part-time basis virtually from the start. Today he is chairman of the board.

John H. Biggar, Jr., is flanked by his two sons, Jack (left) and Dick.

By 1930 the youngest of the founder's three sons, Howard, had come aboard. For many years thereafter the three ran the business, as their father gradually turned over the reins. John Sr., however, remained active, coming to work every morning right up until his death in 1952, twenty-six years after he launched the company.

Edson, who died in 1960, was with the firm for thirty-four years and Howard served for forty-eight years, until his death in 1978.

In the meantime, another generation of Biggars had come along to keep the family banner flying. In 1958, after college and business school, John Jr.'s son, John H. Biggar III, known as Jack, became a full-time member of the team, though he too had started out on a less formal basis, doing odd jobs around the store beginning at about age fourteen. Edson's son, Boyd, joined the firm in 1961 and served until his untimely death in 1967 at the age of thirty-two.

By 1940 the Pasadena store had been expanded on the west, to the corner of El Molino Avenue, on the south side of Colorado Boulevard.

Today Jack is president of the J.H. Biggar Furniture Company and his younger brother, Dick, who joined in 1968, is executive vice-president. Thus, the three-man management team that once comprised John Jr. and his two brothers is now made up of John Jr. and his two sons.

Although neither Edson's nor Howard's direct descendants are active in the operation of the business, all three branches of the family share ownership of the real estate, which includes the Pasadena and Woodland Hills stores, and a Pasadena warehouse.

Today the headquarters of the J.H. Biggar Furniture Company is exactly where it was when it opened its doors in 1926—at 680 East Colorado Boulevard. Back then, however, there was a mere thirty-seven feet of frontage and the entire store occupied 5,500 square feet. In 1937 Hines Grocery Company, which occupied the other half of the building, relocated and Biggar took over the space, doubling in size.

In 1940 it acquired the adjoining building, on the southeast corner of Colorado and El Molino, adding an-

This sketch appeared in a newspaper ad on July 26, 1926, announcing the opening of the store on the following day.

other 15,000 square feet. Over the years the Pasadena store has continued to expand, a total of seven times, with the latest addition occurring in 1973.

Growth was also taking place in other directions, as new stores were added. There was a store in Pomona from 1950 to 1980, and one in Santa Ana from 1952 to 1986. The Woodland Hills store opened in 1978, followed by the Irvine store in 1983. The firm's other facility, a large East Pasadena warehouse, has been in operation since 1953. The company plans continued expansion in the future.

Pasadena has meant far more to the Biggars than simply a place to operate a successful business. Community service has been a family tradition right from the start. Jack and Dick are the third generation in the Rotary Club of Pasadena and John Jr. has been a Kiwanian since 1931, serving one year as president of the Pasadena club. Membership in the University Club of Pasadena has also been a family tradition for three generations.

Founder John H. Biggar, Sr., remained active in the business until his death in 1952. Photo circa 1950

Centennials play a large role in the Biggars' lives. Jack is a member of the Pasadena Centennial Coordinating Committee, planning the celebration of the city's 100th birthday in June 1986. The Pasadena Young Men's Christian Association also celebrates its centennial in 1986, and serving as president of the Metropolitan Board of the YMCA at that time will be Dick Biggar. Dick was also president of the Pasadena Junior Chamber of Commerce in 1973.

Another major centennial celebration also looms on the Pasadena horizon in the near future. The 1989 Rose Parade will be the 100th produced by the Pasadena Tournament of Roses Association and slated to be president that year is Jack Biggar. If tradition is followed and he is elected to that office in January of 1988, he will be the tournament's second president named Biggar, his father having served in that same capacity in 1958.

Only a handful of sons have followed in their fathers' footsteps. In Jack's case, it was a direct result of following his dad's advice as well. He had just joined the firm, in April 1958, when John Jr. suggested: "Get involved with the Tournament of Roses." Ten years later Dick received that same advice and has also been an active member ever since.

Reproduction of a painting of John H. Biggar, Jr., by Norman Rockwell. Rockwell was a float judge when Biggar was Tournament of Roses president and surprised him with this painting.

Numerous other community organizations have benefited from Biggar family participation, including the Pasadena Boys' Club, the American Red Cross, Huntington Memorial Hospital, and the Pasadena Chamber of Commerce.

There have been many changes in Pasadena, and in the furniture business, since John H. Biggar, Sr., opened his store. In those early days a bed sold for $7.50 and a good day's sales was $100. The staff of three now numbers about 100, several of whom have been with the business for thirty years or more.

One thing hasn't changed, however, and that's the company's operating philosophy. It was first stated in an advertisement dated July 26, 1926, inviting Pasadenans to the next day's opening. It read in part: "only high-grade furniture and dependable merchandise—very distinctive styles and correct prices."

Sixty years later the Biggars wouldn't change a word of it.

HAHN & HAHN

Pasadena was in its infancy when Benjamin W. Hahn arrived from Chicago in 1887. Less than one year earlier the city had been incorporated and seemed a good place for a young man bent on becoming an attorney.

In those days that meant "reading" the law in attorneys' offices, which Hahn proceeded to do. After passing the required exam, he was admitted to practice on April 3, 1891, opening his first office in the Wetherby & Kayser Building on Colorado Boulevard.

Benjamin W. Hahn, founder.

Edwin F. Hahn, four years younger, had followed his brother to Southern California, where he attended Pomona College, graduating in 1898. Moving into Benjamin's office, he studied law and was admitted to practice in 1899. On September 1 of that year the partnership of Hahn & Hahn was born.

Except for a brief period when the name was changed to Hahn, Hahn and Landreth, it has remained Hahn & Hahn, with at least one member of the family continuously among its active partners.

Herbert L. Hahn, Benjamin's son, joined the firm in 1917.

In its early days the firm moved several times, from the Vendevort Building on South Raymond, to the Union Bank Building at Raymond and Colorado in 1902, then to the Parkway Building at Colorado and Arroyo in 1907, and, ten years later, to the Boston Building at Raymond and Union.

In March 1906 a second office was opened, in Los Angeles, manned primarily by Benjamin Hahn, while Edwin remained in Pasadena. The former had shown an early interest in politics and, in 1902, had been elected to the State Senate, representing Pasadena and environs.

A third member of the family joined the firm in 1917, when Benjamin's son, Herbert L. Hahn, fresh from Stanford Law School, moved into the Pasadena office. A few months later his career was interrupted by the outbreak of World War I. Herbert served in the U.S. Army Infantry until 1919, when he rejoined the firm.

Edwin Hahn was appointed a Judge of the Superior Court of Los Angeles County in 1921. The following year he was elected to a six-year term and was reelected in 1928. In 1934 he retired from the bench and rejoined the firm, where he remained until his death in 1951.

In 1920 Benjamin Hahn closed the Los Angeles office and joined his son in Pasadena. Another brief move, to the Central Building on North Raymond, followed and, on November 1, 1924, the firm relocated to what is now known as the Security Pacific Building, at Colorado and Marengo. It was destined to remain there for forty years.

Edwin F. Hahn, founder.

That move also marked the beginning of the growth from a small family-oriented firm to a relatively large general practice. Several new associates were added during the mid-1920s, joined in 1927 by Edwin F. Hahn, Jr., eldest son of Edwin.

Stanley L. Hahn, the youngest son of Edwin F., is a partner. He joined the firm in 1936.

Benjamin Hahn died in 1932, and four years later a new partnership was formed, in which Allyn H. Barber, Joseph G. Pyle, Edwin F. Hahn, Jr., and Louis R. Vincenti became partners with Herbert Hahn. Shortly thereafter Stanley L. Hahn, the youngest son of Edwin F. Hahn, joined the firm. A half-century later he is the only remaining family member.

For many years a third generation of Hahns was represented. Richard G. Hahn, grandson of Benjamin and son of Herbert, became the sixth member of the family to practice law with the firm. He joined Hahn & Hahn in 1949, remaining until his retirement in 1984.

On November 1, 1964, exactly forty years after its last move, the firm relocated to its present quarters in the Mutual Building at 301 East Colorado.

Herbert Hahn, who was most responsible for the firm's growth to approximately twenty attorneys, retired in 1978 and passed away on June 16, 1983, at the age of eighty-nine. His career, like those of his father and uncle, was marked by a dedication to the community in which he lived and worked. Much of his time was devoted to Huntington Memorial Hospital and California Institute of Technology, on whose boards he served as trustee for many years.

Stanley Hahn's career has been marked by years of community service as well. Active in the YMCA and the Pasadena Tournament of Roses Association, he served as president of the latter, presiding over the New Year's Day festivities in 1963.

Yet Stanley was not the first Hahn & Hahn partner to be tournament president. In 1948 Louis Vincenti had served in that post. Vincenti later left the firm to join one of its clients, Mutual Savings and Loan Association, serving as vice-president, president, and, later, as president and chairman of Wesco Financial Corporation, Mutual's parent company.

Over the years Hahn & Hahn has conducted a broad general practice, with the exception of criminal work. There is a strong emphasis on such traditional fields as estate planning and corporate law, with substantial trial work, in state and federal courts.

Many current clients, their businesses, and families have been served by Hahn & Hahn for sixty years and more, a tribute to the philosophy of integrity, hard work, and community involvement developed by its founders and passed along to today's members of the firm. As Herbert Hahn was fond of saying, "We owe a great deal to this community and it's up to each one of us to put something back."

The offices of Hahn & Hahn shortly after the firm was established in 1899.

DATATAPE INCORPORATED

Although the exact name, Datatape Incorporated, only goes back to 1983—when Eastman Kodak purchased the Datatape Division of Bell & Howell and incorporated it as a wholly owned subsidiary—the firm has a long and distinguished history in Pasadena.

It was a part of a company founded as Consolidated Engineering Corporation (CEC) on March 1, 1937, by Herbert Hoover, Jr., son of the thirty-first President of the United States, as an affiliate of United Geophysical Corporation. CEC's function was the design and development of geophysical instruments for United. Hoover, an engineer and a Stanford graduate, had launched the latter company in 1935 to engage in geophysical exploration for oil.

In 1938 CEC introduced the first experimental model of a commercial-type mass spectrometer. Modified and improved versions of this instrument are still used today in analyzing complex gas and light liquid measures. The first of these spectrometers was sold to Atlantic Refining Company in 1942, and within a short time the vast majority of U.S. refineries had purchased the product.

Consolidated began a long association with U.S. government agencies in 1940, when it signed its first contract with what was then the U.S. Army Air Corps. As World War II began, CEC equipment was being used in testing the prototypes of many of the aircraft that would play a vital role in America's victory. In September 1944 the company received the first of its three Army/Navy "E" awards for production excellence. Participating in the award ceremony was ex-President Hoover himself.

One of CEC's original staff members was Philip S. Fogg, who was destined to play a major role in the firm's future. He served as its first treasurer, then was named executive vice-president in 1941. By that time the number of employees had grown to eighty, and gross income had reached a new high of $164,000. The following year that figure nearly tripled, to $470,000, and the company had 156 employees.

CEC began to separate itself from United Geophysical Corporation in 1942, and by 1945 had completed its severance. Herbert Hoover, Jr., sold his CEC interests to concentrate entirely on United. CEC conducted its first public stock sale; and Fogg was appointed president and chairman of the board.

Philip S. Fogg served Consolidated Engineering Corporation with distinction for many years as treasurer, executive vice-president, president, and chairman of the board. In 1948-1949 he was president of the Pasadena Chamber of Commerce.

Under his leadership CEC continued to grow and prosper. The tenth-anniversary year, 1947, saw the organization pass the million-dollar level in revenues and the $100,000 level in net profit for the first time. By the following year the firm exceeded $2 million in revenues, and after-tax profits were $250,000. There were 280 people on the payroll.

CEC moved into new, 25,000-square-foot facilities at 620 North Lake Avenue in January 1947, marking the fourth move in the ten-year history of the fast-growing enterprise. That space also soon proved inadequate, and in 1950 the company broke ground for a 70,000-square-foot plant in the Hastings Ranch area of Pasadena. It was occupied early in 1951, but by the end of that year had exceeded its capacity—requiring the reuse of the Lake Avenue facility to handle overflow.

By this time the well-established firm's common stock had been listed on both the American and Pacific Coast stock exchanges. From fewer than 1,000 shareholders at the time of the listings in 1950, there were more than 3,500 by year-end 1953. Revenues during that time climbed from $2.8 million to $14 million, and after-tax earnings jumped from

$291,000 to more than $2 million.

In 1953 the number of employees passed 1,000, making CEC Pasadena's largest employer. This period of rapid growth was also marked by the opening of branch offices nationwide. New products were continually being added; for example, in 1952 CEC had acquired the Vacuum Equipment Department of Eastman Kodak—renaming it Consolidated Vacuum Corporation—and offered a complete line of high-vacuum products, with headquarters in Rochester, New York.

Ironically, a major portion of CEC itself, after a number of changes in its corporate structure and name, would be acquired by Eastman Kodak in 1983.

In 1955, to better reflect the expanded scope of its activities, CEC changed its name to Consolidated Electrodynamics Corporation. In that same year the company introduced a new product line that was to have a major impact on its future. Called Datatape, a magnetic tape recording system that collected test data from airborne vehicles for ground analysis, it had undergone two and a half years in research and development and was the organization's largest development project to date.

In 1959 CEC, now a New York Stock Exchange-listed company with annual revenues of more than $40 million, began merger negotiations with Bell & Howell Company. The merger, involving an exchange of $44 million of stock, was completed in 1960. Phil Fogg remained as president and chairman of the board of CEC, which became a Bell & Howell subsidiary, and was named vice-chairman of the board of the parent corporation.

Fogg relinquished the presidency of CEC in 1961, but remained as vice-chairman until his retirement in 1965. He had guided the once-tiny Pasadena firm as it grew to become a major industrial complex, known and respected around the world. However, it was by no means his only accomplishment.

In 1954 Fogg and several associates had purchased an obscure Illinois operation called the Siegler Corporation, and in 1962 they ac-

An aerial view of the Consolidated facility and the surrounding area as it looked in 1954. Hastings Ranch is at the upper right. The dirt road behind the drive-in theater is now Rosemead Boulevard.

In September 1983 the Space Shuttle made its seventh flight into space. Playing a key role in the photography equipment used on the mission were Datatape Incorporated's magnetic tape recorder and digital encoder.

quired the Lear Company. By 1970 the merged company, Lear, Siegler, Inc., had more than fifty divisions and close to $600 million in revenues. Fogg served as a director and chairman of the executive committee.

The entrepreneur also had a distinguished record of service to Pasadena. He was an active member of the Pasadena Tournament of Roses Association and president of the Pasadena Foundation for Medical Research. He took a great interest in the local municipal planning process, and was one of a four-member panel that drafted a twenty-year blueprint for Pasadena's progress.

Fogg served as president of the Pasadena Chamber of Commerce during its 1948-1949 fiscal year, and in 1950-1951 was president of the Rotary Club of Pasadena. He also served for a number of years as a director of Security Pacific National Bank.

The dawning of the space age saw CEC very much involved. The "Datatape System" introduced in 1955 had received widespread acclaim throughout the aerospace community, while still in the developmental stage. A year later, with testing successfully completed, the first airborne recorders were delivered to Edwards Air Force Base to be used in testing jet aircraft.

Datatape played a key role in the Mercury spacecraft program, which would send American astronauts to frontiers beyond this planet. So it was that, on May 5, 1961, as Alan B. Shepard, Jr., was launched into space aboard Mercury I shouting "Man, what a ride," a Datatape recorder weighing less than nine pounds was measuring the responses of both the astronaut and his spacecraft and transmitting them to eighteen tracking stations around the world.

Twenty years later, on April 12, 1978, America's Space Shuttle made its first successful flight into orbit, and Datatape was again heavily involved. From NASA's space-flight center in Houston came a letter of congratulations to Datatape president Russell W. Frame. It read, in part: "On behalf of NASA and the Space Shuttle program, please allow me to express our congratulations and sincere appreciation for your company's participation in the first Space Shuttle launch. One of your MARS-2000 flight-tape recorders was installed in each of the solid rocket boosters used on the flight, and they survived launch, boost, reentry, water impact, and recovery operations in excellent

The arrow in this photo indicates location of Datatape's recorder (MARS-1428) inside of dome.

The arrow indicates the position of Datatape's MARS-1428 recorder.

condition. Their performance was highly satisfactory during all phases of the flight, and they provided much-needed, high-quality data. . . ."

In the two decades between the first manned space flight and the Space Shuttle, Datatape and its 1973 acquisition, Astro Science Corporation, were heavily involved in many other aspects of the space program. Datatape recorder/reproducers were placed aboard ships in the Atlantic Ocean to record and analyze critical flight-test data of missiles and rockets launched from Florida. When Neil Armstrong became the first man to set foot on the moon, in 1969, a significant amount of his mission's data evaluation and communication relied on Datatape equipment at Mission Control in Houston.

Datatape recorders have been included as part of the instrument ring on the solid rocket booster of every spacecraft used in the Mercury, Gemini, Apollo, and Space Shuttle programs. Despite the rigors they endure, as partially described in the letter above, they not only have performed as designed but are able to be used on subsequent missions.

Today Datatape's business can be summed up as the design, development, manufacture, sales, service, and logistics support associated with sophisticated high-technology data storage and retrieval devices—primarily magnetic-tape oriented—for use in the defense electronics and test instrumentation markets. Its products, however, are by no means limited to those markets. Datatape equipment is used wherever high-quality instrumentation data is required from aircraft engine testing to the measurement of stresses placed upon earth-moving equipment.

In October 1983 the Datatape Division of Bell & Howell was sold to Eastman Kodak, and became Datatape Incorporated, a wholly owned subsidiary. Led by president Russ Frame, a Bell & Howell veteran who became president of Datatape in 1980, the firm occupies more than 250,000 square feet of space on about ten and one-half acres in Pasadena. Although the company has offices in almost all major U.S. metropolitan areas, all manufacturing is done at that location.

The staff of more than 1,000 includes many of Pasadena's top engineers, attracted by this tomorrow-oriented organization that has played a vital role in America's exploration of new technological frontiers. Datatape Incorporated has indeed come a long way from its humble beginnings in 1937 as Consolidated Engineering Corporation.

Messerschmitt-Bölkow-Blohm technicians perform final adjustments and assembly of SPAS-01 satellite at MBB in Ottoburn, West Germany, before the spacecraft was shipped to the Kennedy Space Center.

HUNTINGTON SHERATON

Pasadena was still in its infancy when wealthy easterners, seeking escape from the rigors of snow and ice, discovered that its warm and sunny climate made it an ideal place to spend the winter. Several resort hotels were erected, and in 1906 General Marshall C. Wentworth, who had managed a number of them, decided to build his own.

In January 1907 the ill-fated and only partially completed Wentworth opened its doors but, plagued by inadequate financing and bad weather, lasted a mere six months.

Some time earlier, railroad magnate Henry E. Huntington had moved to Southern California and acquired a large parcel of land on which to build his winter estate. It was located close to the vacant Wentworth Hotel, which soon attracted his attention.

Huntington purchased the hostelry in 1911 and hired prominent architect Myron Hunt to redesign and complete it. Hunt changed the entrance location and added the top two floors and the beautiful redwood footbridge. Renamed the Huntington, it reopened on January 8, 1914, with well-known hotel operator Daniel M. Linnard as manager.

Linnard managed the hotel, with one brief interruption, until 1923—when he turned the reins over to his son-in-law, Stephen W. Royce. In 1920, at his father-in-law's suggestion, Royce had acquired an interest in Pasadena's Vista del Arroyo Hotel for $15,000—which he sold a year later for $75,000.

Royce's arrival marked the beginning of a new era for the Huntington. One of the young man's earliest moves was to open the hotel on a year-round basis, rather than only for the winter season. He also installed a swimming pool, one of the first in Pasadena. His trademark was personal attention to every guest, and soon the Huntington—known for its elegance and charm—became the favorite stopping place for the rich and famous.

The stock market crash of 1929 and the Great Depression that followed brought an end to those golden years. The very people who had flocked to the Huntington were the ones most affected, and for the next several years it took all of Royce's considerable skills to keep the facility afloat.

By the end of the 1930s he had the hotel back on solid ground. Then World War II erupted. Every reservation at the Huntington was cancelled, and Royce began planning to close it. An attempt to sell it to the Army as a hospital was foiled when an architect, with his own plan for an Army hospital nearby, reported that the structure could not withstand an earthquake.

Shortly after that setback the Army did rent part of the hotel for $3,000 a month, enough to keep it open. Near the war's end the Army tried to take over the property permanently, but quick action by Royce averted it.

With world peace restored, the Huntington's fortunes turned upward again—attracting the attention of Sheraton Corporation of America, which purchased it in 1954 and renamed it the Huntington Sheraton. Royce remained as general manager until his retirement in 1969, marking the completion of forty-five years of

The "Grand Old Lady" has been a landmark in Pasadena for eighty years.

Steve Royce guided the destiny of the Huntington for forty-five years.

distinguished service. At his farewell dinner he offered this toast:

This house was built of steel and stone
Of bricks and tiles and piers
And I have loved these sturdy walls
For nearly fifty years.
So here's to you, old friend, my dear
And may you live a thousand years
Just to keep on pleasing guests
As you are checking off the years,
And may I live a thousand too
A thousand—less one year
'Cause I don't want to be around
If you're no longer here.

An important, and what would later prove to be a vital, addition to the facility was made in 1965, when the sixty-room Lanai was constructed just west of the pool.

In March 1974 Sheraton sold the hotel to Keikyu, U.S.A., Inc., part of a major Japanese transportation company. Management of the facility remained with Sheraton.

Early in the 1980s Keikyu decided to launch a multimillion-dollar restoration and reconstruction program, a decision that was to bring about a shocking and unexpected turn of events. A preliminary step in the form of a complete structural study in 1985 revealed that the hotel would be a high risk in the event of a major earthquake. Rather than jeopardize the safety of its guests and employees, Keikyu and Sheraton courageously decided to close the main building immediately. On October 20, 1985, the doors of the "Grand Old Lady," as the hotel had become known, were closed.

For thousands of Pasadenans and others who had grown to love the Huntington and who cherished fond memories of happy times there, it was a tragic blow. The Lanai, however, and the cottages remain open, with a combined capacity of about 100 rooms—and so the Huntington lives on.

The day may indeed come when the lovely old hotel will reopen, reviving the dream of its longtime owner, Stephen Royce: "And may you live a thousand years."

VROMAN'S

Adam Clark Vroman in his office surrounded by the books he loved. This picture was taken about 1900.

Back about 1920 a Vroman's customer wrote in the store's guest book: "A bookstore makes any town a metropolis."

If that assessment is accurate, then it was 1894 when the eight-year-old city of Pasadena became a metropolis. In that year Adam Clark Vroman's bookstore was added to a business district consisting of one hotel, a blacksmith shop, a meat market, and a post office.

Not long before, Vroman had moved to Southern California hoping the mild climate would improve his wife's fragile health. To his great sorrow, she died shortly thereafter, but he decided to remain in Pasadena nonetheless.

A great book lover, Vroman, in partnership with a man named J.S. Glasscock, opened his bookstore, calling it Glasscock & Vroman. That first store was at 60 East Colorado but, as the growing city's business district pushed eastward, Vroman's moved right along with it, to 329 East Colorado in 1920 and to 469 East Colorado in 1937. It remained at the latter location until moving to its present site, at 695 East Colorado, in the early 1950s. In recent years two more stores have been added, one to the west in Eagle Rock Plaza and the other in Arcadia's Santa Anita Fashion Park.

Beside his love for books, Adam Vroman had another passion—photography. He began to travel extensively through the Southwest, camera always at the ready. His favorite subject was the Indians, who came to trust and respect him, and to pose willingly for him.

His reputation and skill with a camera grew rapidly and he left behind for future generations albums filled with mounted photographs of Pasadena and the Southwest. Many of his albums are available for review at the Pasadena Public Library, the Huntington Library, and the Museum of Natural History in Los Angeles.

In 1914 Vroman took a step that would have lasting impact on the bookstore he founded. He began urging a longtime family friend, Allan David Sheldon, to come to Pasadena and work for him.

The timing was perfect. Allan, with his brother, Joel, had recently returned to Seattle after unsuccessfully seeking his fortune in the Alaska Gold Rush. Needing work, Allan came to Pasadena and entered the book business, later to be joined by Joel.

Adam Vroman died two years later, but not without providing for the

The interior of Vroman's first bookstore, as it looked in 1915.

Joel Vroman Sheldon III represents the third generation of his family to run Vroman's.

future of the company and its faithful employees. He was truly a visionary, and through his will he pioneered the concepts of profit sharing and stock option plans. Each employee received a bequest of $100 for each year of service, plus shares of stock and the right to acquire more, based on a combination of responsibility and seniority.

As a result, Allan was able to acquire a majority interest in the firm. By 1922 he had acquired control of the store and ran it with the help of Leslie Hood, another longtime employee who had purchased stock.

Allan continued in charge with his brother, Joel, responsible for finances. The latter's son, Joel Jr., joined the business in the early 1930s, taking over administrative responsibility.

Upon Allan's death in 1953, Leslie Hood became president. Shortly after the elder Sheldon's passing, two other members of the family were hired: Harry, brother of Joel, and Southard "Sud," a cousin.

Some years earlier the company had launched a highly successful wholesale division, distributing books throughout the western United States, and Vroman's School Book Depository program, supplying textbooks to schools and representing publishers worldwide. Joel Jr. and Harry managed the depository, the wholesale division, and the firm's finances, while Sud ran the bookstore.

In 1959 Hood died, leaving the three Sheldons to continue leadership for years to come. On the horizon was young Joel Vroman Sheldon III, being groomed to take over in the future.

Today the organization thrives under the management of Joel III, who became president in 1978. The business has gone through several changes since Harry's passing in 1974 and the deaths of Joel Jr. and Sud in 1982. Joel III modestly claims that "it was a much more complex business back then. Today we do fewer things, but we aim to do them better."

Joel Vroman Sheldon III has not only followed in the corporate footsteps of his family, but in their rich tradition of community service as well. Few are the groups in Pasadena that have not had a Sheldon at or near the top.

Sud Sheldon was president of Kiwanis and Joel Jr. was president of Rotary. The latter also served as president of the Pasadena Merchants' Association and the Pasadena Chamber of Commerce. Harry was also chamber president, making the Sheldons the only brothers to have headed that group during its long history.

The second-generation Sheldons were also active in the Tournament of Roses Association, United Way, Pasadena Beautiful Foundation, the Salvation Army, and numerous other organizations. Joel III has served as an officer and/or board member of Pasadena Rotary, the Pasadena Chamber of Commerce, St. Luke Hospital, and the Pacific Oaks College and Children's School. His lifelong interest in sports is partially reflected in his service as commissioner of the Pasadena Area Youth Soccer Organization.

Joel sums up his philosophy this way: "My focus now and in the future is on running the best book and stationery stores in Southern California, while supporting the city of Pasadena."

That same philosophy guided every member of the Sheldon family down through the years, and it's one Adam Clark Vroman himself would have heartily endorsed.

Pasadenans window shop at Vroman's branch store located at 188 East Colorado. Photo circa 1917

The storefront of Glasscock & Vroman as it looked in 1895.

AMERICAN PACIFIC SECURITIES CORPORATION

Robert L. Johnson has been president and chief executive officer of American Pacific Securities since 1972.

Tracing the roots of American Pacific Securities Corporation takes one back over a half-century, and on a journey of some 3,000 miles, to the city of Rochester, New York. There, Milton C. Powell had been operating his securities business since 1925.

In the early 1930s Powell decided to move to Southern California and opened a Pasadena office of Milton C. Powell, Inc., in the Security Bank Building at the corner of Colorado and Marengo. In 1957 the firm moved to new offices on South Garfield, on the site of what is now part of the Plaza Pasadena.

Robert Louis Johnson, Powell's son-in-law, joined the operation in 1958. A decorated Navy veteran of World War II and a graduate of both Pasadena City College and the University of Southern California, Johnson was planning a career in the securities business—but was aiming at a New York Stock Exchange member firm.

Family circumstances dictated otherwise. The senior Powell was in ill health; and his son, Milton Jr., was on a military leave of absence from the firm. As a result, Johnson agreed to come in on what he called a "look and see" basis, and nearly thirty years later is still there.

Milton Jr. returned to the organization in 1959; and after his father's death in 1960, Johnson and he became partners. The firm's name was then changed to Powell, Johnson and Associates.

By 1966 the company's continued growth required that it find larger quarters, and on July 1 of that year a move was made to its present location in the Mutual Savings Bank Building at 301 East Colorado Boulevard. At the time it had a headquarters staff of six, plus a total of about thirty sales representatives in its six California offices.

By the end of the 1960s Powell, Johnson and Associates had grown to the point where added capital was needed. To meet that requirement the firm became affiliated with American Pacific Holding Company in 1969. After running the companies separately for two years, the economics of a merger became clear. In 1970 American Pacific Securities Corporation was formed, with Johnson as president and chief executive officer.

Milton Powell, Jr., retired from the organization in 1973, and died in 1984.

American Pacific Securities has continued its early record of growth and prosperity. Today the firm has more than 440 employees in seventy-two offices across the United States.

The sales staff of Powell, Johnson and Associates in front of its Garfield Street offices during the early 1960s. Milton C. Powell, Jr., is at the far left, and Bob Johnson is at the far right.

Slightly more than half of the company's business is financial planning for individual and corporate clients. Another 30 percent involves limited partnerships in such areas as real estate syndications, oil and gas ventures, and research and development projects. The balance of the business focuses on securities trading and management for clients. One-time member of the Pacific Stock Exchange, the firm sold its seat as more and more of the business focused on financial planning rather than securities trading.

Johnson, in addition to his day-to-day management of the firm, has been very active in industry groups and is the president of the Broker/Dealers Association of California. He is also a past president of the Pasadena Bond Club, the oldest such organization west of the Mississippi River.

Military service has also had a major role in Johnson's life. He was discharged from active service as a naval officer following World War II, but remained in the United States Naval Reserve for many years—retiring with the rank of captain. During the war his ship, an attack transport, was involved in combat in the Pacific Theater, including the assault on Iwo Jima. After the Japanese surrender, his ship carried the first American troops into Tokyo Bay.

Johnson's community involvement has centered around the Pasadena Tournament of Roses Association, of which he has been a member since 1962. During 1984 he had the distinction of serving as chairman of the Queen and Court Committee, which chose the first black Rose Queen in the event's history. His next assignment was to serve as chairman of the Post Parade Committee, one of the association's largest.

A committed Christian, Johnson serves as president of the Hill Avenue Grace Lutheran Church Choir and teaches a Sunday School class for adults. He and his wife, the former Penny Powell, live in Sierra Madre. They have two children and two grandchildren.

Under Johnson's leadership American Pacific Securities Corporation has come a long way, literally and figuratively, from its beginnings in Rochester, New York, in 1925.

PASADENA PUBLIC LIBRARY

This site, at the corner of Walnut and Raymond, was donated by Charles Legge for the second Pasadena Public Library, completed in 1890.

"The freedom to know is the foundation of our democracy. The mission of the Pasadena Public Library, a basic municipal service, is to be an information center for the Pasadena community in order to preserve and encourage the free expression of ideas essential to an informed citizenry."

The Pasadena Public Library has been fulfilling that mission for more than 100 years.

It began in 1882 with a man named Abbot Kinney. An easterner who had come to Southern California for his health, he had purchased a large parcel of property he called Kinneloa.

A patron of the arts, Kinney began entreating support among local citizens for a library, and on December 26, 1882, the Pasadena Library and Village Improvement Society was incorporated. The organization spent the following year soliciting donations and memberships and in constructing, for $2,300, an 880-square-foot building on Colorado near Raymond Avenue.

On February 26, 1884, the new library opened with a collection of 329 books and some magazines and newspapers. Classics dominated the collection and there were a number of volumes dealing with the evils of liquor and tobacco. The first librarian, Sarah E. Merritt, summed up the book selection policy this way: "... passionate French immorality is never found on these shelves. And you must needs look long to find any ... sensational gush. ..."

Funds were in short supply during those early years, despite a 25-cent monthly fee and a Citrus Fair in 1885 that raised $531. The situation worsened when ambitious society members decided a larger building was needed. A temporary move to 42 Dayton Street had been made in 1886, but there was still inadequate space.

The donation of a site at the southeast corner of Walnut and Raymond by Charles Legge, contingent upon completion by January 1, 1888, of a $25,000 brick or stone building, was offered and accepted. A series of problems arose, however, and the project wound up in foreclosure. By 1889 the society conceded its inability to raise the necessary funds and suggested that the City of Pasadena, incorporated three years earlier, take over. An $8,500 bond issue was approved, and the building was completed. On September 9, 1890, the Pasadena Public Library opened as a free municipal facility.

Nellie Russ succeeded Sarah Merritt as librarian in 1898 and served until 1919. During her tenure three branches were added to keep pace with the exploding population of Pasadena, which in the first decade of the twentieth century had grown from 9,000 to more than 30,000.

When Jeannette Drake became librarian in 1919, the city's population had reached the 45,000 mark—and the library's collection had grown to 68,000 volumes. A long-range expansion plan was adopted; then in 1923 a bond issue to finance a new Civic

The Central Library, located in the Civic Center complex, circa 1927.

Center was approved, consisting of a city hall, central library, and civic auditorium.

Myron Hunt, who had designed the Huntington Library and Occidental College, and his partner, H.C. Chambers, were selected in 1925 as architects for the library. The project was completed in less than two years, and the beautiful new Central Library opened on February 12, 1927. The total cost for the land, building, and furnishings was approximately $856,576.

The Depression years were difficult ones for the library, although the branch system was expanded and improved. Budgets and operating hours were curtailed, and circulation fell.

In 1936, following Jeannette Drake's retirement, Doris Hoit assumed the post of librarian. During her twenty years in office, she led the library to new heights. In 1941 it received ten national first-place awards in categories that included book circulation and number of borrowers.

By 1945 it became clear that existing facilities, consisting of the main library and four branches, would not

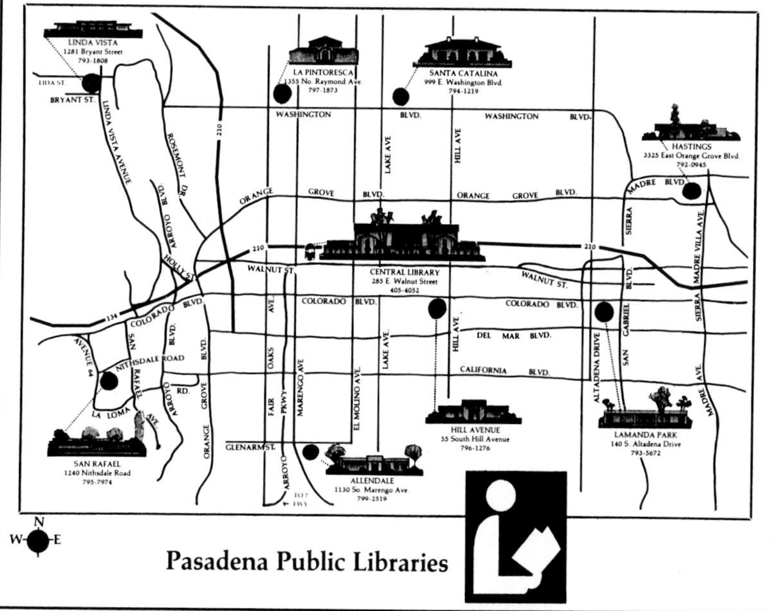

Pasadena in 1963 was declared the "best-read" city in America. This map shows the availability of libraries throughout the Pasadena area.

be enough to serve the projected postwar population. Miss Hoit recommended there be a library within one mile of every Pasadena resident, which meant doubling the number of branches.

Allendale opened in 1951, followed by Linda Vista and San Rafael in 1957, and Hastings in 1959. Although there have been subsequent proposals to consolidate some branches and close or relocate others, no changes have been made; the system continues as it was in 1959, with a central library and eight branches.

Throughout its history the Pasadena Public Library has consistently demonstrated innovation, leadership, and community involvement. It was among the first to have children's and young adults' sections, to allow borrowers to take several books at a time, and to circulate phonograph records. In 1948 it became the first library in the United States to use photocharging and punch-card sorting equipment.

In today's high-technology world, the Pasadena Public Library has continued to lead the way. A fully automated circulation system has been in place for several years and by the end of 1985 the entire card catalog file was on-line. New features will include the public access library service—which allows business data, civic

The Central Library's Main Hall on opening day, 1927.

group directories, volunteer lists, a community calendar, and other data bases to be readily accessible by off-premise personal computers.

Pasadena in 1963 was declared the "best-read" city in America, clear evidence of the affinity that has always existed between Pasadenans and their libraries. Today—with a multimillion-dollar renovation of the Central Library virtually complete, and with a dedicated staff of approximately 120 people at its nine locations utilizing state-of-the-art systems—that affinity, already into its second century, seems certain to continue.

CROWELL DESIGN AND CONSTRUCTION COMPANY

Crowell Design and Construction Company, founded in Pasadena in 1897, has played a major role in the building of the community. Its construction projects include some of Pasadena's most famous and illustrious structures. Among them are the Henry E. Huntington Library and Art Gallery, Pasadena City College, Pasadena Civic Auditorium, Huntington Memorial Hospital, Pasadena First Baptist Church, the Scottish Rite Cathedral, the Pasadena Main Public Library, and the Pasadena YMCA and YWCA.

Robert A. Crowell, son of the founder, remains active in the firm on a consulting basis.

Crowell was the contractor for a major Rose Bowl conversion endeavor in 1931, and has erected more than a dozen buildings on the Caltech campus. The first of these was Throop Hall, constructed in 1910, and another was the magnificent Athenaeum Faculty Club.

William C. Crowell, the company's founder, was born in Nova Scotia in 1871. As a young man, he moved to Seattle, where he worked as a carpenter while attending night school. After moving to Pasadena he launched a business, which he called simply William C. Crowell, Builder. His staff consisted of an estimator, a bookkeeper, and a field crew.

The entrepreneur's first project was building a barn for a Mrs. Smith, for which he did the estimate on the back of an envelope that remains in the possession of his son. Many of his early projects were residences, including one he erected for Michael J. Cudahy (the famed Chicago meat packer) on Bellefontaine Street. Not long ago that home, which had cost $20,900 to construct, was selected as a Showcase House of Design.

An early commercial effort was a six-story office building at the northwest corner of Colorado and Arroyo, where Crowell set up his own headquarters. The structure, newly renovated, is still in use today. In 1918 he constructed new offices for his firm at 495 South Arroyo Parkway, at that time known as Broadway.

In 1930 one of the founder's eight children, Robert A. Crowell, joined the business after earning his civil engineering degree at the University of Washington. The young man had previously worked as a part-time laborer for the company and was one of the carpenters on the Pasadena Library building, which was completed in 1927.

The Depression years caused a temporary interruption in the firm's record of growth and prosperity. At one point Robert Crowell worked for a year without salary, selling his own home to meet his living expenses.

In 1939 the name of the business was changed to Wm. C. Crowell Company, with Robert Crowell as primary owner and manager; however, his father remained active until shortly before his death in 1950.

In the early 1940s the firm moved again, to rented facilities at 170 East

In 1982, on the occasion of the fiftieth anniversary of the Pasadena Civic Auditorium (shown here), the Pasadena Historical Society honored Robert Crowell for his work on that project.

California. It remained there until 1972 when it relocated to 150 South Los Robles, adjacent to the Pasadena Hilton Hotel.

During the organization's early growth years, it basically discontinued residential construction, focusing instead on commercial, industrial, and institutional projects. Nor was its work limited by any means to the Pasadena area. Crowell erected many of the structures on the campuses of the Claremont Colleges, as well as numerous other buildings throughout Southern California.

Pasadena ventures, in addition to those previously mentioned, included the Security Pacific Bank Building at Lake and Colorado, the St. Luke Hospital Maternity Wing, the Community Playhouse School of the Theater, and the California State Unemployment Office on Green Street. The firm demonstrated its versatility in constructing such widely diverse facilities as the Marshall Canyon Golf Course in San Dimas; two wind tunnels, one at JPL and another for Caltech on South Raymond Avenue; a pumping plant on the Colorado River; and 3,800 government housing units during World War II.

The business was incorporated in 1956 as Wm. C. Crowell, Inc., with Robert Crowell as president. He held that post until 1971, at which time Crowell Design and Construction Company was reorganized. Crowell became chairman of the board, succeeded in his former position by Thomas R. Horton. After Horton's death in 1980, Ronald T. Aday, A.I.A., founder and chief executive officer of RTA Architect Planning Interiors, a wholly owned subsidiary of Crowell Design and Construction Company, was named president and chief executive officer. Crowell remains active with the firm on a consulting basis.

The Pasadena Historical Society honored Robert Crowell in 1982, the fiftieth anniversary of the Civic Auditorium, for his work on that project. Several years earlier he had noted that the auditorium had cost one million dollars to build in 1932, but forty years later would have cost at least twelve million dollars.

In 1983 the organization adopted its present name, Crowell Design and Construction Company, to reflect its broadened base of operations and services. The enterprise that had begun as a small building contractor eighty-six years earlier now provided architecture and engineering, construction management, cost control, energy analysis, environmental planning, feasibility studies, site planning, value engineering, construction, space planning, interior design, remodeling and renovation, real estate development, and property management.

Virtually all of those skills are represented in the new building that now houses the firm's headquarters at 350 West Colorado Boulevard. Crowell assembled the land, designed and erected the structure, did the interior design, and manages the facility. Its tenants include a branch of a major commercial bank and several prestigious law firms.

The corporation's ongoing commitment to Pasadena is reflected not only in its new headquarters but in another recent major endeavor, the First Interstate Mortgage Company Building, at Los Robles and Cordova. Of the major projects constructed in the community during the past five years, Crowell's management is proud of the fact that it is the only contractor to have erected more than one of them. In many ways Pasadena may well be called "the city that Crowell built."

Crowell's commitment to Pasadena is reflected in the First Interstate Mortgage Company Building at Los Robles and Cordova.

Another of the firm's major projects constructed in the community is the Wells Fargo Bank Building.

KAISER PERMANENTE MEDICAL CARE PROGRAM

The Kaiser Permanente Medical Care Program had its beginning in a most unlikely place—the Mojave Desert.

The year was 1933. An army of construction workers was laboring in the hot desert sun, building an aqueduct to carry Colorado River water to Los Angeles. To meet the medical needs of the thousands of men, a 27-year-old surgeon named Sidney R. Garfield erected a small hospital, using funds he had personally borrowed.

The doctor's venture met with little acceptance at first, and he teetered on the edge of bankruptcy. Minor injuries were ignored by the workers, who preferred to spend their money on other pursuits. Serious-injury victims were taken, by the contractors' insurance carriers, to Los Angeles for treatment.

Then he and an insurance company executive devised a plan. The concept, which would one day revolutionize the health care profession, was a simple one. The contractors, through their insurance carriers, agreed to pay Dr. Garfield five cents per man per day to cover work-related injuries, with the employees voluntarily paying the same rate if they desired coverage for nonwork-related care.

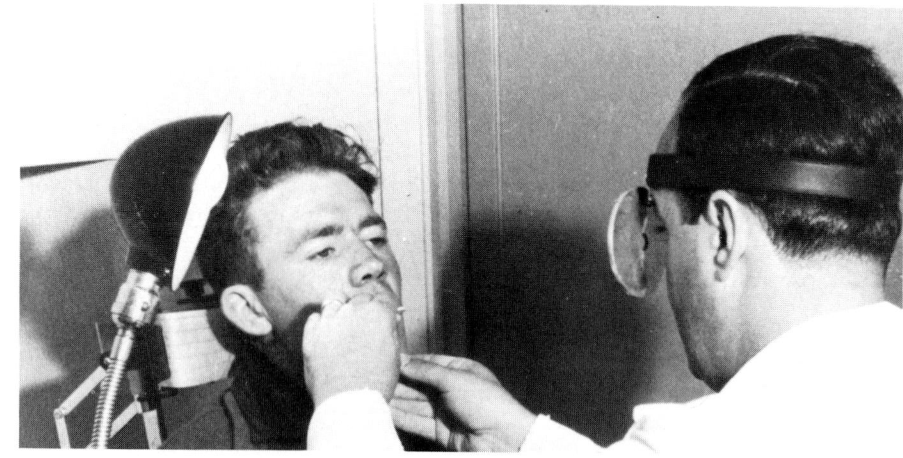

A health plan member being treated by a Kaiser Permanente physician in the 1940s.

The plan was an immediate success for all the parties. Lost man-hours and, thus, labor costs were reduced; the workers had their medical needs met; and Dr. Garfield and his staff were assured of the steady income needed to maintain the program. Before long, two more hospitals were added to meet the demand.

The completion of the aqueduct might well have ended the physician's pioneering venture had the program not caught the attention of visionary industrialist Henry J. Kaiser. In 1938 he asked Dr. Garfield to provide similar facilities and services for the 5,000 workers on his Grand Coulee Dam project in Washington State.

Dr. Garfield agreed and launched the plan at the same rate of five cents per day. Subsequently, the unions made the precedent-setting demand for family coverage, which was granted. The rates, which he later admitted to having taken "out of the air," were fifty cents and twenty-five cents per week for wives and children, respectively.

Again the program was immensely successful, and soon the possibilities of applying it elsewhere became clear. "Toward the end of the project," Dr. Garfield said, "we started dreaming of what we could do with a plan like ours in a permanent community. But the possibilities were remote. So when Coulee was completed, we thought we had come to the end of our journey into medical care."

World War II revived the program when Kaiser wanted to offer it to the workers in his shipyards and steel mills who were striving to meet the needs of the nation's Armed Forces. The coverage of some 200,000 employees and their families was reached during those years. The war's end brought a

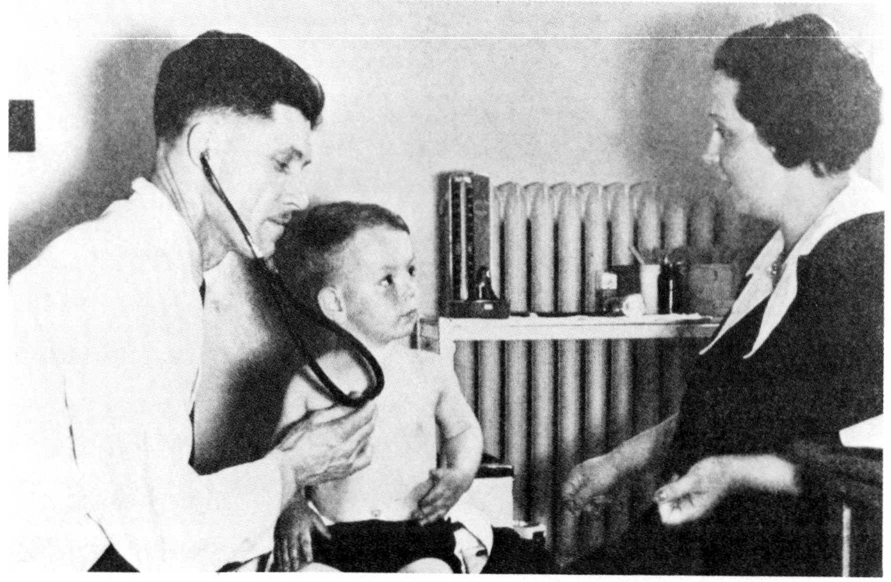

His attention diverted, a young patient is cared for by a Kaiser Permanente physician in the early days of the health plan.

sharp drop in that figure, to about 25,000, and once again the future appeared dim.

This time, however, the dream was to become reality. The advantages of prepaid medical care and group practice had become so obvious that membership was offered to the residents of two California communities, Fontana and Richmond, sites of major Kaiser facilities. The Permanente Foundation—named after Permanente Creek, where one of Kaiser's early ventures was located—was formed to raise the funds needed for existing and future medical care facilities.

Henry Kaiser retained his strong interest and involvement, and in the early 1950s, agreed to allow his name to be used in connection with the program. From this evolved the name Kaiser Permanente Medical Care Program, by which the widely spread and complex organization is generally known today.

The Southern California Region, begun in Fontana, grew rapidly; and during the 1950s, new medical centers were opened in Los Angeles and Harbor City, replacing the old Fontana center. Several medical offices were also established.

The organization was expanding on other fronts as well. In addition to the Northern and Southern California regions, an Oregon-Washington Region had been formed in 1945; then in 1958 Hawaii became the fourth region.

The 1960s brought continued growth, and by 1964 more than one million members had been enrolled. Two new regions—in Ohio and Colorado—opened in 1969, the year membership topped two million. Although no new regions were established during the following decade, membership in the plan passed the three-million mark in 1976.

The Pasadena medical office location on Lake Avenue in the late 1950s.

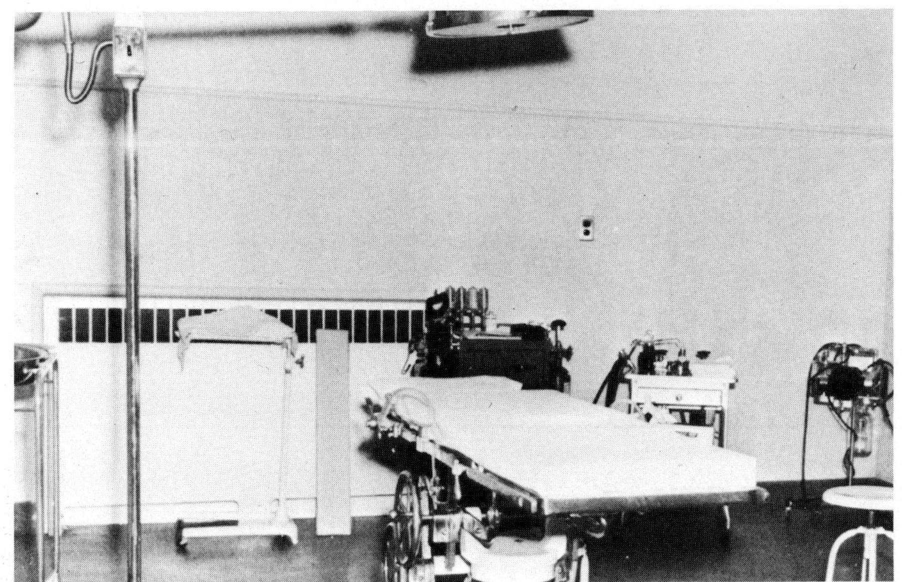

State-of-the-art medical equipment, circa 1940.

By the middle of the 1980s six new regions had been added: Washington, D.C.; Texas; Connecticut; North Carolina; Kansas; and Georgia. The twelve regions were serving 4.8 million members in 29 hospitals and 140 medical offices.

Kaiser Permanente's direct involvement with Pasadena began in 1952, when it opened a medical office on Cordova. In 1985 the organization erected a seven-story headquarters for its Southern California Region at 393 East Walnut Street. There a staff of approximately 1,200 oversee the operations of the most heavily populated of the twelve regions—comprising nine medical centers, thirty medical offices, 2,000 physicians, and 24,000 employees.

On December 29, 1984, an era ended at Kaiser Permanente with the death of its co-founder, Sidney R. Garfield, M.D. While he had retired from management several years earlier, he remained active in the program until his death. In fifty-one years the sagacious physician had seen his "nickel a day" venture grow into a nationwide health care program generating nearly three billion dollars a year in members' dues. Dr. Garfield's dream had not only come true but survives him, transcending his most optimistic expectations.

AMBASSADOR COLLEGE

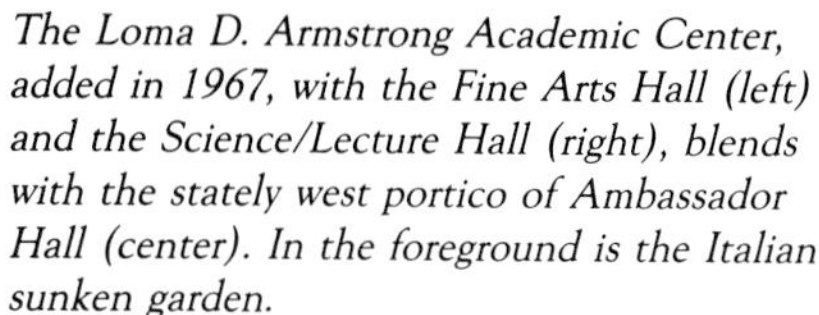

The Loma D. Armstrong Academic Center, added in 1967, with the Fine Arts Hall (left) and the Science/Lecture Hall (right), blends with the stately west portico of Ambassador Hall (center). In the foreground is the Italian sunken garden.

In 1946 Herbert W. Armstrong—pastor general of the Worldwide Church of God, then headquartered in Eugene, Oregon—searched Pasadena for the right location for a college he planned to establish.

Touring a section of the city where several millionaires had built their residences, he discovered the 2.25-acre Fowler estate at 363 Grove Street. A lease with option to purchase was signed on November 27, 1946, and the extensive renovations required to convert a home to a college were begun. The residence was later converted into the library, which today houses over 70,000 volumes.

On October 8, 1947, Ambassador College became a reality as classes got under way. Its motto was—and remains—"Recapture true values." In the first catalog, issued in November 1947, Chancellor Armstrong described its purpose: " . . . at Ambassador we shall put first things first. Character development, self-discipline, the open and investigative mind, cultural and personality development—these are Ambassador's first objectives. . . . These true values, these spiritual laws of life form the true foundation—the beginning of understanding and true education."

During the next few years, as the college grew, neighboring mansions were acquired. In 1949 Mayfair became the first student residence and also housed some classrooms. In 1956 Hulett C. Merritt, who at one time had been the largest stockholder at U.S. Steel, died leaving no direct heirs. The 36-room mansion he had erected, generally regarded as Pasadena's most beautiful residence, was put up for auction and purchased by Ambassador. Renamed Ambassador Hall, it became the main classroom building.

A south wing was added to Ambassador Hall in 1962 to provide additional classroom space. Rapid growth in the mid-1960s dictated a need for even more classrooms, and the Science/Lecture and Fine Arts halls were constructed. Today Ambassador Hall still contains some

Ambassador Hall, once the residence of multimillionaire Hulett C. Merritt, is one of Ambassador College's finest classroom buildings. Since purchasing the estate in 1956, the college has restored the mansion to its original beauty.

The Rosewood Room in Ambassador Hall as it appeared when it was Merritt's living room.

classrooms but also houses the Home Economics Department and a student lounge. The Physical Education Building was completed in 1964, the Student Center in 1966, and the Loma D. Armstrong Academic Center in 1967 (named in honor of Armstrong's wife, who died shortly before its completion).

The Hall of Administration was completed in 1969; and the beautiful Ambassador Auditorium opened in 1974, with an inaugural concert by the Vienna Symphony Orchestra.

Today the Pasadena campus occupies approximately forty-five acres. Its beauty has been recognized on three separate occasions by the Professional Grounds Maintenance Society as one of America's most beautiful campuses. The student body of 650 includes representatives from thirty countries who live and study in a quality environment designed to help them aspire to the college's primary purpose of "recapturing true values," through the development of their character, personality, and intellect.

Ambassador, a four-year liberal arts college, offers a program leading to the bachelor of arts degree, with emphasis on biblical and theological course work. A second campus, located in the beautiful East Texas woods at Big Sandy, was established in 1964 and reopened in 1981 as a junior college.

The grand entrance to Ambassador Hall, lined in Genisaro wood from South America, is typical of the mansion's many exquisite interiors. Ambassador Hall is famous for its rare and beautiful woods, many of them irreplaceable.

The Pasadena campus also houses Imperial School, a private Worldwide Church of God institute for children from kindergarten through grade twelve. Its present enrollment is 470 pupils.

Tuition and housing costs at Ambassador College are kept at a moderate level to allow admission of as many deserving students as possible. Primary funding is provided by the Worldwide Church of God, a fundamentalist, nondenominational, nonproselytizing church that traces its history back to the time of Christ. It is comprised of more than 400 congregations in the United States and 315 others in fifty-five countries.

In addition to its Pasadena headquarters, the church has sixteen regional offices around the world. Its full-color monthly magazine, *The Plain Truth,* is published in seven languages and has a circulation of over eight million. Other publications include *Youth '86* and *The Good News,* a Bible correspondence course, and various literature.

The church also sponsors and produces "The World Tomorrow" program. Begun in 1934, it is now on over 380 television stations and 40 radio stations worldwide.

Herbert Armstrong, who was born on July 31, 1892, in Des Moines, Iowa, became the leader of the present era of the Church of God in 1933 and remains as pastor general today. He continues also as the chancellor of the Ambassador colleges he founded and is chairman of the Ambassador Foundation, which he launched in 1975. Armstrong, who is assisted in his responsibilities by an advisory council of elders, is also editor-in-chief of *The Plain Truth,* which he introduced in 1934.

The church leader also serves as editor of *The Good News* and *Youth '86* magazines, both originated by him, and has authored several books, the most recent, *Mystery of the Ages.* He continues with weekly "World Tomorrow" telecasts, which carry the same theme as the radio programs he initiated in 1934.

Recognized in many nations as an unofficial "ambassador for world peace," Armstrong has traveled throughout the world and numbers the rulers of many countries as his friends. Numerous honors have been bestowed upon the educator, including a magnificent watch presented to him in 1970 by His Majesty King Leopold III of Belgium. It was one of four such watches that had been made by order of Leopold's father, King Albert I, following World War I, to be presented to the four individuals who had done the most to foster world peace.

King Albert had found only three men who matched his criteria—and it was more than a half-century before the fourth worthy candidate would be identified. For Herbert W. Armstrong, it may have been his highest accolade.

AMBASSADOR FOUNDATION

The Ambassador Foundation—established in 1975 by Herbert W. Armstrong, pastor general of the Worldwide Church of God and founder and chancellor of the Ambassador colleges—represents the philanthropic arm of the church. In embracing a wide variety of cultural, educational, and humanitarian endeavors, it expresses the philosophy of Armstrong, its chairman, that character is developed by turning to and living the right way of life, "the way of give."

The cultural centerpiece of the foundation—which is headquartered in Pasadena—is the acoustically perfect Ambassador Auditorium, considered one of the world's most beautiful performing arts centers. On its stage have appeared many of the world's finest performers, including piano virtuosi Vladimir Horowitz and Artur Rubinstein; opera stars Luciano Pavarotti, Marilyn Horne, Montserrat Caballé, Dame Janet Baker, Leontyne Price, and Joan Sutherland; Eugene Ormandy and the Philadelphia Orchestra; Carlo Maria Giulini with the Vienna Symphony, in the April 1974 inaugural event; and Herbert von Karajan and the Berlin Philharmonic.

The materials and furnishings in the 1,262-seat auditorium have been gathered from around the world—Angola, Norway, Hong Kong, Brazil, Burma, Turkey, and several other nations—making it a truly international cultural center.

The foundation's cultural activities are by no means limited to the Performing Arts Series at Ambassador Auditorium, and again reflect its international scope. The enterprises it supports include the King Leopold III Foundation in Belgium, which performs research in the fields of oceanography, primitive cultures, and wildlife; cultural and educational exchanges with the People's Republic of China; the Jerusalem Excavation Project in Israel; and other ventures in Egypt, Great Britain, Japan, Kenya, Jordan, Syria, the Philippines, and Thailand.

In the United States the foundation contributes substantial funding to the Los Angeles Chamber Orchestra, which is the resident orchestra of the Ambassador Auditorium, and—in conjunction with the USC Law School—funds the David Ben Gurion Exchange Professorship. It also sponsors the Herbert W. Armstrong Professorship at USC, a tenured faculty position representing the foundation's continuing interest in constitutional law, especially rights guaranteed by the First Amendment. Numerous other grants are made to deserving cultural, professional, and charitable organizations.

One of the foundation's newer and

Ambassador Auditorium has gained international acclaim as a prestigious center for the performing arts since its grand opening in April 1974. The main theater seats 1,262 people and is designed for the finest acoustical projection and balance.

Herbert W. Armstrong, founder and chancellor of Ambassador College, founder and chairman of the Ambassador Foundation, and pastor general of the Worldwide Church of God. Photo by Desmond Groves

most innovative projects has been the Community Dispute Resolution Center, based in Pasadena. Organized by a group of Pasadenans seeking to mediate disputes as an alternative to the formal and overcrowded court system, it opened its doors in August 1983. Funding for the center's first year of operation was provided by the foundation, which also donated services and supplies. After the completion of its one-year commitment, the foundation (encouraged by the center's results) has continued its support and active participation.

The center uses a three-step process in helping to resolve disputes. The first is fact-finding, where the person requesting assistance outlines the issues in the dispute. If it falls within the center's parameters, a written application is made, for which the applicant pays a five-dollar fee. It is the only charge made, regardless of the length or complexity of the center's involvement.

The other party is then notified and invited to the center for a discussion, where the dispute is often resolved. If not, the mediation process begins, involving a neutral mediator who attempts to arrive at a mutually satisfactory solution. If that step fails, the parties may present evidence to a panel of three arbitrators chosen from a volunteer group of private citizens from the community.

During its first two years of operation, the center helped more than 500 individuals resolve disputes that might otherwise have ended up in court—thus saving them untold amounts of money and time. Of the cases it has handled, the center has satisfactorily resolved nearly 95 percent of them.

The Ambassador Foundation has been a model citizen in Pasadena in many other ways as well. Students in the Pasadena Unified School District have been frequent guests of the foundation, attending and participating in various musical productions. In 1984 alone the foundation made financial contributions to eleven civic organizations in the Pasadena community. Ambassador representatives, from both the foundation and the college, have been very active in serving such community groups as the Pasadena Chamber of Commerce and the Pasadena Tournament of Roses Association.

In Pasadena and throughout the world, the foundation's activities slice through the complexities that divide a world where hatreds, prejudice, and personal ambitions too often rule. By serving the cultural, educational, and humanitarian needs of mankind, the Ambassador Foundation believes it can create in men and women an awareness of their ultimate individual and collective potential for good.

An early view of the east elevation of Villa Merritt Alivier (now Ambassador Hall), the former estate of multimillionaire Hulett C. Merritt.

LAS ENCINAS HOSPITAL

The year was 1886. The little community of Pasadena had just been incorporated as a city when James H. McBride, M.D., arrived from Wauwatosa, Wisconsin. There, six years earlier, he had founded the Milwaukee Sanitarium, devoted exclusively to the care of neuropsychiatric patients. Now he had come to Pasadena to establish a general medical practice.

Dr. McBride was truly a pioneer in the field of psychiatric medicine. Born and raised in the Oregon Territory, he was the son of a physician. Following the completion of his own medical training at New York University's Bellevue Medical College, he worked in various hospitals, where he specialized in neuropsychiatry.

He had also served as president of the American Academy of Medicine and the American Neurological Association. In 1880, when he founded the Milwaukee Sanitarium, Sigmund Freud was a 24-year-old medical student.

The original water tower, 1864.

Not long after launching his Pasadena medical practice, Dr. McBride again decided to start a private hospital. His search for a suitable location ended in 1902, when he spied the Sunny Slope Rancho, a 1,300-acre parcel owned by Leonard Rose, founder of the nearby community that bears his name—Rosemead. Dr. McBride purchased twenty-nine acres, part of the rancho's arboretum, for $27,000. Many of the arboretum's trees still grow today on the hospital's beautifully landscaped grounds.

The land Dr. McBride bought reflected the influence of the Rose family. Its western boundary was Rose Street (now San Gabriel Boulevard). Del Mar Boulevard, the northern boundary, was then called Blanche Street after one of Rose's daughters.

With the site in hand, Dr. McBride set about building a team to staff his new hospital. Within a short time he had recruited four prominent and highly skilled physicians. They were Norman Bridge, president of the board of trustees at Throop College of Technology (now California Institute of Technology); Henry G. Brainerd, former dean of the faculty at the University of Southern California

Nurses and allied staff around 1910.

A view of the main entrance to Las Encinas Hospital in 1925.

School of Medicine and superintendent of Los Angeles General Hospital; Walter J. Barlow, a former vice-president of the American Medical Association; and Merritt B. Campbell, former superintendent of the California State Hospital at Patton.

In February 1904 the five doctors incorporated the Southern California Sanitarium for Nervous Disorders, the forerunner of today's Las Encinas Hospital. As their motto, and as their guiding principle in treating patients, the founders selected the phrase: "Not just to live but to enjoy living." The Latin version, "Non Est Vivere Sed Valere Vita," is inscribed above the main entrance, as honored in practice today as it was in 1904.

That philosophy guided the design and construction of the new facility, which still today retains the appearance of a gracious nineteenth-century country estate in Great Britain, a distinct departure from the typical hospital building.

The original main building, consisting of two stories and a basement, is still in use, although it has undergone frequent remodeling and expansion. Many other buildings have been added as the hospital has grown. Among the earliest additions were staff residences, built partially to solve the problem of commuting to what was a remote location "out in the countryside."

That carefully cultivated "homelike" atmosphere has not only aided in patient care and treatment but has made the facility a real home for many staff members.

Dr. Stephen Smith II, destined to succeed Dr. McBride as medical director, arrived in 1910 and would spend the rest of his life there. In 1912 he married a staff member and the couple moved into a recently built cottage on the grounds where, three years later, a son, Stephen III, was born. Like his father, he too would one day serve as medical director.

Dr. McBride retired in 1919 and was succeeded by Stephen Smith II, who remained as medical director until his death in 1947. Under his leadership the hospital continued to grow and prosper. Many of his innovative programs helped bring the hospital

The lobby of the administration building, circa 1940.

international recognition. His tenure was also marked by the selection of two staff members who would play major roles in the hospital's future, and by a name change, in 1929, to Las Encinas Sanitarium. The Spanish word "Encinas" is the name of one variety of oak tree on the grounds. The term "for Nervous Disorders" was deleted, as it reflected a limitation in patient care that was no longer valid.

Typical patients' accommodations in 1950.

In 1923 Dr. Smith hired the hospital's first female doctor, Anna Ethel Fanson. In residency at Los Angeles General Hospital, she had been invited to an interview with Dr. Smith, which involved a considerable walk from the end of the trolley line.

Her efforts proved to be well worth it, for all parties. Much impressed with her record (and possibly her stamina), Dr. Smith immediately offered her a job. Thus began a relationship with the hospital that would end with her retirement in 1973, a half-century later. Her career was an illustrious one and she maintained her close ties with Las Encinas until her death in 1978.

The second key person Dr. Smith hired was his longtime friend, Dr. Charles W. Thompson. The two men had known each other since childhood and had served briefly together as young physicians on the staff at Kalamazoo State Hospital in Michigan. It was Dr. Thompson who would become the hospital's third medical director, following the death of his old friend in 1947.

A swimming pool and restful patio are among the many recreational facilities that also include a tennis court, putting green, golf driving range, and badminton court.

The board of directors' room in the 1960s with two still-familiar staff members, Eric Thompson, M.D. (standing, center), and Kenneth Nash, M.D. (right).

As was the case with his predecessor, Dr. Thompson's administration was marked by virtually continuous growth, expansion, and improvement. A new unit for the treatment of patients in need of more intensive psychiatric treatment and observation was built. Larger and completely remodeled facilities were completed to house the dietary/kitchen operation and the Occupational/Recreational Therapy Department. The main building was once again enlarged, providing a board of directors' meeting room and much-needed office space.

It was also during Dr. Thompson's leadership years that Las Encinas was licensed as an acute, as well as a general, medical facility and, once again, underwent a name change. In 1960 the board adopted the present name, Las Encinas Hospital, to more fully reflect the scope of the services provided.

Dr. Thompson retired in 1965. He had served as medical director for eighteen years and was only the third man to have led the hospital during its 61-year history. His successor was the son of the man he himself had succeeded.

Stephen Smith III had grown up on the grounds of the hospital he was now chosen to lead. A 1943 graduate of Cornell Medical School, he married a classmate, Dr. Harriet Hull, shortly thereafter. Called into military service, he was sent overseas. His wife came to Pasadena to await his return and to serve on the Las Encinas staff, under her father-in-law.

After his discharge, Stephen Smith completed his residency at Boston's

Las Encinas Hospital, located on twenty-five acres of tree-shaded gardens and rustic charm in old Pasadena, affords patients special care in a very private setting. It is over eighty years old and still ahead of its time.

Peter Bent Brigham Hospital and pursued his own career for several years before joining the Las Encinas staff in 1954.

Dr. Smith served as medical director until 1980, when he retired. He continued to serve as chairman of the board of directors until his death in 1983. During his administration the hospital achieved the greatest growth in its history. It became one of only two private hospitals in California licensed as both a general and acute medical facility, as well as a general and acute psychiatric facility.

In 1978 a limited internship program was begun for students from nearby schools, including California State University at Los Angeles and Fuller Theological Seminary. The following year, as the hospital celebrated its seventy-fifth anniversary, a Volunteer Services Department was started which, in its brief history to date, has made a major contribution to the care and comfort of the patients, helping them "not just to live but to enjoy living."

Another major project got under way in 1979. It was the groundbreaking for a facility that would make a longtime dream come true for Stephen Smith III. That dream was to build a different kind of retirement center, one that would cater to the needs of older adults seeking a gracious living environment while maintaining some degree of independence and self-reliance.

The result was The Oaks of Pasadena, consisting of ninety-two rental units in two two-story buildings on the northeast section of the hospital property. The units range from studio size to two-bedroom, two-bath apartments, all equipped with kitchens. Other amenities include a swimming pool, saunas, a barbershop and beauty salon, and a fine restaurant-style dining room for residents who choose not to prepare their own meals.

The Oaks is a separate corporation but is staffed by hospital personnel. Though specifically not a convalescent facility, The Oaks does provide emergency medical care for its residents via 24-hour physician coverage at the hospital.

Dr. Samuel Youngman became the hospital's fifth medical director in 1980. Though he would serve only two years, two events of major significance took place during his administration. In 1981 the hospital adopted a new policy, allowing nonstaff physicians in the area to admit and follow patients at Las Encinas, both on an inpatient and outpatient basis. The move has done much to cultivate the hospital's relationship with the local medical community.

In 1982, after seventy-eight years as a privately owned and operated entity, the hospital was acquired by two major, reputable, publicly owned companies in the health care field. In November of that year Hospital Corporation of America (HCA), the nation's foremost owner and operator of private hospitals, acquired 75 percent of the stock. The remaining 25 percent was purchased by Beverly Enterprises, headquartered in Pasadena and the nation's largest operator of nursing homes.

By the start of 1983 HCA had its own management team in place, including Edward J. Mullen as executive director. His new team is committed to maintaining the traditions of Las Encinas Hospital as a quality-care facility in a unique setting, and to continue to develop superior, specialized psychiatric programs.

The oldest and most important tradition at Las Encinas, its approach to patient care, remains its top priority—"Non Est Vivere Sed Valere Vita."

HUNTINGTON MEDICAL RESEARCH INSTITUTES (HMRI)

The Huntington Medical Research Institutes (HMRI), while affiliated with Huntington Memorial Hospital in medical research, is a separate and distinct organization. Formed on January 1, 1982, HMRI represents an amalgamation of medical research activities, including the former research laboratory of the hospital.

The first of these entities, the Pasadena Foundation for Medical Research, was incorporated in 1952 to conduct cancer research. Eight years later the Pasadena Neurovascular Foundation was established, specializing in studies of the brain.

The latter group joined with the Research Department of Huntington Hospital in the late 1960s to form the Huntington Institute of Applied Medical Research. In 1978 that organization began a close working relationship with the Pasadena Foundation for Medical Research, which led to their combining in 1982.

Since that time HMRI has pioneered in developing a major diagnostic tool called magnetic resonance imaging, or MRI. Its development was an outgrowth of the institutes' neurosurgical and cancer research programs. The next step was the formation of a magnetic resonance spectroscopy laboratory for chemical analysis of living tissue. The spectrometer allows researchers to conduct biochemical studies of patients without resorting to X-rays or any other type of radioactivity. As of January 1986 the imager had scanned more than 7,000 patients, making it the world's leader in clinical experience in the field.

Originally developed to aid in brain studies, magnetic resonance (MR) technology is now being applied to the diagnosis of heart disease. In addition to the whole-body imager, two smaller spectrometers have been set up to study laboratory specimens. More than 150 physicians from over seventy medical centers have used the facilities of the MR Laboratory for education and research purposes.

Formed on January 1, 1982, the Huntington Medical Research Institutes represent an amalgamation of medical research activities, including the former research laboratory of the Huntington Memorial Hospital.

The Huntington Institute of Applied Medical Research was formed in 1960.

Huntington Medical Research Institutes is one of some sixty independent organizations of its kind in the United States. From its research programs have come numerous products that are saving lives and improving health. Scientists from around the world come to HMRI to work, compare notes, and collaborate on projects at the cutting edge of medical science.

The executive director of HMRI is William Opel, who worked at the Pasadena Foundation for Medical Research and later became its executive director; he has served in that post at HMRI since the 1982 merger.

One of HMRI's most successful products has been the Pudenz VP (ventricular/peritoneal) Shunt used in the treatment of hydrocephalic infants. Named for its inventor, Robert

H. Pudenz, M.D., a specialist in hydrocephalus, the shunt has saved the lives of thousands of children. Dr. Pudenz is considered one of the men most responsible for the emergence of HMRI as a leader in the field of medical research.

Other major contributors have included George S. Sharp, M.D.; C. Hunter Shelden, M.D.; Richard J. Bing, M.D.; William F. Agnew, Ph.D.; Donald Rounds, Ph.D.; and the late Leland G. Hunnicutt, M.D. Dr. Hunnicutt, who died in 1984, was a founder of the Institute of Medical Research of the Huntington Memorial Hospital. He had served on the hospital's medical staff for forty-six years and was its president in 1949.

Dr. Sharp, a graduate of Harvard Medical School, is a radiotherapist and surgeon, specializing in head and neck surgery. He has been a pioneer in the cancer research field. Dr. Shelden, who graduated from the University of Pennsylvania and also studied in Germany, was a resident in neurosurgery at the Mayo Clinic. He was also on staff at Bethesda Naval Hospital in Maryland, where he did joint research on head injuries with Dr. Pudenz. After leaving Bethesda, the two established a neurosurgical practice in Pasadena.

Dr. Bing, former head of the internal medicine residency program at Huntington Hospital, has been a pioneer in the diagnosis of heart disease and is a recognized expert in heart physiology. Dr. Agnew is a leading researcher in neural prosthetics, utilizing electronics in the nervous system to restore varying degrees of mobility to the paralyzed. Dr. Rounds heads the cell biology laboratory and specializes in the use of lasers in medicine. He has been active in this field since 1963, utilizing one of the first lasers ever built.

Three separate laboratory buildings in Pasadena currently comprise the Huntington Medical Research Institutes. The first, at 99 North El Molino Avenue, was the original site of the Pasadena Foundation for Medical Research. The structure at 734 Fairmount Avenue, adjacent to Huntington Memorial Hospital, formerly housed the hospital's research department. The third, at Pico and Fair Oaks, contains the magnetic resonance imaging and spectroscopy labs and other facilities.

In the not-too-distant future, Huntington Medical Research Institutes hopes to combine all its laboratory facilities in a single new building—enabling it to operate even more effectively as it continues to open new frontiers in medical research.

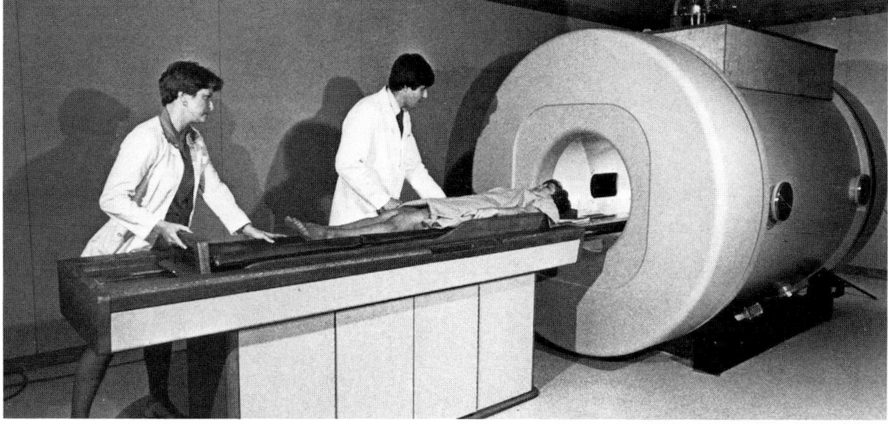

HMRI has pioneered in developing a major diagnostic tool called magnetic resonance imaging, or MRI. By January 1986 the imager had scanned more than 7,000 patients under the guidance of William G. Bradley, M.D., Ph.D.

The cell biology laboratory is located, and the Interleukin-2 studies and prostate research are carried out, at the institute's 99 El Molino location.

SOUTHERN CALIFORNIA GAS COMPANY

Southern California Gas Company and its predecessors have been serving Pasadena since the late nineteenth century. In October 1886, shortly after the city's incorporation, the *Star* noted: "Soon the city gas works will be in full blast. . . . Pasadena is full of the spirit of prosperity, and is making the most of it."

At about the same time, the Los Angeles *Evening Express* reported from Pasadena that: "The gas men are whooping it up lively and expect to supply the Raymond (Hotel) by the first proximo and the city within a couple of weeks thereafter." The newspaper's prediction proved to be accurate, as gas service began in mid-November.

The city's first gas public utility, Pasadena Gas and Electric Company, was short-lived, lasting from May 5 to November 17, 1886, when financial difficulties forced its reorganization as Pasadena Gas and Electric Light Company. In 1889 control of the operation was acquired by Thaddeus S.C. Lowe. Although better known for his railway system and for the mountain that bears his name, the entrepreneur was a pioneer in the gas industry and had earlier formed the Lowe Gas and Electric Company in Los Angeles.

He operated his newly acquired Pasadena firm as part of the Los Angeles company until 1896, when financial problems brought about by the bankruptcy of his Mt. Lowe railway system led to his forming the Pasadena Consolidated Gas Company. Nevertheless, Lowe's financial problems continued, and in 1903 control of the enterprise was obtained by Pacific Lighting Company, which in 1890 had also acquired Los Angeles Gas Company. In 1909 Pacific Lighting merged the two utilities as Los Angeles Gas and Electric Corporation.

Natural gas supplied by the company burned brightly in the Olympic torch above the Los Angeles Coliseum for both the 1932 and 1984 Olympic Games. This photo was taken just prior to the 1984 Games.

The first gas plant in Pasadena was on Raymond, north of Glenarm as were the three large tanks, or "holders," which stored the manufactured gas. The first business office was at 25 East Colorado. In 1906 it was moved to 64 North Raymond.

The type of gas supplied in those early years was manufactured in various ways. Much of it was coal gas; so-called "water gas," a process developed by Lowe, was also used. Most of the communities in Southern California were served by small local companies. In 1909 large deposits of natural gas, a fossil fuel, were discovered and a gradual conversion to this much cleaner fuel began.

As pipelines were built to carry the natural gas, the need for small local firms diminished and a number of mergers began to take place. By 1925 there were four major companies serving most of Southern California. Pacific Lighting Company—which already owned one of them, Los Angeles Gas and Electric—soon acquired the other three, the last of which was Southern California Gas Company. By 1929 the area was being served by one large system.

On March 31, 1930, a new district office was opened in Pasadena. The structure (at the northwest corner of Garfield and Ramona) was designed to blend with other Civic Center buildings, which included the new city hall and the Central Library. Con-

The Pasadena office opened in the Civic Center on March 31, 1930.

structed in the Italian Renaissance style, it cost about $275,000.

In 1937 Pacific Lighting sold its electric properties to the City of Los Angeles, and merged Los Angeles Gas and Electric and Southern California Gas into a single organization, under the latter name. The company grew rapidly, keeping pace with the Southern California population boom. In 1953 the firm designated Pasadena as the headquarters of its recently formed Northeast Division, serving several communities in the San Gabriel Valley. It was the utility's eleventh division, and included about 113,000 customers.

The giant gas tanks that had been familiar sights on Raymond Street for decades, began to disappear in 1957. The last one, which had a capacity of six million cubic feet of gas, was removed in 1962.

Southern California Gas Company celebrated its 100th anniversary in 1967. It traced its origins to a day in 1867 when, for the first time, Los Angeles' Main Street glowed with the light from forty-three gas lamps, courtesy of the Los Angeles Gas Company. A century later Southern California Gas had become one of the largest distributors of natural gas in the world. With thirteen operating divisions, it stretched from Fresno on the north to the Mexican border on the south, and from the Pacific Ocean to the California-Arizona border.

The Pasadena headquarters on Ramona, which has been in continual use for more than a half-century, has been frequently remodeled in an attempt to keep up with many changes including the area's growth. Adjoining property was acquired, and an annex was erected in 1968 to house additional offices. By the end of that year the Northeast Division had approximately 194,000 meters connected.

In addition to the Ramona Street facilities, the company maintains an operating base at Foothill and Rosemead boulevards. Its 300 employees in Pasadena are divided almost equally at the two locations. Since 1968 the number of meters in the San Gabriel Valley has virtually doubled, to 385,000. Of those, about 44,000 are in Pasadena—a far cry from the fewer than 5,000 that were connected at the time Pacific Lighting acquired its first Pasadena operation back in 1903.

Throughout its century of service to Pasadena, the Southern California Gas Company has been a good neighbor. Its representatives have participated actively in literally dozens of community and civic organizations, and it has been a frequent contributor to worthwhile local causes. Typical of the organization's involvement has been its work with the Pasadena Tournament of Roses Association. Through participation in this activity, excellent relations have been developed and maintained throughout the years.

The gas company's teams and wagons were familiar sights to Pasadena residents in the early 1900s.

The Southern California Gas Company shows off its product in the 1910 Pasadena Rose Parade.

GEORGIANA RODIGER CENTER, INC.

"Be all that you can be" may be the opening of an enlistment jingle, but for Georgiana Rodiger, Ph.D., those words describe her work, her philosophy, and her life. As the founder of the facility that bears her name, she strives to meet the needs of children and adults in ways that help them be all they have been created to be. The Rodiger Center's programs deal with death, learning disabilities, parenting, personal growth, eating disorders, mid-life crisis, and many other key issues. All of the center's work encourages new ways of being in the world that allow people to become more confident, competent, and productive.

At the Rodiger Center, learning-disabled children, often intellectually gifted, are guided through developmentally based tasks to increase their cognitive capacity. They learn to move so that they can move to learn. Through sensory motor integration, better thinking, planning, and problem solving are made possible so students can handle schoolwork more effectively.

For three years Dr. Rodiger directed the Rodiger School to provide an intensive combination of sensory motor integration with traditional academic studies. The Christopher School, a related program, was for students in the middle grades who enjoyed planning their own learning opportunities.

Psychological support and training in parenting skills were also provided as part of the school. A variety of therapies helped the youngsters deal with feelings of failure and low self-esteem.

The Candlelighters of Pasadena, sponsored by the Rodiger Center, has had a profound impact in Southern California. As a group for parents whose children have died or are suffering from life-threatening illnesses, Candlelighters offers support. During their weekly meetings at the home of co-founders Jim and Pat Schlanser, grieving and frightened parents share their stories and encourage one another. Candlelighters is an organization of hope and new beginnings.

A third Rodiger Center program offers therapy for those who are captured by the devastating eating disorders of bulimia and anorexia. For two years Dr. Rodiger led a weekly dream association group in her home so that these troubled individuals could explore the roots of their self-abusive behavior. Currently much of Dr. Rodiger's private psychotherapy practice is devoted to equipping these severely disturbed men and women with skills needed for productive lives.

Georgiana G. Rodiger, Ph.D., executive director of the center that bears her name.

Affordable psychological counseling is a consequence of the newest Rodiger Center program. Outstanding marriage, family, and child counselor interns and trainees now work under the supervision of Dr. Rodiger. With her guidance, they assist individuals and families in exploring their inner worlds and interpersonal relationships.

Dr. Rodiger, known by those with whom she works as Georgie, comes from a background where service to people is a priority. Tracing her heritage, one finds Dr. Benjamin Rush, who signed the Declaration of Independence and founded the first mental hospital in the United States. Another ancestor, Hiram Sibley, put the telegraph across the country and engineered the purchase of Alaska through his friend, Congressman Seward, so that Sibley could put the

Members of the Candlelighters of Pasadena enjoy a celebration.

telegraph through Alaska to Europe. Her grandfather, Harper Sibley, was international president of the YMCA, USO, and many other groups. He was also national president of the United States Chamber of Commerce. Her grandmother, Georgiana Sibley, was very active in many phases of church work, lecturing extensively throughout America as head of United Church Women. Both grandparents were delegates to the founding of the United Nations in 1945.

Dr. Rodiger's father, the Reverend Charles Leslie Glenn, was rector of Christ Church in Cambridge, Massachusetts. He later served at St. John's Church in Washington, D.C., and then as canon of the Washington Cathedral. Her mother, also named Georgiana, who later became Mrs. Jack Hardy, was active in the National Red Cross, was vice-president of the National Girl Scout organization at nineteen, and served on the Los Angeles School Board for twenty years. Many people enjoyed a television program that she hosted called "Cavalcade of Books."

Dr. Rodiger received her bachelor of arts degree in psychology from Pomona College, and then served as a professional field director with the Pasadena Area Girl Scout Council.

She married attorney William Rodiger and they raised five children, Georgiana IV "Christy," William Jr. "Biff," James, and twins Margaret and John. Dr. Rodiger led Scout troops, worked with the PTA, and directed youth choirs. She was an active board member of the Visiting Nurses' Association, the PTA, the United Way Agency Operations, the Sierra Madre Girl Scout Council, the Community Planning Council, the Junior League, the Pasadena Child Guidance Clinic, and Hospice.

Dr. Rodiger was on the founding board of St. George's Church in La Canada and the director of its church school program. She taught adult-education classes—"Journey in Faith"—at All Saints' Church and is still very involved leading retreats and preaching at many area churches.

In 1968, two years before the courts ordered the Pasadena schools to desegregate, Dr. Rodiger spearheaded the "Washington Project," designed to alleviate the racial and educational problems that were causing serious unrest at Washington Junior High School. For her efforts, she received the Newton D. Baker Certificate of Recognition from the United Community Funds and Councils of America.

Dr. Rodiger received her master of arts degree in marriage, family, and child counseling from Fuller Theological Seminary in 1975 and her doctoral degree in clinical psychology from Fuller Graduate School of Psychology in 1980. She worked at the Pasadena Community Counseling Center, and completed her internship in the psychiatric division of Children's Hospital in Los Angeles.

While at Fuller, Dr. Rodiger traveled throughout California teaching cognitive development programming in all the state hospitals and putting on many workshops for regional centers and school districts. She was on a team led by Clara Lee Edgar, Ph.D., supported by the State Department of Mental Health.

Dr. Rodiger listens to a student who is delighting her classmates with a song.

Dr. Rodiger encourages three children who are working on rocking boards blindfolded to enhance their sensory motor development.

Dr. Rodiger is highly regarded as a teacher and a speaker. As part of the Rodiger Center outreach program, she talks with many groups on a variety of subjects, including sensory motor integration for cognitive development, eating disorders, families and death, relationships, Christian living, and wholeness in a fragmenting world. Students have benefited from her expertise at Chaffey College, La Verne College, Pacific Oaks College, the Rosemead School of Psychology, and Fuller Theological Seminary.

The Rodiger Center is still evolving. As a need is presented to Dr. Rodiger, she evaluates it and where possible expands the work of the center to incorporate a new program. There is only one criterion for inclusion: a heartfelt need with an unwavering hope. The center, born in response to hurting people, will continue to answer the call of the Pasadena community.

LYTLE ROOFING COMPANY, INC.

Gary B. Outzen, president and sole stockholder of Lytle Roofing Company, Inc., estimates that someone from his firm has been on the roof of nearly every building in Pasadena. To substantiate his claim, he has records on file dating back to 1922, the year the enterprise was founded.

The operation was originated by John W. Lytle, as John W. Lytle Roofing Company. The founder was an Iowa farmer whose son had come to Southern California and was working as a salesman for Johns-Manville. Unimpressed with the quality of the roofing work he saw, he convinced his father to relocate and launch the new venture, which naturally used Johns-Manville products.

The senior Lytle saw additional opportunities and soon branched out into residential construction—building many custom homes in Pasadena, San Marino, and throughout the San Gabriel Valley. In 1955 he decided to retire, and sold the company to his son-in-law, Terry Chambers. Under Chambers' leadership it soon became one of the largest roofing firms in Southern California, and also specialized in sheet-metal work and air conditioning.

In June 1959 Chambers was offered a position with the Pasadena Tournament of Roses Association and sold the roofing operation to three longtime Lytle employees—Carl Outzen, Fred Hansen, and Ralph Paglia. Chambers' career with the tournament was destined to be a brief one. During the 1960 tournament, his first after joining the staff of the association, he met Grand Marshal Richard M. Nixon, who was then serving as Vice-President of the United States. Chambers left his tournament post to work for Nixon and would later become associated with another future President of the United States, Ronald Reagan.

The three new owners incorporated the business as Lytle Roofing Com-

A Lytle residential roofing project.

This 1956 photo shows the staff of John W. Lytle Roofing Company in front of the original location at Walnut and Sierra Madre.

pany in 1959. Two years later Paglia died, leaving half of his stock to each of his two associates. Outzen sold his interest to his son, Gary, in July 1980; in 1982 Hansen sold his stock to his son-in-law, Jarold Ray.

As a boy, Gary Outzen had worked with his father in the roofing business. Launching out on his own, he began buying old houses and rehabilitating them. He then went to work with United Parcel Service, where he remained until he joined Lytle in January 1980. Both his father and Hansen had wanted to retire for some time, and had put the company on the market two years earlier. Gary was well aware of the organization's fine reputation, and—six months after joining the company—he acquired his father's stock.

On April 1, 1985, Gary Outzen purchased Jarold Ray's interest and became the sole shareholder, although Ray remains active in the company. A third generation of Outzens is now following in the footsteps of father and grandfather. Gary's son Tim, who joined the operation in 1980, is in sales; Tim's younger brother, Tod, works on one of the roofing crews.

The Lytle Roofing Company has come a long way since it was launched by a farmer from Iowa back in 1922. The firm now has more than 100 employees and a fleet of more than two dozen trucks. It provides full roofing and reroofing services; a complete sheet-metal shop; and is a licensed general contractor, enabling it to do structural repair and alterations. The company also has full-time repair and maintenance men—covering California, Arizona, and Nevada—for several large corporations.

Many of the Pasadena area's finest and most famous structures have been roofed or reroofed by Lytle. They include the California Institute of Technology, Huntington Memorial Hospital, the Jet Propulsion Laboratory, and the Huntington Library.

In July 1985 a new affiliate, Lytle Solar Company, was established, with William J. Kelso as president and Gary Outzen as secretary/treasurer. Ironically, the circumstances that led to the formation of this organization were similar to those that brought Lytle Roofing into existence. Having rebuilt, repaired, or inspected the vast majority of roofs in the Pasadena area, Lytle employees noted that much of the solar installation work they had seen was done by firms with no roofing expertise, and that roof damage often resulted.

Convinced his own people could do a better job, Outzen decided to start the new venture—which sells and installs a full line of top-quality solar equipment and also offers a complete line of conservation devices, such as computer thermostats and solar windows. The company shares space with Lytle Roofing at 2948 East Walnut Street, which has been at that location since 1970.

The corporation's original location was at Walnut and Sierra Madre. In 1958 it moved to Daisy and Walnut. When the City of Pasadena acquired that property in 1970, Lytle moved to its present location.

Both Gary Outzen and his father have been active in the Pasadena community. Carl Outzen has been a member of the Rotary Club of Pasadena since 1973, and his son since 1980. Gary has participated in Boy Scout activities for many years, and the company is a longtime member of the Pasadena Chamber of Commerce.

A company crew works on a commercial building in Pasadena.

BUSHNELL, DIVISION OF BAUSCH & LOMB

Romance plus a love for travel had much to do with starting David P. Bushnell down a career path quite different than he had originally planned. During the early 1930s Bushnell was studying mechanical engineering at Pasadena's California Institute of Technology when he decided to take some time off and see the world. Withdrawing his life savings of $700, he set sail for Europe—which he toured by bicycle—and then went on to the Middle East, via tramp steamer.

Seven months later Bushnell returned home determined to enter the field of foreign trade. He established D.P. Bushnell & Company—importing and exporting such commodities as oil, cement, and chemicals—with headquarters in Los Angeles. The outbreak of World War II ended that venture, and he then went to work in the finance department at Lockheed.

While in Japan on his honeymoon, Bushnell was drawn to the field of precision optical instruments, in which the Japanese were making great strides. In those days a pair of binoculars sold for considerably more than the average American could afford.

Bushnell became convinced that an excellent market could be developed in the United States for reasonably priced binoculars. Before leaving Japan late in 1949, he purchased 400 binoculars that he planned to sell during the upcoming Christmas season. When the shipment failed to arrive on time, the quick-thinking businessman placed himself in the mail-order industry. A single ad brought such response that he sold every binocular.

The entrepreneur began his new business at 43 East Green Street in Pasadena. The prompt response to his ad confirmed his belief that there was a large untapped market for reasonably priced binoculars, and he set about designing his own. Determined to give people what they wanted, he carefully researched the market, consulting with sportsmen and athletic heroes such as Tom Harmon, who helped him design his product line.

Bushnell quickly established a reputation not only for lower prices but also for the high quality of his binoculars. Soon he added telescopes, riflescopes, and other items—and before long he was the dominant figure in the field of sports optics. By 1959 much larger facilities were needed, and Bushnell moved his booming business to its present site at 2828 East Foothill Boulevard. The 47,500-square-foot lot had once been the location of a pony track, and the original stable is still used for storage.

A new 15,000-square-foot building was constructed on the property, where the company's products were designed, warehoused, and shipped.

David Bushnell remained the sole owner of the company until 1971, when he sold it to Bausch & Lomb Incorporated of Rochester, New York, known throughout the world for its top-quality, high-precision products.

David P. Bushnell launched his binocular business from this shop at 43 East Green Street in Pasadena.

He remained with the company he founded for two years, and then retired. The tiny enterprise he had begun in 1949 now had more than 100 employees.

The founder attributed his success primarily to his philosophy of "finding out what people want and reacting accordingly." He frequently ran questionnaires in sportsmen's magazines, designing his products according to the responses. A firm believer in the principle that a satisfied customer is a company's best means of advertising, he usually provided even more than his buyer expected; as a result his firm grew to become the market leader in sports optics.

The reputation and financial strength that Bausch & Lomb brought to Bushnell has enabled it to become the world's largest sports optics company. It not only enjoys overall dominance but has half or more of the world market in each of its three lines: binoculars, riflescopes, and telescopes.

Bushnell products have been to even more places than their much-traveled founder. They have been virtually everywhere man has visited, including the top of Mount Everest. They were the first binoculars in space, for use as secondary sighting systems, and it has long been the policy of the corporation to donate its products for expeditions to the far corners of the world.

Although some of Bushnell's top-of-the-line products cost as much as $1,400, many others are within reach of the average American consumer. Telescopes start at about $100, while riflescopes can be purchased for as little as $13.95. Good-quality binoculars, the item that launched the company, can be obtained in the $50 range. Quality at an affordable price, David Bushnell's original concept, continues as the cornerstone of the company's marketing philosophy.

Bushnell is often credited with bringing binoculars within the price range of the average American.

JACOB MAARSE FLORIST INC.

It seems natural, and perhaps inevitable, that a young man whose family had been in the floral business since the middle of the nineteenth century would make his way halfway around the world to Pasadena, the City of Roses. Born in Aalsmeer, Holland—an internationally known floral center where his family had been in the business since the 1850s—Jacob Maarse attended the Aalsmeer Horticultural School, apprenticed in Germany and Switzerland, and worked for a short time in the family nursery before departing for the United States.

He was nineteen years old when he arrived in New York, where he intended to seek fame and fortune. After spending a few months there, a visit to California to see an uncle who was a violinist with the San Francisco Symphony convinced him that the West Coast had more to offer than its eastern counterpart, and the young man settled in Pasadena. He found a job at Preble's Market, working in its flower shop and, in his words, "doing a little bit of anything and everything."

Maarse remained at Preble's for fifteen years, taking on ever-increasing responsibilities in the store's floral operations. In 1966 he decided to step out on his own, and Jacob Maarse Florist was born. His first shop was at the corner of Euclid and Green. The shop had four employees, including the founder and his wife, Clara, whom he had met while they were both studying at Occidental College. Married in 1957, they have raised two sons and two daughters, and have worked side by side since starting their business. Jacob directs his attention to floral design; Clara is in charge of finances.

In 1969 the City of Pasadena acquired the property to allow for the expansion of the Civic Center, and Maarse was forced to find another location. It was a critical time. The company had been in operation for just two and a half years and was beginning to make some progress. Maarse felt it was important to find space fairly close by. He learned of the availability of a building at the northwest corner of El Molino and Green, four short blocks away.

While the location was tempting there were shortcomings, and Maarse was advised to look elsewhere. The structure had been built in 1928 for an automobile agency and seemed ill-suited for any other purpose. Its 23,000 square feet, high ceilings, and cement floors seemed less than ideal for a flower shop. Ignoring the advice he had received, Maarse was able to obtain a mortgage loan and purchased the property from Symes Cadillac.

Jacob Maarse, founder of the Pasadena floral business that bears his name.

It has proven to be a wise choice, and may well be the world's most unusual flower shop. In the showroom where Cadillacs once sat on display may now be found magnificent floral arrangements and unique giftware from all over the world. The large service area is now used for storage and, most important, for covered parking facilities to accommodate the customers who come from throughout Southern California to meet their floral needs.

The staff of four has now grown to more than forty, who serve the customers drawn by Maarse's reputation as one of the nation's most innovative floral designers. Other florists, both here and abroad, often come to him for advice. In 1984 he was given the prestigious assignment of being one of the float judges for Pasadena's world-famous Tournament of Roses.

The success Maarse has enjoyed has made little, if any, change in the outlook or life-style of this genial Hollander. Three times a week he arises by 3 a.m., in order to be at the Los Angeles flower market an hour later. Back in the shop by 9 or 10, he remains until 6 p.m. He spends three other days each week in the shop, from 8 to 6. There are also numerous weddings, funerals, banquets, receptions, and other functions, the most important of which always get his personal attention. His reputation is such that, during the Nixon presidential years, he provided the floral arrangements for nearly all the functions held at the so-called Western White House.

Two or three times every year, Maarse returns to Aalsmeer on business. He receives shipments from there twice each week, and feels it is important to maintain close personal contact. The Aalsmeer Flower Market, which was started by his grandparents and others as a cooperative in about 1920, now occupies the largest building under one roof in the world. The 75-acre structure could encompass fifty football fields.

Maarse's oldest son, Hank John, a business graduate of the University of Southern California, is now learning the floral business. A second son, Glenn Jacob, is a student at the University of California at Berkeley and has also shown some interest, but has made no commitment to date.

The Maarse daughters have other career plans. The older plans to become a psychologist and is pursuing a Ph.D. in that field, while the younger is a student at Loyola Law School. Both are graduates of the University of Southern California.

Regardless of how many of the Maarse offspring follow in the footsteps of their parents and grandparents, Jacob Maarse Florist remains very much a family operation. Most of the staff have been with the shop for more than five years, and both Jacob and Clara work hard at maintaining a family atmosphere. Often, when seasonal demands for flowers mean long hours, Clara will prepare a home-cooked meal for forty or more employees.

Well-treated themselves, the Maarse employees show the same kind of consideration to customers— many of whom return again and again to what is certainly one of the world's unique flower shops.

This building was constructed in 1928 to house an automobile agency. Today it is the unique home of Jacob Maarse Florist Inc.

CHRISTIE, PARKER & HALE

The Pasadena law firm of Christie, Parker & Hale practices intellectual property law. Specifically, the firm specializes in patent, trademark, copyright, trade secret, and unfair competition law, including the procurement of patents, trademarks, and copyrights for clients, litigation concerning the enforcement or defense of such rights, licensing, and overall client counseling.

The firm was organized on June 1, 1954, by James B. Christie, Robert L. Parker, and C. Russell Hale. Christie came to California in 1943 after practicing law with a New York City firm. In 1946 Parker graduated from law school after a career as a chemist with Union Oil Company, and he joined Christie at that time. Hale came to California to attend Stanford engineering school; later he graduated from law school and was employed in New York. He joined the Christie firm in 1951 when it occupied offices in the Lloyds Bank Building at Madison and Colorado.

All three founders had scientific backgrounds before beginning the practice of law: Christie in mining and mechanics, Parker in chemistry, and Hale in electronics.

Christie, Parker & Hale supplements legal research with computer searching of extensive data bases.

At its inception, the firm's primary client was Consolidated Engineering Corporation, founded in Pasadena in 1937 by Herbert Hoover, Jr., and expanded into the city's largest employer by a prominent Pasadenan, Philip S. Fogg. However, the law firm rapidly expanded its clientele to include many other industrial companies throughout Southern California.

In 1966 the expanding law firm moved to larger quarters in the Union Bank Building at 201 South Lake Avenue. Further growth to its present size of twenty-two attorneys necessitated a move early in 1985 to its current quarters in the Wells Fargo Bank Building at 350 West Colorado Boulevard, in which the firm has an ownership interest.

In the tradition of the founders, every attorney in the organization has a degree in some branch of engineering or science (many of them advanced degrees) as well as a law degree, and most have worked in their areas of technical expertise before going into legal practice. Their specialties include such fields as electrical, chemical, and mechanical engineering; electronics; computer sciences; chemistry; nuclear physics; materials science; thermodynamics; naval architecture; and biology. This broad range of scientific and engineering disciplines is essential to meet client needs because of the complex nature of the firm's practice.

Having a professional graphics department is somewhat unusual for lawyers, but important for the firm's patent practice.

Rapid technological advances made in recent years have introduced added complexities. Computer science and software, for example, require considerable attention.

Partners and associates appear in court across the United States, usually in federal courts. Cases can be very complex and may take months or years to complete. In a landmark case, the firm succeeded in persuading the U.S. Supreme Court to overturn a long-standing legal principle that prohibited a licensee from challenging the validity of a licensed patent. This one case was in various state and federal courts for nine years.

All of the firm's attorneys are registered to practice before the United States Patent and Trademark Office, and also to appear before other government agencies, such as the U.S. Customs Service and the International Trade Commission.

Much of the firm's practice today is international. International situations involving patents or trademarks require considerable expertise because laws vary widely from country to country. Christie, Parker & Hale not only is involved with the representation of American clients overseas, but has a number of foreign clients that it represents in the United States.

Other areas of specialization include taxes concerning intellectual property, trade name infringement, false advertising, franchising, and related business matters. Because many other areas of the law are peripheral to the firm's specialties, it works closely with many law firms throughout the world.

Members of the Christie, Parker & Hale firm have long taken an active part in local community affairs. Some of them belong to the Pasadena Tournament of Roses Association. Other organizations in which they actively participate include Rotary, Kiwanis, Chamber of Commerce, Jaycees, Boy Scouts, and the YMCA. Professional activities include the American Intellectual Property Law Association, various national, state, and local bar associations, and technical societies. Many have led seminars in their specialties.

In 1984 the firm established a branch office in Newport Beach to provide service for its increased client base in the Orange County high-technology region. However, the firm's headquarters remains in Pasadena because of its long association with the Crown City.

Although James Christie and Robert Parker are deceased, the founding firm name has been retained.

Modern equipment and a skilled support staff enable the firm to provide rapid service to its clients.

Every vantage from the firm's offices is memorable. They include the Norton Simon Museum, seen here from the main conference room.

MIKE BROWN GRANDSTANDS, INC.

January 1, 1985, was a historic day for Mike Brown Grandstands, Inc., and for Mike Brown himself. On that morning he and his company had provided more than 80,000 seats for spectators at the 96th Annual Tournament of Roses Parade in Pasadena. It was the first time the 100,000 mark had been reached, and it almost certainly represented the largest temporary portable-seating installation in the history of the world.

Mike's introduction to the grandstand business came when he was eleven years old. A native Pasadenan, the youngster had a newspaper route along Colorado Boulevard. In those days Rose Parade seat sales were handled by individuals stationed at each location. One fateful December morning Mike found a box of tickets on the street, and turned them in to Kelly Seating Company. For his honesty he was given six front-row seats in the grandstand in front of the Elks Club, still one of the choicest viewing locations.

The main grandstands, where thousands watch and cheer as the Rose Parade turns the corner from Orange Grove Boulevard (foreground) onto Colorado Boulevard.

Mike's honest deed was to have a far greater impact on his life: It marked the start of a lifelong infatuation with the Rose Parade; and also developed within him an awareness of temporary grandstand seating. Little did he dream, however, that one day he would be providing seats for many millions of people.

As soon as Mike graduated from high school, he went to work for a man named Jack Milne, who owned and operated a motorcycle store on East Colorado Boulevard. More important, the businessman was a pioneer in the use of portable grandstands. He had been the first American to win the world's speedway championship, and frequently provided temporary seating for racing events. Milne Brothers Grandstands also provided some seating for the Rose Parade.

One day in 1958 a Los Angeles school called to ask if the organization ever rented its portable Rose Parade stands to other groups. The school wanted temporary stands for an upcoming football game. Mike Brown, who took the call, put the question to his boss. Milne's response was that if Mike wanted to handle it himself, he could use the stands and they would split the profits.

Mike Brown became the owner of the company—which had undergone a series of name changes—in 1959, and incorporated it as Mike Brown Grandstands, Inc., in 1964. In its early days the firm had a mere 800 seats available, but that figure grew to 4,000 within five years and today

Extra seating was provided by Mike Brown Grandstands for the Pepperdine University Swim Stadium during the 1984 Summer Olympics.

The Marvin Hagler-Thomas Hearns world middleweight title fight setting at Caesars Palace, Las Vegas, Nevada, in 1984.

United Production Services did all the staging for the Rolling Stones 1981-1982 world tour.

exceeds 100,000. Events for which it provides seating include football games, boxing matches, golf tournaments, auto races, concerts, circuses, rodeos, and, of course, parades.

The Rose Parade is the company's major ongoing event and presents some unusual logistic problems. Dozens of locations are involved, and, except for two sites, local ordinances prevent the start of construction before November 15. The two exceptions are the Elks Club stands, where it all began for Mike Brown, and the VIP stands on Orange Grove Boulevard.

After November 15 construction begins on whatever vacant lots are available, which change from year to year. The last stands to be built are on business properties, so as to minimize the negative impact on customer traffic. Leases must be negotiated with forty or more landlords, some on a long-term basis and others annually. Each grandstand must be approved by the City of Pasadena, which conducts the most thorough inspection of any authority with which the company deals. Mike Brown considers the Pasadena inspectors the most qualified because of their many years of experience, and credits them with not only keeping his firm's standards high but in helping it maintain an accident-free record for more than thirty-five years. "Their inspection process has kept us in business," he says.

The removal process begins almost as soon as the Rose Parade ends. All stands must be removed by January 15 and the sites restored to their original condition.

That kind of pressure stood the company in good stead during the 1984 Olympics in Los Angeles. Through an affiliate, United Production Services, Inc., the company did all the staging for the opening and closing ceremonies. For the latter event everything had to be done within a fifteen-hour span. As competition ended, forty-six trucks were standing by in the parking lot of the Los Angeles Coliseum to begin the massive job. Earlier, rehearsals for the project had been held at nearby Aviation High School, the very same school that Mike Brown had provided seating for a quarter of a century earlier.

Mike Brown Grandstands was the official supplier for the 1984 Olympic Games, and provided seating at every venue. At Santa Anita Race Track, 35,000 seats were installed for the equestrian events. For the modern pentathlon and shooting events, a mere 250 seats were installed—causing a few logistic problems for Olympic organizers when 15,000 fans arrived.

Other major events for which the company provides seating include the Hollywood Christmas Parade, the Long Beach Grand Prix, and world championship boxing events at Caesars Palace in Las Vegas. United Production Services does all the staging of Rose Bowl events and for the worldwide tours of such musical stars as Bruce Springsteen, Fleetwood Mac, and the Rolling Stones.

The annual Rose Parade remains Mike Brown's favorite. The passion that first bloomed in the heart of an honest eleven-year-old boy is as strong as ever. While 100,000 spectators sit in his stands on New Year's morning, Mike is involved as one of the hundreds of white-suited volunteers making certain that not one of those spectators is disappointed.

JACOBS ENGINEERING GROUP INC.

Jacobs Engineering Group Inc. officially traces its origins back to 1947, but for founder Joseph J. Jacobs, Ph.D., its roots lie in the Lebanese traditions of his forebears. Both of his parents had been born in Lebanon and had come to the United States at an early age. The Lebanese (descendants of the ancient Phoenicians) had inherited a tradition of trading, of being in business for oneself.

Joseph Jacobs' father went into business for himself and, for a time, prospered. He taught his son other traditions of the trader, such as the importance of pride, reputation, and integrity—characteristics that would mold the younger man's own life and career.

Jacobs graduated from the Polytechnic Institute of Brooklyn (now Polytechnic University) in the midst of the Great Depression and was unable to find work. Offered a teaching fellowship at his alma mater, which paid $300 per year, he accepted it and earned a few extra dollars teaching night classes.

After obtaining his master's degree Jacobs found a job as a research engineer, and continued teaching at night while working toward his doctorate. A new fellowship grant enabled him to quit his job and concentrate on his studies. In 1942, at the age of twenty-six, he received his doctorate in chemical engineering from the Polytechnic Institute. A few days later he married Violet Jabara.

Jacobs was hired by Merck & Company in New Jersey, where he was involved in the development of two substances destined to make major impacts on the world. One was penicillin and the other, DDT. He left Merck when he was offered a position with a small, family-owned company in Northern California, called Chemurgic Corporation. There he began to learn the many and varied disciplines needed to operate a successful business.

By 1947 the traditions of his culture burned so strongly within him that they could no longer be ignored. Determined to start his own consulting firm, he chose Southern California as his base of operations and moved his family to Altadena. To augment his consulting practice, the entrepreneur served as a manufacturers' representative for capital equipment for the process industries. The name he chose for his business was Jacobs Engineering Co.

By the mid-1950s four people were involved in sales, and the consulting practice had become too large for Jacobs to handle alone. He hired a young engineer named Stan Krugman to join him, and today gives him much of the credit for the early success of the business. Working together, they handled consulting assignments for many major firms, including Kaiser Aluminum.

It was Kaiser that motivated the young company to broaden its scope. A large alumina plant was in the planning stage, and Kaiser needed someone to design it. Jacobs and Krugman assembled a team of about twenty people to meet Kaiser's needs. Many of that group remain with Jacobs Engineering today.

The rapidly growing company was

Joseph J. Jacobs, Ph.D., founded Jacobs Engineering Group Inc. in 1947.

The first offices owned by Jacobs Engineering were at 837 South Fair Oaks Avenue.

incorporated in 1957, and in 1960 received its first contract to design and construct a large plant. Construction was a field Joseph Jacobs had avoided, believing it would impair the professionalism of his engineering profession. Reluctantly, he agreed to do what so many of his competitors had already done and, in his own words, "found out quickly that all the myths were untrue. Engineers have no monopoly on professionalism."

More design/build contracts followed, and by 1962 there were about 150 people on staff. In 1967 the firm, which had primarily been serving California and the Southwest, decided to expand to other areas of the country. The first of what would become several decentralized offices was opened in New Jersey.

The organization went public in 1970—not because of a need for added equity but as a means of rewarding its loyal employees, through stock options and other methods. That same year, while retaining its original offices at 837 South Fair Oaks, the company expanded some of its operations to 10 Congress Street. In 1975 Jacobs purchased its present headquarters building at 251 South Lake Avenue, which it later sold and has leased back on a long-term basis.

In 1974 Jacobs merged with The Pace Companies of Houston, intending to keep the two operating entities separate under a new firm called Jacobs Engineering Group Inc. That later proved to be impractical, and today there is a single operating corporation; however, the new name was retained.

The enterprise that its founder began as a one-man consulting business now has close to 2,000 employees, with offices throughout the United States and several foreign countries. Its work has taken it to such faraway places as the People's Republic of China and Jordan's Dead Sea. Closer to home, it designed and constructed the beautiful Corporate Center building, the firm's next-door neighbor on South Lake Avenue.

Jacobs' worldwide operations are conducted from this building at 251 South Lake Avenue, which has been the firm's headquarters since 1975.

In 1983 the achievements of Dr. Joseph J. Jacobs were recognized when he was chosen as the forty-third recipient of the prestigious Herbert Hoover Medal. Previous recipients of the award, given to engineers for civic and humanitarian achievements outside of their profession, have been such men as Alfred P. Sloan, Jr.; Charles F. Kettering; and Dwight D. Eisenhower. Among Dr. Jacobs' achievements are his years of service to his alma mater, Polytechnic University, where he is chairman of the board. He is also on the board of trustees of Harvey Mudd College.

Jacobs Engineering Group Inc. is today one of the top twenty firms in its field and is still headed by its founder as chairman, chief executive officer, and president. He is quick to give much of the credit for its success to his associates, but, understandably, is proud of what his company has become. Jacobs sees it as having developed a personality of its own, which he describes as "pride without arrogance; professionalism without being hidebound; integrity without self-righteousness; and daring without foolhardiness."

That description suits the organization, and its founder as well.

Jacobs Engineering moved some of its operations to this facility at 10 Congress Street in 1970.

BURROUGHS CORPORATION

Like the City of Pasadena, Burroughs Corporation is 100 years old. The first meeting of stockholders was held on January 23, 1886, in St. Louis, Missouri. The name of the new business was American Arithometer Company, changed in 1905 to Burroughs Adding Machine Company, in honor of its ace-founder, William Seward Burroughs.

At that first meeting, it was stated that the organization was established " . . . for the purpose of manufactur-

Each Burroughs machine is rigorously tested before leaving the factory, as this 1908 advertisement stresses.

ing machines for the use of bankers, insurance companies, railroad companies, merchants, brokers, and others in the prosecution of their business and for making and keeping correct and accurate accounts of their business transactions. . . ."

William Burroughs was still in his twenties when the enterprise was launched, with initial capital of $300. The funds were depleted long before the first machine was begun, but the young inventor kept going. His first two models were failures. A third worked well for him, and fifty machines were built. Untrained operators, however, were unable to make them perform accurately. Burroughs personally threw each of the fifty machines out a second-story window and started all over again. Finally, he perfected his invention and the little company was on its way.

That first product, a straight adding and listing machine, constituted the firm's entire "line" and sold for $475. Burroughs and his co-founders of American Arithometer, Thomas Metcalfe, R.M. Scruggs, and William R. Pye, were jubilant. It was the first step in the fulfillment of a prediction made by Burroughs in 1884: "Someday there will be one of these machines in every city bank in the land, and that means over 8,000 machines sold."

Burroughs' invention would prove to be successful beyond his wildest imagination. In 1895 an independent organization, Burroughs Adding Machine and Registering Company Ltd., was formed in Nottingham, England, and licensed to produce and market a version of the machine Burroughs had developed that tabulated in English currency. Three years later full manufacturing facilities were established outside the United States for the first time, also in Nottingham.

Unfortunately, William Burroughs would get but a foretaste of the growth and success of his company. In 1898, at the age of forty-one, he died.

In 1904 the firm's headquarters was relocated to Detroit, Michigan, and a year later the name was changed to Burroughs Adding Machine Company. In 1908 it purchased the British operation, and in 1911 produced the first machine that could subtract as well as add.

As the 1920s began, Burroughs had 12,000 employees worldwide; in 1924 its stock was listed on the New York Stock Exchange. Its first portable adding machine, weighing twenty pounds, made its debut in 1925—the following year the one-millionth machine was produced.

By the time the organization reached the half-century mark in

Burroughs acquired the Electro Data Company in Pasadena in 1957. The plant is located on Sierra Madre Villa and employs 400 people.

1935, that original product "line" of one machine had grown to 450 and included manual and electric adding machines, bookkeeping machines, and typewriters. When World War II erupted, the company's production was restricted to military needs. It produced the Norden bombsight, which made accurate, high-altitude bombing possible. For its war efforts Burroughs received the coveted Army/Navy "E" Award.

With the Allied victory the firm once again turned its attention to its primary purpose of transforming relevant technologies into useful, dependable machines. The age of electronics was dawning, and Burroughs was at the forefront. In 1950 it introduced the first Sensimatic accounting machine with a programmed control panel, considered the greatest advance in accounting machines in a quarter of a century.

The company changed its name to Burroughs Corporation in 1953, to reflect its growing diversification, particularly in the field of electronics. A few years later Burroughs built the world's first operational transistorized computer, which was used in guiding the launch of the Atlas Intercontinental Ballistic Missiles. Later versions of this computer guided every launch in the Mercury and Gemini programs of manned space flights. Today these systems are on display at the Smithsonian Institution in Washington, D.C.

At about that same time, a Pasadena firm called Electro Data Company was producing computer systems. Impressed by the technology, Burroughs acquired the company in 1957, and has played a major role in Pasadena's economy ever since. The plant—located on Sierra Madre Villa—employs 400 people who design and develop Burroughs' V Series computer systems, primarily for use in the financial community. Engineers in that facility developed the corporation's B 5000 computer, considered in 1961 a decade ahead of its time.

The Burroughs' V Series computer system is designed and developed at the Pasadena facility.

The Pasadena plant is part of a worldwide network that includes operations in 100 countries and 65,000 employees. Engineering and manufacturing operations include 64 major facilities in 13 countries and 1,200 marketing and support offices. Revenues reached the billion-dollar level in 1972, doubled that figure five years later, and have now reached the five-billion-dollar mark.

William Seward Burroughs' century-old invention has spawned a giant electronics-based information systems organization serving customers in key industry sectors—including financial, manufacturing, government, education, health care, airlines, hospitality, distribution, and services. As the firm begins its second century, its objective remains as it was when William Burroughs filed his first patent application in 1885—to use technology to solve human problems making business more cost-efficient.

SEE'S CANDIES

It often comes as quite a surprise to even longtime local residents to learn that world-famous See's Candies began in Pasadena, in 1921.

The home has long been known in the neighborhood as Mrs. See's house. It's located at 462 South Marengo Avenue between California and Colorado boulevards, just south of the Pasadena Center and the Plaza Pasadena.

The See's Candies story in California began in this post-Victorian bungalow-style home designed in 1904 by noted architect C.W. Buchanan. Research by the Pasadena Historical Society uncovered the fact that, in the city directory of 1921, the house was listed as the residence of Charles A. See, son of Mary See. It was in the kitchen of that home where Mary See made candy for her family and friends.

Mary See died in 1939, but her picture still adorns every box of See's candies sold.

Charles A. See, who began making candy in 1921 using his mother's recipes.

In that same year—when Mary See was sixty-seven years old—her son began making candy for sale, using many of her recipes and putting her photograph on the cover of his candy boxes. He opened the first See's Candy Shop at 135 North Western Avenue in Los Angeles and soon afterward opened another shop closer to home, at 396 East Colorado Boulevard in Pasadena. As the city expanded eastward this shop eventually closed, and another that opened at 803 East Colorado Boulevard later became one of the original tenants in the Plaza Pasadena. A second local shop is in the Hastings Ranch Shopping Plaza, at 3641 East Foothill Boulevard.

Among the earliest corporate records are the minutes of a meeting held on June 8, 1922, which note the location of the first three shops—the third being in Grauman's Theater Building at Sixth and Hill streets in Los Angeles. The photo of Mary See, who died in 1939, is still on every See's candy box, and hers is certainly one of the most recognized faces in the world.

By 1986, as Pasadena celebrated its 100th anniversary and See's commemorated its own 65th birthday, the little company that was born in a Pasadena kitchen had grown to what is widely recognized as the premium retailer of quality candies in the confectionary industry, with some 220 shops across the United States, and from Hawaii to Hong Kong.

The U.S. shops are company owned, and operated by See's own locally hired and trained employees. The three shops in the British Crown Colony of Hong Kong, which in part is due to be merged into the People's Republic of China by 1997, are operated under a special licensing arrangement with a longtime business associate of See's.

The Hong Kong staff, who are mostly of Chinese heritage, have been trained with the help of See's supervisors sent to Hong Kong, and the quality control on which the company prides itself is assured by direct air shipments from See's candy-making facilities in South San Francisco.

On Main Street of Disney World in Florida, See's candies are featured in a special confectionary center, where employees have also been trained with the help of See's supervisors to serve customers with candies that have been sent fresh from See's Southern California candy-making facilities on La Cienega Boulevard in Los Angeles. Depending on their location, all See's Candy Shops receive kitchen-fresh candies either by air or in refrigerated vans.

How could an operation of such range and magnitude have reached out so far fom a modest home on Marengo Avenue? When did the See family arrive in Pasadena? Where did they come from?

Mary See was of Dutch-English de-

During World War II the ingredients for quality candy were in short supply, so customers waited in long lines for their favorite See's products.

scent. She was born in Gananoque, on Howe Island, Frontenac County, Ontario, Canada, on September 15, 1854. She married Alexander See, with whom she had three children. One of them, Charles, studied pharmacology. A natural entrepreneur, he soon opened two drugstores in an Ontario mining town. When they were later destroyed by a forest fire, he started over again as a chocolate salesman.

After his father died Charles immigrated with his family to Southern California, where they settled into their home on Marengo and, not long afterward, began See's Candies. His business and sales experience, plus his entrepreneurial spirit and commitment to quality, would stand him in good stead as he guided the company through both lean and prosperous times for twenty-eight years.

During the 1920s the business grew steadily, with a focus on quality and the grandmotherly image of Mary See, backed by shrewd marketing. During the Depression years of the 1930s, Charles See cut his prices from eighty cents to fifty cents per pound. He told his landlords: "Lower rent is better than no rent; reduce the rent and we'll survive together." To increase volume, ice cream was also sold in the shops, although that has long since been discontinued.

This house, at 462 South Marengo in Pasadena, once belonged to the See family. It was from the kitchen of this home that See's Candies was launched.

Despite the Depression Charles See was determined that the enterprise would not only survive but expand. In 1936 he sent Edward G. Peck, who had been with the company since 1931, to Northern California to begin a subsidiary. The new operation was to make candy for new shops in that part of the state. It also placed the firm on the scene when, in 1939, the San Francisco World's Fair opened. See's Candy Shop, with its tempting displays, quickly became one of the fair's major attractions.

In the difficult years of World War II, with supplies greatly limited, Charles See was determined that the company's hard-earned reputation for only the highest quality candies would not be compromised by the use of inferior ingredients. See's curtailed production and kept its shops open only a few hours each day, resulting in long, never-to-be-forgotten lines of eager customers. When the day's supply was gone, the remaining customers were uged to buy war bonds.

A Sacramento police chief, who sent officers to keep one block-long line of See's customers from interfering with traffic, also had the foresight to instruct his own secretary to get in line.

Charles See, who became identified as a leader in business and community service activities in the greater Los Angeles area and throughout California, was active in helping stage the 1932 Olympics in Los Angeles. He established family homes in Beverly Hills and on Catalina Island, but always maintained a Pasadena candy shop and his interest in the community.

On November 6, 1949, See died at his home in Beverly Hills, after a long illness. In an obituary the *Los Angeles Times* described him as a man who "built a three-man candy store into a chain of 78 establishments employing more than 2,000. . . . "

The founder was succeeded as president by his oldest son, Laurance A. See, who had literally grown up in the business. He joined the company following his graduation from Stanford University in 1934 and, except for military service during World War II, remained with it until his death. It was he who made the decision that tied See's to California shopping-mall growth, a decision that led to the establishment of the firm's shops in major malls across much of the United States, including the Plaza Pasadena.

Like his father, Laurance See was a Pasadena booster and a supporter of the Tournament of Roses Parade. By the time of his death in 1969, See's had won many awards for its Rose Parade floats.

Charles B. "Harry" See, who was born the year the company was launched, took over the leadership following his brother's death. He gave the corporation increased momentum, reaching out to Hawaii and other new marketing areas. He chose as president Charles N. Huggins, who had come to top management under Edward Peck—the man who had begun the Northern California operations.

In 1972 Harry See sold the family-owned company to Blue Chip Stamps. It is now a part of the Berkshire Hathaway Corporation, headed by Warren Buffett—the nationally known financial genius who has played a key role in helping put together the multibillion-dollar acquisition of the American Broadcasting Company.

Under Charles Huggins' direction See's has enjoyed its greatest period of growth, combining tradition and the skills of the individual candy maker with all the quality controls, high-tech advances, management techniques, and human and product resources available. Ingredients for See's candies are sought out wherever the quality is best—nuts from California, pineapple from Hawaii, chocolate from Africa and Venezuela, and maple sugar from Canada. Quantity Order

During the Great Depression See's reduced its prices from eighty cents to fifty cents per pound, enabling the candy company to survive.

and Mail Order divisions of the organization send See's candies around the world. Substantial quantity discounts are offered for company gift giving, employee group purchasing, and church and club fund raising.

Quality-control testing begins with the ingredients as they are received and continues through the finished piece of candy. The corporation's laboratories in Los Angeles and South San Francisco utilize the highest possible scientific technologies. Facilities include a full pathological laboratory for microbiological tests and a chemical laboratory, where organoleptic tasting tests are made. Even the degree of gloss of the chocolate can now be tested by instrumentation.

Candy making, too, has been advanced by automation and innovation, but never at the sacrifice of See's traditional formulas. Candy making by skilled hands remains of highest importance. Where mechanization has been added, it has been to improve consistency, flavor, and sanitation levels. In the latter area See's has received the Food and Drug Service Honor Roll Award for "Consistent Sanitation Achievement" annually for the past thirty-six years.

The organization is equally renowned for the quality of service consistently provided by its friendly sales people who work in the familiar and sparkling white and black shops.

Mary See's own integrity and concern for quality came through during a rare interview late in her life. She was at the International Hotel in Gananoque, Ontario, on the occasion of her eighty-third birthday, September 15, 1937. The local newspaper referred to her as a woman "who is known from one end of the American continent to the other, as well as in other countries due to the fact that her photograph occupies a prominent place on all boxes of See's candy. . . . "

The noble lady replied quite simply that she was "proud to have her picture on the candy boxes," and that she felt it made a statement to See's customers "about the care and thoughtfulness that went into the making of the candy."

On July 31, 1939, a few weeks before her eighty-fifth birthday, Mary See died while visiting her daughter in Gananoque, and is buried in the community where she was born. However, the business that grew out of her candy recipes lives on, and flourishes. The Pasadena home where it all began lives on as well. It has been completely restored, and converted into quality offices, in keeping with the rich history of the house and of the area.

In noting the long relationship that exists between Pasadena and See's, president Huggins says: "We deeply appreciate what Pasadena means in the history of See's Candies, and we are proud to continue to serve the community through our shops in the Plaza Pasadena and in East Pasadena. With all our growth and success, we still like to think of ourselves as an individual candy shop serving its own community."

See's candy making combines the tradition of Mary See with the latest technology.

Delivery vehicles used by See's during its early days. The motorcycle driver pictured is Hugh Fry, who was later to become general manager of See's, Los Angeles.

HERBERT HAWKINS REALTY COMPANY, INC.

Herbert Hawkins, founder of the real estate company that bears his name, sold his first home in the San Gabriel Valley in 1946 when he was twenty-four years old. The sale price of the house was $14,500.

He formed Hawkins Realty with his mother, and after buying her interest in the early 1950s incorporated it as Herbert Hawkins Realty Company, Inc., a name that would become synonymous with residential real estate in Pasadena and the surrounding communities.

Hawkins' first office was in Temple City. Within a few years new branch offices were opened in Arcadia and San Gabriel. In 1960 the company opened its first Pasadena office, at 1155 East Green Street. It was later moved to Union Street and Oak Knoll Avenue.

During the mid-1960s Hawkins purchased a building at 232 North Lake Avenue, where the company's executive offices are still located. From that headquarters Preston Hawkins, who succeeded his father as president, oversees the operations of an organization that now includes real estate offices throughout Southern California, four escrow offices, a mortgage banking firm, a real estate school, and an insurance agency.

The company's growth has been swift and steady. Not long after that first sale, Herbert Hawkins' firm was selling homes at the rate of one every day. When the first Pasadena office opened, sales jumped to more than 100 per month, and eventually topped 600 per month. As the firm celebrates its fortieth anniversary, it has passed the 150,000 mark in the number of properties sold, averaging some 312 sales for every one of those 480 months.

It was the opening of the first branch office that would eventually determine the management style of the Herbert Hawkins Realty Company. At first the founder tried running it as a separate entity, with both offices managed by him. By the time the next office opened, he had recognized the advantages of a centralized operation, a move that he credits for enabling the firm to expand as rapidly as it has.

Herbert Hawkins (left), founder and chairman of the board, with son, Preston, president, giving out awards at the 1985 Awards Dinner Dance.

Today all advertising, bookkeeping, listings, and other functions are conducted by specialists in the central office—with daily messenger service to each of the branch offices. When the escrow operation was established in 1961, the same management principle was instituted, as it was with the insurance firm and mortgage company that opened shortly thereafter.

In January 1980 Hawkins suffered a heart attack and turned the reins of the company over to his son, Preston, who was named president. However, the founder—who ran the business for more than thirty years—remains as chairman of the board. Throughout his career he was extremely active in community and professional organizations, serving as a member of more than twenty local realty boards,

Left to right: Bruce Miller, vice-president, general counsel, and manager of the South Arcadia office; Preston Hawkins; and Jim Papararo, manager of the Alhambra office and vice-president/general manager of the company, on the occasion of the 1984 Awards Breakfast.

Herbert Hawkins, standing in the background, overseeing a training class in 1956.

the California Association of Realtors, and the National Association of Realtors.

Herbert Hawkins served both as a regional vice-president and as education committee chairman of the California Association of Realtors, and as a member of the California Real Estate Commissioner's Advisory Committee. Highly committed to higher educational standards in his profession, he taught real estate courses in UCLA's extension program and in local adult education programs, and was on the President's Advisory Committee at the University of California.

The realtor's activities have by no means been limited to the real estate field. He was on the development committee at Pasadena's Fuller Theological Seminary and chairman of the Building Committee of the Metropolitan YMCA in Pasadena. Hawkins has been an active member and frequent speaker in the Christian Business Men's Committee, USA, and is a former chairman of the board of trustees of Lake Avenue Congregational Church. He is a member of the board of directors of World Vision International, where he has served for fifteen years.

Preston Hawkins was still in high school when his father put him to work painting some of the firm's offices and performing messenger duties. While in college he worked for a local title company, and began selling houses in Pasadena following his graduation from the University of Southern California in 1973.

Entering Pepperdine University Law School in 1975, Preston Hawkins received his law degree in 1978. While at Pepperdine he also handled the mortgage company's marketing operations. After passing his bar examination in 1978, he joined his father in the administration of the firm and was named president in January 1981. A member of both the California and Federal bar associations, he provides the organizations with sound legal guidance.

Preston Hawkins is also following his father's example of community involvement. He is a member of the Rotary Club of Pasadena, the Caltech Associates, and the University Club of Pasadena. He serves on the boards of directors of the Pasadena Chamber Orchestra, the Harambee Christian Family Center in Pasadena, the board of visitors of Pepperdine University Law School, and the Audit Committee of Wycliff Bible Translators.

His commitment to Pasadena is not only the result of his father's good example, but of his own heritage. He was born and raised in the community, as was his mother, whose own parents had been Pasadenans for many years. Today this third-generation Southern Californian is at the helm of the San Gabriel Valley's largest independent real estate firm, with many clients who represent the third generation of families who have purchased homes from Herbert Hawkins Realty Company, Inc.

Herbert Hawkins recognized the advantages of a centralized operation, a move that he credits for enabling the firm to expand as rapidly as it has. Photo circa 1962

CITY OF PASADENA

It was a significant year in America. In New York Harbor the Statue of Liberty was dedicated; in Columbus, Ohio, the American Federation of Labor was launched; and in Washington, D.C., Grover Cleveland became the first U.S. President to be married in the White House, taking as his bride the daughter of his former law partner.

It was a significant year in Pasadena, California, as well. The state itself was a mere thirty-six years old, the thirty-first of what were then thirty-eight states. Its governor was George Stoneman—elected three years earlier—who was from the unincorporated community of Pasadena, one of eight that comprised the San Gabriel Township.

The year was 1886, and for a majority of the residents in that tiny community there was trouble. As in the famous Meredith Wilson lyrics, it was trouble with "a capital 'T' and that rhymes with 'P' and that stands for 'pool.'" Two years earlier one Jerome Beebe had opened a pool hall in the center of town, to which he soon added a saloon. Attempts to have it closed came to naught, as the residents had no legal standing and were powerless to act.

Incorporation as a city seemed to be the answer, and an application was presented to the Los Angeles County Board of Supervisors. It was approved, and the boundaries drawn, on May 13, 1886. The new city, comprised of 5.114 square miles, was bounded on the west by the Arroyo Seco, on the north by Mountain Street, on the east by a line slightly east of Lake Avenue, and on the south by Columbia Street. Attempts to include Altadena and South Pasadena within the boundaries proved fruitless when those communities demurred.

An election was held on June 7. Of the 229 votes cast, 179 favored incorporation, while 50 were opposed. The official date of incorporation was June 19, and a slate of five trustees was chosen to govern the affairs of the new city. They were H.J. Holmes, the only holdover from the San Gabriel Orange Grove Association, who was named chairman; R.M. Furlong; M.M. Parker; E. Turner; and E.C. Webster.

During those early years city officials lived a rather nomadic existence. The first city hall was established on June 23, 1886, on the second floor of a building at 33 East Colorado Boulevard. Within two months it was moved to Fair Oaks Avenue and Green Street, and five months later to the Carleton Hotel at 25 East Colorado Boulevard. On February 26, 1887, it moved again, to the Central School Building on South Raymond Avenue. A mere eight months old,

The corner of Fair Oaks Avenue and Colorado Boulevard looking north toward the mountains, circa 1928.

Photo of city hall during construction taken immediately after the forms were removed and before the stucco finish was applied. Photo circa 1927

the city government was now in its fourth home.

City hall remained at the South Raymond location for nearly three years, moving to a corner of Fair Oaks Avenue and Union Street in December 1889. It would not leave that intersection for thirty-eight years, although it did move from the northwest corner to the southwest corner in 1893 and then to the northeast corner in 1903 where it remained for nearly a quarter of a century.

As Pasadena grew, changes in the form of its government were also needed. A new charter was adopted in 1900, after suffering defeat five years earlier. It called for a mayor-council system. Fifteen freeholders were elected and Martin W. Weight became the city's first official mayor.

In 1904 the city completed the first of what would be more than seventy-five annexations, bringing North Pasadena within its boundaries, followed in 1906 by East Pasadena. Geographically they were the largest areas Pasadena has ever annexed, more than doubling its size to approximately 11.25 square miles. Nearly fifty years passed before the city doubled again.

A charter amendment brought still another form of government to Pasadena in 1913. A city commission was elected with R.L. Metcalf as chairman. That structure lasted a mere eight years. In 1921—as the city celebrated its thirty-fifth birthday—Pasadena adopted its fourth type of government, calling for a city manager and a board of city directors. It is the basic system that remains in effect today. One change of major significance took place in 1980 that divides the city into seven districts. Each district elects one city director, replacing the citywide elections that had prevailed for almost sixty years.

One of the earliest actions taken by the board of directors was the appointment in 1922 of a City Planning Commission, destined to have a major and immediate impact. The commission drew up a plan that featured a new civic center to be comprised primarily of a new city hall, the public library, and the civic auditorium. In 1923 voters approved a $3.5-million bond issue, and the project was launched.

A competition was held to select a city hall architect. The winning design was submitted by a San Francisco firm, Bakewell and Brown, which had earlier designed the city halls in San Francisco and Berkeley. The city board rejected the firm's first proposal, which featured a bell tower rather than the more traditional dome the directors favored. The final design was influenced by three famous domed structures: the Church of Santa Maria della Salute in Venice, Italy; the Hotel des Invalides in Paris; and St. Paul's Cathedral in London.

A building permit was issued on January 15, 1926, and construction began six days later. The structure, completed in October 1927 and occupied by the city staff on November 11, cost slightly more than $2.3 million. It has served the city and its people well for nearly sixty years and is recognized as one of the nation's most distinctive public buildings.

City officials check the controls on a newly installed semaphore traffic signal in Pasadena's central city. Photo circa 1920

Today the 100-year-old city of Pasadena has approximately 125,000 residents within its twenty-three square miles. Governing a community of this size requires a city staff of about 1,400 and an annual budget of $170 million. Despite its growth Pasadena remains very much as it was described more than a half-century ago by Dr. Edward L. Thorndike of Columbia University. Ranking Pasadena first among 310 U.S. cities with populations of 30,000 or more, Thorndike called it a city where the "general goodness of life is greatest."

Early Pasadena firemen pose in Central Park in front of the Green Hotel (right) and the Doty Block (left).

MIJARES MEXICAN RESTAURANT

Few indeed are the restaurants that can boast of a history spanning more than six decades. Fewer still are those with a founder who has remained active throughout that span.

Fitting this description is Mijares Mexican Restaurant. It was begun in 1920 by a young but already twice-widowed mother of three named Jesucita Mijares. Born in Guadalajara, she was married while in her teens and, shortly thereafter, found herself a widow with an infant daughter. She remarried, and in 1920 came to the United States with her husband and their young son, Joe.

The young couple settled in Pasadena in a home at South Raymond Street and Fillmore Avenue, where a daughter was born to them. While Jesucita was carrying their third child, her husband was fatally shot during a robbery.

Once again tragedy had struck in the life of Jesucita, but it only seemed to make her stronger. She was twenty-seven years old with three little ones to feed, and was determined not to let them down. She began making tortillas in her home at Fair Oaks and Pico. Her fame quickly spread; and before long she was supplying restaurants and grocery stores with her homemade product.

Now almost ninety years of age, Jesucita Mijares resides next door to the restaurant and, with a daily visit, keeps an expert eye on operations.

This home at South Raymond Street and Fillmore Avenue was where Jesucita Mijares began making tortillas to supply to restaurants and grocery stores in the area.

To help make ends meet Jesucita began taking in boarders. One of them was Antonio Mijares, whom she married in 1931. The family, consisting of Jesucita, Antonio, and four children, then moved to 626 South Fair Oaks, where they continued their flourishing tortilla business. There two more children were born, Alice and Hilda.

During World War II Jesucita purchased property at Palmetto Drive and Pasadena Avenue, the former site of a Japanese nursery. In 1949 the Mijares family moved there, continuing their tortilla business and opening a small delicatessen. It would not remain small very long.

Jesucita's skills as a cook, plus the experience she had gained feeding her boarders, stood her in good stead as the little delicatessen soon became a full-fledged restaurant, serving the finest Mexican foods. Rooms and patios were added to accommodate the growing crowds, and all the family members worked there in some ca-

The new Mijares Mexican Restaurant opened in April 1981 at the original site, 626 South Fair Oaks Avenue.

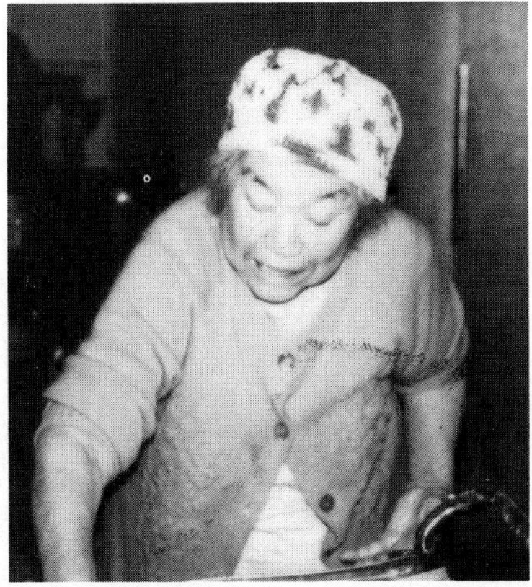

Jesucita Mijares making tamales at the restaurant's old site before the 1979 fire.

pacity. The kitchen, of course, was where Jesucita spent most of her time, preparing the dishes that were bringing fame to Mijares Mexican Restaurant.

By 1979, when the restaurant was thirty years old, Alice Mijares Recendez was running the day-to-day operation, although her mother was on hand every day to prepare her specialties. Then, in December, a fire swept through the restaurant, causing widespread damage estimated at about $45,000. The fire was set by a burglar in an effort to cover his tracks.

The comfortable old patio before the fire in 1979.

As severe a blow as it was, the destruction proved to be no more than a temporary setback for the Mijares family and its indomitable matriarch. The decision to rebuild and reopen the restaurant was made, a process that would take several years. In the interim a search was begun for another location, and in April 1981 a new Mijares Mexican Restaurant opened—at the corner of Washington and Allen. Considerably smaller than the original, it nevertheless provided the now-famous Mexican fare for its many aficionados.

Meanwhile, the rebuilding process went on at 145 Palmetto Drive, and in March 1984 the original Mijares Mexican Restaurant reopened. To the delight of its longtime patrons, the style of the old structure was retained—with its comfortable dining areas, both inside and out. While the basic floor plan remained the same, a number of modern improvements were made and a full-service bar was added.

Another major improvement was an increase in seating capacity from 125 to about 240. The Washington and Allen location has thirty-six seats and does a lot of take-out business. Both restaurants are open seven days a week, serving lunch and dinner.

Alice Mijares Recendez continues to oversee the operations of both restaurants, aided by a staff of about forty, some of whom have been with the business for thirty years or more. A third generation of the family is now involved as well.

And what of Jesucita Mijares, who came to this country as a young widow so long ago? Today, as she nears her ninetieth birthday, she is still going strong. The tragic deaths of her husbands could not stop her. Nor could the fire that swept her restaurant—though it did hospitalize her with smoke inhalation.

Age may have slowed her down a little, but she is still in the restaurant every day, preparing some of her famous specialties and keeping her expert eyes on the chefs. She still lives right next to the restaurant, and her home is always open to the many visitors and old friends who come to call. For Jesucita Mijares, "mi casa es su casa" is more than a motto—it is a way of life.

LAKE AVENUE CONGREGATIONAL CHURCH

The City of Pasadena was a mere nine years old when a small band of women formed the Lake Avenue Union Sunday School. The date was October 27, 1895. Meetings were held in a car barn at Lake Avenue and Orange Grove.

William Waterhouse, the mayor of Pasadena, was one of the earliest members and, with several others, wanted to add a church. He personally donated property at Lake and Maple. On November 25, 1896, the thirty-five charter members of Lake Avenue Congregational Church held their first worship service.

The Reverend Allen Hastings, whose family members still attend the church, was called to become the first pastor, on January 1, 1897. Ill health forced him to resign the following year, and he was succeeded by Stephen G. Emerson. The latter served until 1908, and under his leadership the sanctuary that would later be called the Old Corner Church was built in 1905. Its cost was $14,000, including furnishings.

James H. Lash followed Emerson, and during his first year church members donated $291 to foreign missions. It began a tradition that has grown to more than one million dollars annually. In 1917 Angelo E. Shattuck became Lake Avenue's fourth pastor, serving until 1921.

That year, the church's twenty-fifth anniversary, saw the dawn of a new era—one that the next thirty-eight years would see it develop into a major force for world Christianity. It was the era of James Henry Hutchins. For his first sermon to the 200 members of his flock, he chose the text: "For we preach not ourselves, but Christ Jesus the Lord; and ourselves your servants for Jesus' sake," from St. Paul's Second Epistle to the Corinthians. His thirty-eight years as senior pastor epitomized that philosophy. Under his leadership sixteen Sunday School departments were organized—serving children, youths, and adults. Today nearly 3,000 persons participate in Sunday School classes each week.

The Old Corner Church, 1905.

Service to the community has always had a high priority at Lake Avenue Congregational Church. During Dr. Hutchins' tenure eleven Christian Endeavor societies were formed, helping to bring the message of God's love to the citizens of Pasadena. In 1932, while the Great Depression raged, the three-story Maple Street Educational Building was erected, providing sorely needed classroom space.

Lake Avenue Congregational Church has always maintained close ties with Fuller Theological Seminary. When Dr. Charles E. Fuller founded the seminary in 1947, the facility was housed at the church until its own campus was built in 1953. Many of Fuller's staff and students today have active roles in the Lake Avenue family.

By 1950 the congregation had grown to more than 1,500 members, and the Old Corner Church was bursting at the seams. A building program was launched, and in October 1951 a new sanctuary—seating nearly 1,000 people—was dedicated.

One of the first Women's Fellowship groups gathers in front of the Old Corner Church.

Dr. Hutchins retired in 1958; however, he remained active in the church for another quarter of a century, until his death on March 24, 1984. His successor, Dr. Raymond C. Ortlund, was installed on November 1, 1959. Dr. Ortlund's twenty years of leadership were marked with the continued growth of the church, and before long even the new sanctuary became too small for the congregation. A second service was needed, and then a third. Another large building, to house offices and classrooms, was erected, and named Hutchins Hall. Sunday morning services were broadcast on a local radio station and, via the facilities of the Far East Broadcasting Company, to other parts of the world.

It was under Dr. Ortlund's ministry that the church's traditional three priorities were formalized. Simply stated, they are: Love God; Love the family of God; and Love the world. Those priorities have been expressed in many ways, not only in service to Pasadena but via the hundreds of missionaries who have gone forth from Lake and Maple to "the uttermost parts of the earth."

Dr. Ortlund resigned in 1979; and on January 1, 1981, eighty-four years to the day after calling its first pastor, Lake Avenue Congregational Church welcomed its seventh, Dr. Paul Cedar. His message has been the same as that of his predecessors—the good news of the gospel of Jesus Christ.

In 1984, as membership passed the 3,500 mark, the need for larger facilities became evident if Lake Avenue was to remain faithful to its ministry to the community and to the world. Plans for a major new sanctuary seating 3,000 were drawn, and members pledged more than eleven million dollars to enable the project—which includes classroom and office space, and additional parking facilities—to get under way.

The new facilities will mark the dawn of yet another new era for Lake Avenue Congregational Church. From its modest beginnings nearly a century ago it has grown to become one of the largest churches in America and a major force for Christianity throughout the world. Today, as always, the focus is on people and on service. The new facilities will enable the church to reach its goals for 1990, which include meeting the needs of senior citizens, equipping 1,000 members for effective community ministry, and preparing 100 or more members a year for professional Christian ministry.

Like the city of Pasadena itself, Lake Avenue Congregational Church has a rich history; and the two have often been intertwined. William Waterhouse may have been the first of the community's leaders to worship at Lake Avenue, but countless others have followed in his footsteps. It has been a richly rewarding relationship on both sides, one that seems likely to continue for another century or more.

Currently over 3,000 people each Sunday come to worship the Lord at the Lake Avenue Congregational Church.

An artist's rendering of the new sanctuary, to be completed by early 1988.

PATRONS

The following individuals, companies, and organizations have made a valuable commitment to the quality of this publication. Windsor Publications and the Pasadena Chamber of Commerce gratefully acknowledge their participation in *Pasadena: Crown of the Valley.*

Ambassador College*
Ambassador Foundation*
American Pacific Securities Corporation*
J.H. Biggar Furniture Company*
Mike Brown Grandstands, Inc.*
Brown, Winfield & Canzoneri, Inc.
Burroughs Corporation*
Bushnell, Division of Bausch & Lomb*
Christie, Parker & Hale*
City of Pasadena*
Crowell Design and Construction Company*
Crown Fence and Supply Company*
Datatape Incorporated*
Fedco Membership Department Stores
Hahn & Hahn*
Herbert Hawkins Realty Company, Inc.*
Preston & Carrie Hawkins
Hill Avenue Grace Lutheran Church
Huntington Medical Research Institutes (HMRI)*
Huntington Memorial Hospital*
Huntington Sheraton*
Jacobs Engineering Group Inc.*
Tom Joyce Realty
Kaiser Permanente Medical Care Program*
Lake Avenue Congregational Church*
Las Encinas Hospital*
Licher Direct Mail, Inc.*
Lytle Roofing Company, Inc.*
Jacob Maarse Florist Inc.*
Meguiar's Inc.
Mijares Mexican Restaurant*
Mutual Savings and Loan Association*
The Parsons Corporation
Pasadena Municipal Employees Association
Pasadena Public Library*
Provident Investment Counsel, Inc.*
Georgiana Rodiger Center, Inc.*
See's Candies*
Southern California Gas Company*
Thorson GMC Buick, Inc.
Vroman's*

*Partners in Progress of *Pasadena: Crown of the Valley.* The histories of these companies and organizations appear in Chapter VIII, beginning on page 201.

Bibliography

Only a few of the sources consulted are listed below. Many of them are standard published works available in the Pasadena Public Library, which can serve as a valuable introduction to Pasadena history. More interesting, however, are the many primary sources, manuscripts, clippings, scrapbooks, newspaper and magazine articles, which give a fuller, more immediate, view of Pasadena's history. Most of these are preserved in the Huntington Library in San Marino, in the Pasadena Historical Society Library, and in the Archives of the California Institute of Technology. At the Huntington are the papers of many prominent Pasadenans, including Dr. Thomas Balch Elliott, Jeanne Carr, Theodore Parker Lukens, Grace Nicholson, Charles and Myra Saunders, Clara Burdette, Myron and Virginia Pease Hunt. Caltech's Archives contain papers of scientists associated with the institution, including those of Robert Andrews Millikan, George Ellery Hale and Theodore von Kármán. The Pasadena Historical Society Library holds a number of manuscripts related to early Pasadena history, including lists of the first settlers and first housebuilders, the diary of Thomas Finley Croft, an account by Mary Agnes Crank of early ranch life and one by Marion Parks on the first Pasadena post office and scrapbooks compiled by A.L. Hamilton and by Milton Brenner. Also useful are the annual Tournament of Roses booklets published alternately by the *Pasadena Daily News* and the *Pasadena Star* during the years 1900 to 1920 and *California Southland,* a periodical published in Pasadena from 1918 to 1928. Oral histories collected by the Pasadena Oral History Foundation are available at the Pasadena Public Library and the Historical Society Library. An almost complete file of Pasadena newspapers is maintained on microfilm at the Pasadena Public Library.

General Sources

Arnold, Ralph, and Shoop, C.F., eds. *Pasadena in the Gay Nineties.* Pasadena: A.H. Cawston, 1955.

Carew, Harold D. *History of Pasadena and the San Gabriel Valley.* 3 vols. Chicago: S.J. Clarke, 1930.

Chapin, Lon F. *Thirty Years in Pasadena.* Los Angeles: Southwest Publishing Co., 1929.

Crocker, Donald W. *Within the Vale of Annandale. 3rd ed.* Pasadena: Typecraft, 1975.

Page, Henry Markham. *Pasadena: Its Early Years.* Los Angeles: Lorrin L. Morrison, 1964.

Pineda, Manuel and Perry, C. Caswell. *Pasadena Area History.* Pasadena: Historical Publishing Co., 1972.

Pinney, Joyce Y. *A Pasadena Chronology, 1769-1977.* Pasadena: Pasadena Public Library, 1978.

Reid, Hiram Alvin. *History of Pasadena.* Pasadena: Pasadena History Co., 1895.

Robinson, John W. *The San Gabriels.* San Marino: Golden West Books, 1977.

Wood, J.W. *Pasadena, California. Historical and Personal.* Pasadena: J.W. Wood, 1917.

Chapter One

Bean, Lowell John, and Smith, Charles R. *Handbook of North American Indians.* Vol. 8: *California.* Washington: Smithsonian Institution, 1978.

Buwalda, John. *Geology of the Raymond Basin.* [Pasadena: Pasadena Water Department,] 1940.

Dakin, Susanna Bryant. *A Scotch Paisano in Old Los Angeles: Hugo Reid's Life in California, 1832-1852.* Reprint. Berkeley, Los Angeles, London: University of California Press, 1978.

Johnston, Bernice Eastman. *California's Gabrielino Indians.* Los Angeles: Southwest Museum, 1962.

Rose, L.J. Jr. *L.J. Rose of Sunny Slope, 1827-1899.* San Marino: Huntington Library, 1959.

Weber, Francis J., ed. *The Pride of the Missions: A Documentary History of the San Gabriel Mission.* Los Angeles: Timothy Cardinal Manning, 1979.

Chapter Two

Baur, John E. *The Health Seekers of Southern California, 1870-1900.* San Marino: Huntington Library, 1959.

Elliott, Thomas Balch. *Papers.* Manuscript. Huntington Library, San Marino, California. (This collection contains letters of Daniel M. Berry and a brief history by Elliott of the founding of Pasadena.)

Farnsworth, R.W.C., ed. *A Southern California Paradise.* Pasadena: Farnsworth, 1883.

Garey, Thomas A. *Orange Culture in California. Appendix on Grape Culture by L.J. Rose.* San Francisco: Pacific Rural Press, 1882.

Giddings, Jennie Hollingsworth. *I Can Remember Early Pasadena.* Los Angeles: Lorrin L. Morrison, 1949.

Raitt, Helen and Wayne, Mary Collier, eds. *We Three Came West.* San Diego: Tofua Press, 1974.

Raymond, Arthur E. *A Gentleman of the Old School: Walter Raymond and the Raymond Hotel.* Pasadena: Pasadena Historical Society, 1983.

Rhoades, William Lauren. *The History of the Famous Sierra Madre Villa Hotel.* Typescript. Sherman Library, Corona Del Mar.

Saunders, Charles Francis. *The Story of Carmelita: Its Associations and Its Trees.* Pasadena: A.C. Vroman, [1928.]

Second Annual Citrus Fair of the San Gabriel Valley. [Los Angeles:] Times-Mirror Co. 1885.

Chapter Three

Bridges, Amy T. *Diaries.* 1882, 1886-1887. Manuscript. Huntington Library, San Marino, California.

Carpenter, Thomas D. *Pasadena: Resort Hotels and Paradise.* Pasadena: Castle Green Times, 1984.

Dumke, Glenn S. *The Boom of the Eighties in Southern California.* San Marino: Huntington Library, 1970.

Hendrickson, Joe and Stiles, Maxwell. *The Tournament of Roses: A Pictorial History.* Los Angeles: Brooke House, 1971.

Holder, Charles Frederick. "The Rod and Gun in Southern California," *The Raymond and Its Surroundings.* Boston: n.p., [ca. 1888].

______________. "History of the Tournament of Roses," *Pasadena Daily News.* Tournament of Roses edition [1905].

Seims, Charles. *Mt. Lowe: The Railway in the Clouds.* San Marino: Golden West Books, 1976.

______________. *Trolley Days in Pasadena.* San Marino: Golden West Books, 1982.

Chapter Four

Adams, Walter S. "Early Days at Mt. Wilson," *Publications of the Astronomical Society of the Pacific,* 54 (Oct. 1947), 213-304.

______________. "The Founding of Mt. Wilson Observatory," *Publications of the Astronomical Society of the Pacific,* 66 (Dec. 1954), 266-303.

Andersen, Timothy, et al. *California Design 1910.* Los Angeles: California Design Publications, 1974.

Batchelder, Alice Coleman. *Coleman Chamber Concerts 1904-1944.* Pasadena: Coleman Chamber Music Association, 1945.

Book of the Crown City and Its Tournament of Roses. Pasadena: Pasadena Daily News, 1907.

Buwalda, Imra. "The Roots of the California Institute of Technology," *Engineering and Science,* (Oct-Dec. 1966).

Cartland, Earl F. *Study of Negroes Living in Pasadena.* Master's thesis, Whittier College, 1948.

Decker, Donald M. and Mary L. *Reflections on Elegance: Pasadena's Huntington Hotel Since 1906.* Laguna Niguel: Royal Literary Publications, 1984.

Gaut, Helen Lukens Jones. "Description of Pasadena Sewer Farm," *Annual Report of the Auditor 1904-1905.* Pasadena: City of Pasadena, 1905.

Light and Power Utility: History and Worth. Pasadena: 1969. Pasadena Municipal Light and Power Department.

Makinson, Randell L. *Greene and Greene.* 2 vols. Salt Lake City and Santa Barbara: Peregrine Smith, 1977, 1979.

Wight, Peter B. "Bungalow Courts in California," *Western Architect,* 28 (Feb. 1919) 16-24.

______________. "California Bungalows," *Western Architect,* 27 (Oct, 1918) 92-99.

Winter, Robert. *The California Bungalow.* Los Angeles: Hennessey and Ingalls, 1980.

Chapter Five

Damon, George. *Some Preliminary Suggestions for a "Pasadena Plan."* Pasadena: Woman's Civic League, 1915.

Dobyns, Winifred Starr. *California Gardens.* New York: MacMillan, 1931.

Eighty-One Years of Public Education in Pasadena. Superintendent's Annual Report. Pasadena City Schools, June 1955.

Green, Harriet L. *Gilmor Brown. Portrait of a Man—and an Idea.* Pasadena: Burns Printing Co., 1933.

MacGowan, Kenneth. *Footlights Across America. Towards a National Theater.* New York: Harcourt, Brace and Co., 1929.

Muntz, Jan Furey. "The Rose Bowl," *Myron Hunt, 1868-1952. The Search for a Regional Architecture.* Santa Monica: Hennessey and Ingalls, 1984.

White, Leonard D. "C. Wellington Koiner, Manager of Pasadena," *The City Manager.* New York: Greenwood Press, 1927.

Wright, Helen. *Explorer of the Universe: A Biography of George Ellery Hale.* New York: E.P. Dutton, 1966.

Chapter Six

Brienes, Marvin, "Smog Comes to Los Angeles," *Southern California Quarterly,* 58 (Winter 1976) 515-532.

Cottrell, Edwin A. *Pasadena Social Agencies Survey.* Pasadena, 1940.

Goodstein, Judith. "Science and Caltech in the Turbulent Thirties," *California History,* 60 (1981) 229-243.

Hoffman, Abraham, "Angeles Crest: The Creation of a Forest Highway System in the San Gabriel Mountains," *Southern California Quarterly,* 50 (Sept. 1968), pp. 309-345.

Koppes, Clayton R. *JPL and the American Space Program.* New Haven: Yale Univ. Press, 1982.

Mayo, Morrow. "Croesus at Home," *The American Mercury.* 27 (Oct. 1932) 106, pp. 230-236.

Thorndike, Ralph. *Your City.* New York: Harcourt, Brace, 1939.

Chapter Seven

Chronology of Urban Renewal in Pasadena. Pasadena: Community Redevelopment Agency, 1965.

Coplans, John. "Diary of a Disaster," *Artforum.* (Feb. 1975) 28-46.

Development Fact Sheets. Pasadena: Pasadena Redevelopment Agency, 1980.

Hulburd, David. *This Happened in Pasadena.* New York: Macmillan, 1951.

Oliver, Robert W. *An Economic Survey of the City of Pasadena.* (Pasadena:) Stanford Research Institute, 1959.

Schaffer, Paul A. "Pasadena Establishes an R-R Zone," *American City.* (April 1960) 103.

"The Best-Read City in the U.S.A.: Pasadena," *McCall's* 90 (April 1963) 40, 181.

Townsend, Dorothy. "Pasadena's Crown City Image Tarnished," *Los Angeles Times.* April 29, 1969.

INDEX

PARTNERS IN PROGRESS INDEX

Ambassador College, 234-235
Ambassador Foundation, 236-237
American Pacific Securities Corporation, 226-227
Biggar Furniture Company, J.H., 214-215
Brown Grandstands, Inc., Mike, 256-257
Burroughs Corporation, 260-261
Bushnell, Division of Bausch & Lomb, 250-251
Christie, Parker & Hale, 254-255
City of Pasadena, 268-269
Crowell Design and Construction Company, 230-231
Crown Fence and Supply Company, 204-205
Datatape Incorporated, 218-221
Hahn & Hahn, 216-217
Hawkins Realty Company, Inc., Herbert, 266-267
Huntington Medical Research Institutes (HMRI), 242-243
Huntington Memorial Hospital, 208-211
Huntington Sheraton, 222-223
Jacobs Engineering Group Inc., 258-259
Kaiser Permanente Medical Care Program, 232-233
Lake Avenue Congregational Church, 272-273
Las Encinas Hospital, 238-241
Licher Direct Mail, Inc., 206-207
Lytle Roofing Company, Inc., 248-249
Maarse Florist Inc., Jacob, 252-253
Mijares Mexican Restaurant, 270-271
Mutual Savings and Loan Association, 212-213
Pasadena Chamber of Commerce and Civic Association, 202
Pasadena Public Library, 228-229
Provident Investment Counsel, Inc., 203
Rodiger Center, Inc., Georgiana, 246-247
See's Candies, 262-265
Southern California Gas Company, 244-245
Vroman's, 224-225

GENERAL INDEX
Italicized numbers indicate illustrations.

Acuranga, 14, 20
Adams, Charles Gibbs, *116,* 154
Adams, Mary, *116*
Adams, Walter S., 114
Addams Hull House, Jane, 99
African Methodist Episcopal congregation, 40, 97, 98
Aleupkinga, 14
Alexander, J. Turner, 179
Allen, Robert S., 157
Almonds, 34, 37
Alpine Tavern, 87, *89*
Alps of America, 89
Alter Memorial Association, Edna P., 99
Amateur Athletic Union, 149
Ambassador Auditorium, 177, *188*
Ambassador College, 177, 188
American Legion, 136
Anaheim, 26
Anderson, Carl D., 164, *176,* 176
Anderson, Hugh, 168
Andrews, Dana, 172
Angeles Crest Highway, 163
Angeles Forest Highway, 163
Annual Report of the Pasadena Public Schools, 66
Aoki, T., 167
Apricot growing, 34
Architects, 150, 151
Armstrong, Alfred C., 89
Arroyo culture, 120, 186
Arroyo Park Committee, 106
Arroyo Seco, 10, *11,* 14, 21, 22, 48, *117, 186,* 198
Arroyo Seco Parkway, 160, *161,* 168
Arroyo Vista Guest House, 70
Art Loan Exhibition, 42, 93, 98
Associated Charities, 99
Atchison, Topeka and Santa Fe Railroad, 58
Automobile Club of Southern California, 119, 163
Automobiling, 116, *116*

Baker, John, 32, 38
Bakewell and Brown, 136
Baldwin, E.J., "Lucky," 10, 20, *45,* 46, 119, 192
Baldwin, Mrs. Anita, 119
Baldwin, Roger, 156
Ball, Benjamin F., 49, 50
Banbury, Jessie, 31
Banbury, Thomas, 70
Bandini, Arturo, 49, *49,* 99
Bandini, Helen Elliott, *49,* 113
Bandini, Ralph, *49,* 99
Bangs, Emma C., 70
Baptists, 40
Barker, George H., 127
Barthé, Richmond, *177*
Bashford, Katherine, 153
Batchelder, Ernest, 110, *110,* 113, 120, 139, 172
Batchelder Music Collection, Alice Coleman, 173
Baur, John, 43, 45
Beadle, George W., *176,* 176
Beautification, 67, 104
Beechnuts, 37
Bennett, Parsons and Frost, 135
Berry, Daniel M., 26, 27, *27,* 28,

29, 32, 44
Berry, Fred, 26
Better Government League, 157
Bischoff, Franz, 120
Black community, 97, *97,* 98, *142,* 177, 179, 180
Blacker, Robert R., 116, 127
Blinn, Edmund, 127
Board of Trade, 68, 69, 96, 134, 163
Bohr, Niels, 164
Boom of the Eighties in Southern California, The, 59
Boosting Committee, 135
Bootlegging, *145,* 146
Bowen Court, *123,* 123
Brenner, Milton, 157
Bresee, Phineas, 110
Bridge, Norman, 116
Bridges, Amy, 53, 59, 61, 64, 67, 70
Bristol, Albert O., 28, 32
Brooks, Mrs. E.W., 107
Brooks, Noah, 114
Brookside Park, 102, *107,* 160
Brookside Plunge, 98
Brown, Benjamin Chambers, 120
Brown, Gilmor, 139, *140,* 141
Brown, Jason, 48, *48*
Brown, John, 43, 48
Brown, Owen, 48, *48*
Browning, Robert, 113
Browning Club, 113
Brown Trail, 48
Brown vs. Board of Education, 179
Building boom, 63, 64
Building Department, 173
Bullock's, 168
Bundy, May Sutton, 129
Bungalowland, *128*
Burdette, Clara, 126, 133
Burdette, Robert, 126
Burnham, Daniel, 133, 135
Busch, Adolphus, 95, 96, 104, 106, 124, 125
Busch, Mrs. Adolphus, *105*
Busch Gardens, *94,* 104, 106, 144
Butternuts, 37

Cabrillo, Juan Rodriguez, 12, 14
Calder, Alexander Stirling, 120
California Colony of Indiana, 26, 31
California Craftsman bungalow, *122*
California Fair Employment Practice Commission, 179
California for Health, Pleasure and Residence, 26
California Institute of Technology, 40, *80,* 164, *165,* 165, 166, 167, 173, *198*
California-Panama Exposition, 133
California State Federation of Colored Women's Clubs, 177
Cambell-Johnston family, 50
Campfire Girls, 180
Camping, 46, 48, *49*
Canneries, 54
Carmelita, 35, *35,* 37, 42
Carmelita Park, 145
Carnegie, Andrew, 134
Carpenter, Thomas D., 69
Carr, Ezra, *34,*, 35, 37
Carr, Jeanne, *34,* 35, 37, 42, 67, 68, 124
Carr, William J., 104, 168
Carradine, John, 172
Casa Propia, 31
Castle Green, *184*
Catholic church, 109
Central Park, 101, *101*
Central School, *38, 56*
Chamber of Commerce, 133, 163, 168, 174
Chambers, Harold C., 144
Channing, William, 127
Channing family, *85*
Charleville, John W., 157
Cherry growing, 34
Chestnuts, 37
Chihuahuaita, 99
Chinese American Vegetable Cooperative, 99
Chinese laborers, 34, 57, 58
Chinese settlers, 97, 98, 99
Christian Scientists, 109
Churches, 50, *65,* 97, 109, 136, 168, *193*
Church of the Angels, 50, *193*
Citrus Fair, 40-42
City Beautiful movement, 130, 133, 134
City Hall, *79,* 101, *118,* 134, 136, *184, 199*
Civic Auditorium, *17*
Civic Betterment Survey, 169
Civic Center, *78, 130,* 134, 135, 136, 137, *137,* 144, 176, *195*
Civil War, 98
Clapp, Jennie, *38,* 40
Clapp, William, 28, 40
Clark, Alson, 112
Clark, Stephen Cutter, 149
Clarke, Clinton, 172
Classical School for Boys, 149
Cleveland School, 180
Clune's Theatre, 110
Coate, Roland, 151
Cobb, Lee J., 172
Cogswell, William F., 43, 46
Cogswell, William G., 46
Coleman, Alice, 110, *110*
Coleman Chamber Music Association, 110, 177
Collier, Jennie, 42, 44, *51, 103*
Colorado Boulevard, *195*
Colorado River Aqueduct, 146
Colorado Street, *154*
Colorado Street Bridge, *116,* 117, *185, 186, 187*
Columbia Hill school, 40

Columbia Hill Tennis Club, 84
Comanche Indians, 11
Community Redevelopment Agency, 174, 181
Conference Center, 181
Congar, Orville H., 35, 37
Coolidge, D.W., 96
Corbitt, William, 20
Cornell, Joseph, 176
Cornell, Ralph, 144
Corruption, 156
Cottrell, Edwin, 156
Council, Lucille, 153
Country clubs, 148
Craftsmen, 120
Craig, James, 23
Crane, Richard T., 71, 85
Crank, F. DeW., 31
Crank, James F., 46, 54, 57
Craftsman, The, 120
Cravens, John S., 126
Croft, Thomas, 28, 29, 31, 32
Cruzado, Antonio, 10, 14
Cub Scouts, 180
Culbertson, James, 112
Cultural Festival, *196*
Curlett, Eisen, and Cuthbertson, *63*

Damon, George, 133, 134
Daniels, Gertrude Potter, 114
Davis, William Heath, 20
Dawson, Robert, 157
Defender's Parkway, 144
Delbruck, Max, *176*
Deppe, Ferdinand, *14-15*
Depression, 156, 160, 163
Devil's Gate, 10, 29
Dewey, John, 90, 92
Dibblee, Albert, 20
Dickinson, Emma, 144
Dirac, Paul, 164
Disciples of Christ, 40
Downtown, *181*
Drama League, 139
Draves, Victoria, 169
Dumke, Glenn, 59
Dunbar Hospital, 177
Durand, Henry Calvin, 90, 124, 125

Earley, Thomas, 102
Easton, Louis B., 121, 122
Eaton, Benjamin S., 21, 23, 28, 40
Echo Mountain House, 87, 88
Echo Mountains, 86
Edison Electric Company, 102, 104
Education, *38, 39,* 40, 56, 59, *60, 66,* 66, 67, *80,* 90, *91,* 92, 99, 101, *108,* 108, 109, 110, 114, 149, 165, 166, 167, 173, 177, 180, 181, 188, *198*
Einstein, Albert, *164,* 164
El Centro De Acción Social, 181
El Molino Viejo, 10, 18, *22*
Electricity, 102, 103, 104
Eliot, Charles W., *86*
Elliott, Agnes, *49*
Elliott, Helen, 99
Elliott, Mrs. Thomas Balch, *49*
Elliott, Thomas Balch, 25, 26, *27,* 27, 28, 31, 32, 99, 114
Elliott, Whittier, *49*
Employment Bureau, 158
Episcopalians, 40

Fair Oaks, 23
Fair Oaks Businessmen's Association, 174
Fair Oaks Ranch, 98
Farland, J.L., 84
Farrand, Beatrix, 153
Farwell, Arthur, 110
Fenyes, Adalbert, *124-125,* 127
Feynes, Eva, *124, 125,* 127
Feynman, Richard, *176,* 176
Fig growing, 34
Filberts, 37
Fire department, 64, 65
First Baptist Church, 136
First Church of Christ Scientists, 109
Fleming, Arthur, 112, 114, 116, *121,* 126, 134, 145, 164
Fletcher, Calvin, 31, 32
Flintridge Riding Academy, 148
Font, Pedro, 14, 15
Football, 144
Foothill Freeway, 174
Forman, Deward S., 166, *168*
Fowler, William A., 176
Fraser, Robert J., 106
Fremont School, 99, 180
French, Stuart, 144
Friends Meetings, 109
Friendship Baptist Church, 97
Friends of the American Way, 167, 168
Fruit trees, 20
Fulton, Robert, 157
Furlong, R.M., 58

Gabrielino Indians, *11,* 11, *12,* 12, 13, 14, 16, *17,* 18
Gamble House, 128, *192-193*
Gardner, Halbert P., 157
Garfias, Manuel, 21
Garfield, Mrs. James A., 119, 126
Garfield School, 67, 99, 180
Garner, George, 177
Gartz, Kate Crane, 112, 153, 156
Gaut, Helen Lukens, 113
Gell-Mann, Murray, *176,* 176
Giddings, Eugene, 48
Giddings, Jennie Hollingsworth, 40, 46, 47, 48
Gill, Irving, 153
Glaser, Donald, 176
Golf, 84, *85*
Goodhue, Bertram, 80, 153
Goslin, Willard, 173
Government, 132
Graham, Margaret Collier, 42, 44,

51, 103
Graham, Martha, 172
Grant, Ulysses S., 43, 46
Grape growing, 37
Green, George G., 71, 89
Green, Lewis M., 71
Green, Perry M., 32, 42
Greene, Charles Sumner, 121, 127
Greene, Henry Mather, 121, 127
Green Hotel, 71, *72,* 72, *73, 77, 85, 92,* 110, 128, 129, 148, 160
Grey, Elmer, 114
Griffin, Edna, 179
Griffin, John S., 21, 23, 28
Grinnell, Elizabeth, 113
Grogan, Alexander, 23
Grogan Tract, 23
Guggenheim Aeronautics Laboratory, 166
Guillén, Eulalia Pérez de, 19
Gutenberg, Beno, *165,* 165

Hale, George Ellery, 112, *113,* 114, *115,* 116, 134, 135, 139, 165, 172
Halfway House, 47
Hall, Peter, 157
Hall of Justice, 136
Hamilton, Arthur L., 157, 161
Harbert, Elizabeth Boynton, 114
Harkness, Lamon Vandenburg, 124
Harris, Roy, 110
Harrison, Benjamin, 72
Harrison, William, 177
Hastings, Charles C., 40
Hastings, Charles Houston, 37
Hastings Ranch, 37, 173
Hayes, Rutherford B., 72
Health Seekers, The, 43
Heckman, Jo, *180,* 184
Heineman, Alfred, 104, 121, 122
Heineman, Arthur, 121, 122
Hertrich, William, 128
Hickory nuts, 37
Hicks, Corinne Bush, 177
Highlands of Pasadena, The, 71
Hill, Raymond, 49
Hillier, Edward B., 157
Hillmont, 191
Hilton Hotel, 181
Hiney, Harlan, 77
Hispanic population, 97, 99, 180, 181
Hispanic Society, 99
History of Pasadena, 49, 62
History of the San Gabriel Orange Grove Association, 26
Hokan tribe, 11
Holden, Charles, 40
Holden, William, 172
Holder, Charles Frederick, 43, *43,* 71, 81, 96, 112, 113, 122
Hollingsworth, L.D., 40
Holmes, Henry J., 58, *115*
Holmes, Joseph, 97
Home Owner's Protective Endeavor, 174
Hopi Indians, 11
Hopkins, Caspar T., 49
Hopkins, Mark, 46
Hopkins, Una Nixon, 113
Horse-car trolley lines, 65
Hotel Fairmont, 148
Hotel Green, 71, *72,* 72, *73, 77, 85, 92,* 110, 128, 129, 148, 160
Hotel Huntington, 117, 128, 129, *148,* 148, 160, 173
Hotel Maryland, 128, *129,* 129, 148, 160
Hotel Raymond, 52, *59,* 70, 71, 99, 128, 129, *147,* 160
Hotels, 71, *72,* 72, *73, 77, 85, 92,* 110, 128, 129, 148, 149, 160, 181
Hunt, Mrs. Myron, 119
Hunt, Myron, 114, 128, 129, 136, 144, 153, 157, 158
Hunt, O.D., 143
Hunt, Virginia, 157
Hunt and Grey, 153
Hunting, 48, 49
Huntington, Arabella, *135*
Huntington, Collis P., 46
Huntington, Henry E., 65, 112, 127, 128, 134, *135*
Huntington Hospital, 173
Huntington Hotel, 117, 128, 129, *148,* 148, 160, 173
Huntington Institute of Applied Medical Research, 173
Huntington Library and Art Gallery, 10, 134, *198*
Huntington Memorial Hospital, 173
Huntington-Sheraton Hotel, *194*
Hurlbut, Edwin F., 31, 124
Hutton, A.W., 28

Incorporation, 58
Indiana Colony, 40
Indian revolt, 16

Jackson, Fred W., 157
Jackson, Helen Hunt, 35, 42, 43
James, George Wharton, 76, 112, *113*
Japanese citizens, 97, 167, 168
Japanese Union Church, 168
Jawlensky, Alexander, 172
Jeffers, Robinson, 112
Jet Propulsion Laboratory, 169, 173, *198*
Johnson, Joseph, 112, 127
Johnson, Reginald, 151
Johnston, Mrs. Albert Sidney, 23
Jory, Victor, 172
Judson, William Lees, 120

Kaufmann, Gordon, 152
Kaufmann's Athenaeum, Gordon, *150*
Kawai, Toichiro, 167
Kee, Yuen, 40

Kee's laundry, Yuen, 98
Kellogg Laboratory, 166, 167
Kewen, Edward J.C., 22
Kimball, Nathan, 26
Kinneloa, *36,* 37, 46
Kinney, Abbot, *33, 36,* 37, 40, 43, 46
Kitson, Ruggles, 189
Klee, Paul, 172
Koiner, C. Wellington, 103, 133, 134, 157, 158, 169
Kuranaga, F.T., 167

La Casita del Arroyo, 158, *158*
La Miniatura, 153
La Pintoresca Hotel, 144
Lacy Park, 10
Lake Vineyard, 22
Lake Vineyard Ranch, 84
Lake Vineyard Water Company, 101
Lamanda Park, 21
Lauritsen, Charles C., 165, 167
Lawn Bowling, *146*
Lazarus Laughed, 139
Lee, George E., 157
Lee, Sammy, 169
Legge, Charles, 93
Leighton, Frank, 79
Leupp, Francis, 114
L'Hermitage ranch, 23
Liberty Loans, 19
Library, 42, 93, 134, 172, 173, *189*
Library Association, 93
Library Park, 101, *189*
Lichtenstein, Roy, 176
Lime growing, 37
Linda Vista, 10, 50
Linnard, Daniel Moore, 128, 160
Lippincott, J.B., 102
Lipscomb, William N., 176
Liquor regulation, 58, 59
Literary figures, 112
Literary Society, 42
Littlefield, J.H., 70
Little Switzerland, 128
Live Oak Park, 32
Locke, Mrs. R.C., 44
Long Beach earthquake, 189
Long Beach Freeway, 174
Los Angeles and San Gabriel Valley Railroad, 54, *56,* 56, 57, *57*
Los Angeles Basin, 11
Los Angeles House, 54, *55*
Los Angeles Music Center, 177
Los Robles Ranch, 72
Lowe, Thaddeus Sobieski Constantine, 76, 86, *86,* 87, *87,* 88, 89, *89,* 90, 92, 93
Ludwigshafen, 168
Lukens, Theodore Parker, 62, *64*
Lukens House, Theodore P., *192*
Lummis, Charles F., 85, 113
Lutes, John, 157

MacArthur, Douglas, 159
McGroarty's Easter Pageant, 148
McKinley School, 149
McMillan, Edward D., 176
McMurray, Donald, 152
McNally, Andrew, 89
Macomber, A. Kingsley, 127
Macpherson, David J., 86
Maher, George Washington, 127
Malina, Frank J., 166, *168*
Mann Building, Horace, *108*
Mannheim, Jean, 112, 120
Mariné, Juan, 19, 21
Markham, Henry H., *62,*, 93
Marston, Sylvanus, 121, 151
Masonic Temple Block, *61*
Matthews, J.M., 72
Mature, Victor, *141*
Maude, Frederick Hamer, *16, 29, 68*
Mayo, Morrow, 156
Memorial Park, *196*
Mercereau, John Drake, 117
Merriam, Frank, 160
Merritt, Hulett C., 90
Methodist congregation, 97
Mexican-American War, 23
Mexican laborers, 34
Mexican Revolution, 99
Micheltorena, Manuel, 21
Midwick Country Club, 84, *146,* 149
Millard, Alice, 153
Millikan, Clark, *166*
Millikan, Robert, 116, 164, 167, 172
Millionaires' Row, *90,* 96, 124, 126
Mische, Emil T., 106
Mission San Carlos Borromeo, 16
Mission San Gabriel, 16, 17, 18, 19, 20
Mission San Juan Capistrano, 18
Monk, Henry G., 23, 49
Monk Hill, 10, 23
Monk Hill School, 66
Morgan, Julia, 135
Morgan, Thomas Hunt, 165
Morris, William, 92, 120
Morrison, Fannie, 139
Morris Orchestra, *142*
Mossbauer, Rudolph, 176
Motherwell, Robert, 176
Mount Lowe Railway, *76, 77,* 84, 86, *88,* 129
Mount Lowe: The Railway in the Clouds, 86
Mount Wilson, 86
Mount Wilson Observatory, 28, 114, *115,* 134, 164
Muir, John, 35, 37, 42, 46, 48
Muir Junior High School, John, 108, *108*
Municipal Golf Course, 102, 144
Municipal Light Department, 133, 136, 139
Muscat, 28
Museums, 176

Musical organizations, 110, *111*

National Aeronautics and Space Administration, 173, 198
National Association for the Advancement of Colored People, 98
National Federation of Women's Clubs, 126
National Old Trails Route, 117, 119
National Women's Basketball, 149
Nay, Edward O., 157
Nectarine growing, 34
Neff, Wallace, 150, 151
Negro Tax Payers' and Voters' Association, 98
Nelson, William, *97*
Nicholson Building, Grace, 152, *152,* 177
Nicholson's gallery of Oriental art, Grace, 137, 139
Nobel Peace Prize, 176
Nordhoff, Charles, 26
North Pasadena Water Company, 102
Noyes, Amos, 116

Oak Knoll, 127
Oldenburg, Claes, 176
Old Pasadena, *195*
Oliver, Robert H., 171, 174
Olivewood Tract, 49
Olson, Culbert L., 161, *161*
Olympic Games, 158, 169, 177, 184
O'Neill, Eugene, 139
Opera House, *92,* 93
Operation Junkyard, 173
Oppenheimer, J. Robert, 164
Orange Grove Avenue, *29, 30, 31,* 90, 156, 172
Orange growing, 20, 28, 33, *33,* 34
Orange Tournament, 81
Orbison, Robert V., 143, 156, 157
Orton, Anna B., 39
Orton School, 149
Orton's Classical School for Girls, Miss, *39*
Ota, K., 167
Our Lady of Guadalupe church, 99
Outdoor Art Association, 133
Owen, Robert, 97
Owens, Jesse, 177

Pacific-Asia Museum, 177, *179*
Pacific Electric Railway, 65, *162, 163*
Pacific Telephone Building, 181
Page, Henry Markham, 64, 81
Painter, John H., 49, 50
Painter, John J., 71
Painter Hotel, 71, 84
Panama-Pacific Exposition, 133
Parent-Teacher Association, 133
Park, Eleanor, 172
Parker, M.M., 40, 58, 90
Parker Dam, 146
Parkes, T.W., 88
Parks, 101, *101*
Parsons, John W., 166, *168*
Parsons, Ralph M., 181
Pasadena Academy, 90
Pasadena Art Institute, 139, 152, 172
Pasadena Art Museum 176, 177
Pasadena Association, 157
Pasadena Athletic and Country Club, 148
Pasadena Athletic Club, 158, *159*
Pasadena Block-Aid Committee, 157, 158
Pasadena Centennial, *199*
Pasadena Chronicle, 54
Pasadena City College, 181
Pasadena City College Band, *197*
Pasadena Civic Auditorium, 102
Pasadena College, 110
Pasadena Colony, 42
Pasadena Community Playhouse, 139, *141*
Pasadena Council of Women's Clubs, 169
Pasadena Country Club, 84, 127
Pasadena Daily News, 96
Pasadena Fire Department Orchestra, *159*
Pasadena Garden Club, 106, 158, *158*
Pasadena Hall, 114
Pasadena Heritage, *195*
Pasadena High School, *66,* 67, 108, *108,* 149, 173
Pasadena House, 54, 55
Pasadena: Its Early Years, 64
Pasadena Junior Chamber of Commerce, 163
Pasadena Junior Philharmonic Committee, 189
Pasadena Labor News, 157
Pasadena Lawn Bowling Club, 147
Pasadena Manufacturing Company, 54
Pasadena Music and Art Association, 112
Pasadena Pioneer Society, *103*
Pasadena Playhouse, 110, 172, 177
Pasadena Preferred, 168
Pasadena Presbyterian Church, *65*
Pasadena Preventorium, 158
Pasadena Promotion Board, 96
Pasadena Public Library, 108, 109, *109,* 173
Pasadena Realty Board, 62, 133
Pasadena Redevelopment Agency, 181
Pasadena: Resort Hotels and Paradise, 69
Pasadena Settlement House, 99

Pasadena Star-News, 84, 156
Pasadena Symphony Orchestra, 177
Pasadena Unified School District, 179
Pasadena Vocational School, 149
Pasadena Water Company, 101
Pasadena Water Department, 102
Patton, George S., 112
Pauling, Linus, 176
Payne, Theodore, 144
Peach growing, 34
Pear growing, 34
Pecans, 37
Peck, George, 114
Peebles, Sylvia, 179
Pérez, José, 21
Perkins, Charlotte, 85
Perkins, Gilbert E., 127
Perkins and Stern, 20
Phillips, James, 177
Pine Canyon Dam, 145
Pioneer Bridge, *169*
Place, James, 64
Planning Commission, 135
Playhouse Association, 139, 172
Playhouse School, 139, *140,* 172
Plaza Pasadena, *17, 195*
Plum growing, 34
Polk, Willis, 131, 135
Pollution, 163
Polytechnic School, 149
Pomological Society, 42
Population growth, 96, 132, 172
Porter, A.O., 32
Post Office, 137
Poynton, Dorothy, 158, *159*
Presbyterians, 109
Prince, William, 98
Prisk, Charles, 156
Prohibition, *145*
Proposition 14, 174
Prospect Mount, 23
Prospect Park, *127,* 153
Prune growing, 34
Public Works Administration, 158
Pullman, George M., 127
Pullman, Mrs. George, *147*

Racial incidents, 57, 58, 98
Rainwater, Leo James, 176
Rancho San Pasqual, 19, 21, 22, 23
Rancho Santa Anita, 19
Raymond, Emmons, 59, 70
Raymond, Walter, 49, 69, *147*
Raymond and Whitcomb Travel Agents, 46, 52
Raymond Avenue school, 99
Raymond basin, 10
Raymond dike, *10,* 14, 20, 22
Raymond Hill, 10, 161
Raymond Hotel, *52,* 59, 70, 71, 99, 128, 129, *147,* 160
Real estate boom, 54
Real Estate Exchanges, 62
Recreational programs, 180
Redevelopment, *175*
Reed, McClellan, 157
Reeds, Simeon G., 124
Reid, Hiram, 48-49, 62
Reid, Hugo, 18, 19, 20, 23, 45, *193*
Reid, Victoria, 19, 20, *193*
Religion, 40, 50, 90, 97, 98, 109, 136
Reservoir, The, 42
Residences, 124-129
Resorts, 54
Reyes, Stephen, 180, 181
Rhoades, William Porter, 46
Richter, Charles F., *165,* 165
Ridgway, Hamilton (Harry), 54, 55, 62, 93, 191
Ripley, Clinton B., 54, 55
Robinson, John W., 48, 125
Robinson, Charles Mulford, 133
Robinson, Jackie, 179
Robinson, Mack, 177, 179
Robinson Park, Jackie, *196*
Rockefeller Foundation, 165
Roehrig, Frederick L., 71, 121, 124
Roosevelt, Franklin Delano, 158, 160
Roosevelt, Theodore, 106, *106*
Rose, Guy, 112, 120
Rose, Leonard J., *19,* 20, 23, 26, 120
Rose, Leonard, Jr., 20
Rose Bowl, 160
Rosemeade ranch, 21
Rosenbaum, Moritz, 40
Rose Parade, *143,* 197
Rose's Sunny Slope Brandy, 20
ROTC, 119
Rowland, Francis F., 43, 81
Royal Raymond, *52,* 54, 70
Ruskin, John, 92
Russ, Nellie, 108, 109, *109*

St. Andrews Church, 109
San Bernardino, 26, 27
Sánchez, José, 18
San Gabriel Mission, 10, 11, *13,* 14, 17, 19, 20, 46
San Gabriel Mission church, *16*
San Gabriel Mountains, 48
San Gabriel Orange Grove Association, 28, *30,* 31
San Gabriels, The, 48
San Gabriel Valley, *8,* 10, 27, 33, 46
San Pasqual Ranch, 10, 21, 22, 23, 28, 35
San Rafael hills, 10
San Rafael Ranch, 50, 84
Santa Anita Race Track, 167
Santa Anita Ranch, 19, 20, 23, 26, *45*
Santa Fe Railroad, 59
Saunders, Charles and Mary Channing, 85
Savoy Theater, 139
Scandal, 156

Scherer, James A.B., 112, 114, 116, 119
Scheyer, Galka, 172
Scott, Randolph, 172
Scott, Reuben, 98
Scoville, C.B., 112
Sears, Fred, 67
Segregation, 98
Seims, Charles, 86
Sepulveda, Enrique, 21
Serra, Junipero, 14
Serra, Richard, 176
Settlement House Association, 181
Shakespeare Club, 112, 133
SHARES, 168
Sheraton Corporation, 173
Shimanouchi, Y., 167
Shockley, William, 176
Shorb, J. De Barth, 22, 28
Shorb's winery, 46
Showcase House, *189*
Siemer, Chris, 187
Sierra Madre College, 40
Sierra Madre Villa, 43, 46, 70
Sierra Madre Villa Hotel, 21, 43, *44,* 98
Silk culture, 37
Simon, Norton, 177
Simon Museum of Art, Norton, 177, *178*
Sinclair, Upton, 112, 156, 160
Sisitcanongna, 14
Smith, Apollo M.O., 166, *168*
Smith, George, *41*
Smith, Kristina Kaye, 180
Snowball, McDougall, 84
Society of Friends, 40
Sommerfeld, Arnold, 164
Southern California Gas Company, 137
Southern Pacific Railroad, 56
South Fair Oaks Avenue, *41*
South Marengo Avenue, *78*
South Orange Grove Association, 172
Southwest Protective and Improvement Association, 172
Spangler, et al vs. Board of Education, 179
Spanish exploration, 12, 14
Spanish heritage, *142*
Sperry, Roger W., 176
Sphinx Ranch, 98
Staats, William R., *115,* 127
Staats House, *151,* 152
Stafford, E.H., 84
Stanford Research Institute, 173
Stanton, Sally, 161, *161*
State Employment Relief Commission, 158
Stetson, Charles Walter, 34, 85, 93
Stevens, Frank D., 58
Stewart, Albert, 157
Stickley, Gustav, 120
Stickney, Susan, 112
Stickney Memorial School of Fine Arts, 112, *112*
Stimson, George, 126
Strain's Camp, *47*
Street, Arthur Edmond, 50
Street of a Thousand Palms, *154*
Street widening, *138,* 139
Stuart, W.C., 124
Sunnycrest, 126
Sunny Slope Vineyard, *19,* 20, 21, 26, 33, 46
Switzer, Perry, 48
Switzer's Camp, 163
Switzer's Falls, 48
Sylvan Square, 32

Taft, William Howard, *94*
Takei, Esther, 168
Temin, Howard M., 176
Tennis, 81, 84, *85*
Thiene, Paul, 153
Thompson-Glickman, Loretta, 179, *180,* 184
Thorndike, Ralph, 156
Throop, Amos G., 90, *91,* 92
Throop College of Technology, 116, 119
Throop Hall, 80, *120*
Throop Memorial Universalist Church, 90
Throop Polytechnic Institute, 28, 90, *91,* 92, 114, 115
Throop University, 40, 90
Thum, William, 102, 106
Titleyville, 99
Tolman, Richard, 164
Torrance, J.S., 127
Tourism, 48, 54, 59, 67, 70, 119, 156
Tournament of Roses, 40, *74-75,* 81, *82-83,* 143, 144
Tournament of Roses Association, 133, *190*
Tournament Park, 149
Townes, Charles, 176
Toypurina, 16
Traffic violations, 146
Transportation, 65
Trolley cars, *77*
Tuesday Evening Club, *83*
Turner, Edson, 58

United States Forest Service, 163
Universalist Church, 90
University of California Building Survey Committee, 149
Unjust Competition Act, 104

Valley Hunt Club, *50,* 81, *84*
Van Pelt, Garrett, 151, 152
Van Pelt, Helen, 153
Vawter, Mrs., 35
Vedder, William H., 101, 106
Villa-Parke Neighborhood Center, *180*
Vineyards, *19,* 20, 21, 26, 33, 46, 50
Vista del Arroyo Hotel, 128, 129,

149, *149,* 160
Volstead Act, 146
Von Kármán, Theodore, 165, 166, *167,* 167

Wachtel, Marion Kavanaugh, 186
Wadsworth, Hiram, 134, 135
Walker, Francis J., 157
Walker, Patrick, 157
Walker's Spanish Troubadours, Fred, *142*
Wallace, Joseph, 54
Walnuts, 20, 34, 37
Warhol, Andy, 176
War Savings Stamps, 119
Washington Elementary School, 149
Washington Junior High School, 149
Waterhouse, William, 102
Webster, E.C., 58
Webster Hotel, 71
Webster School, Daniel, 149
Weight, Martin H., 101
Whittaker, James T., 177
Whittlesey, Charles, 128
Wight, Peter B., 121
Williams, Romayne "Barney," 54, 55, 62, 191
Wilson, Benjamin D., 21, 22, *22,* 23, 28, 29, 31, 38, 40, 42, 46, 49, 59, 60
Wilson, Robert D., 176
Wilson Lake, 10, *10*
Wilson School, *60,* 66
Wilson's Lake Vineyard Tract, 40
Wilson's Trail, 46
Wineries, *19,* 20, 21, 26, 33, 46
Wise, William J., 157
Wolfskill, William, 20
Women's Christian Temperance Union, 59
Women's Civic League, 126, 133, 134
Women's Hospital, 181
Wood, John W., 101
Wooster, Philander G., 62
Works Progress Administration, 155, 156, 158, 160
World War I, *118,* 119, 132
World War II, 160, 164, 172
WPA Guide to California, 155, 156
Wright, Frank Lloyd, 127, 153
Wrigley, William J., 126
Wrigley House, *126*
Wrigley mansion, *190*

Yerkes, Charles, 134
YMCA, 135, 136
Yoch, Florence, 153
Yocum, J.D., 50
Young, Robert, 172
Yount, George, 9, 10, 14
Your City, 156
YWCA, 135, 136

Zalvidea, José María de, 17, 18

About the Authors

Author Ann Scheid earned her bachelor's degree at Vassar College and her master's degree at the University of Chicago. She has also studied at the universities of Munich, Stockholm, and Oxford, and taught for two years at UCLA. In 1976 Ms. Scheid began working for the City of Pasadena Architectural and Historical Building Survey and is now a Senior Planner and Coordinator of the City of Pasadena's Architectural and Historical Inventory. Her publications include works for the University of Chicago Press and Caltech, and numerous articles for publications such as the Pasadena Heritage Newsletter and the *Pasadena Star News.* She is also the principle author of a publication on old Pasadena, the historic commercial center. The author is a member of Pasadena Heritage, and is on the board of trustees of the Pasadena Historical Society. She has served as a tour guide and a frequent lecturer on Pasadena history.

Corporate historian Robert J. Kelly is editor of the *Pasadena Journal of Business,* the biweekly publication of his Pasadena-based communications firm, Kelly, Peck & Associates, Inc. A much published writer, Mr. Kelly has ghosted several articles on corporate financial planning that have appeared in national and regional journals such as *The Journal of Commercial Bank Lending* and the *ABA Banking Journal.* Active in many community organizations, Mr. Kelly is vice-president and director of the Pasadena Chamber of Commerce, and is a member of the Tournament of Roses Association and Pasadena Rotary.

THIS BOOK WAS SET IN
GOUDY, PALATINO, AND CARTIER TYPE
PRINTED ON 70-LB. MEAD ENAMEL OFFSET
AND BOUND BY
WALSWORTH PUBLISHING
COMPANY

The snow-covered San Gabriel Mountains provide a picturesque backdrop for this early Pasadena photograph, taken on a crisp winter day in the 1920s. Courtesy, The Huntington Library

PASO MAR
RST NATIONAL BANK, COR. FAIR OAKS & COLORADO STS.
ORANGE GROVE AVE
LIVERY FEED STABLE
JARVIS PHOTOGRAPH GALLER